CakePHP 1.3 Application Development Cookbook

Over 60 great recipes for developing, maintaining, and deploying web applications

Mariano Iglesias

[PACKT] open source *
PUBLISHING   community experience distilled

BIRMINGHAM - MUMBAI

CakePHP 1.3 Application Development Cookbook

First published: March 2011

Production Reference: 1030311

Published by Packt Publishing Ltd.
32 Lincoln Road
Olton
Birmingham, B27 6PA, UK.

ISBN 978-1-849511-92-6

www.packtpub.com

Cover Image by Javier Barria (Javier.Barria@cwpanama.com)

Credits

Author
Mariano Iglesias

Reviewers
Nick Baker
Sam Sherlock
Jeff Smith
Mark Story

Acquisition Editor
Sarah Cullington

Development Editor
Reshma Sundaresan

Technical Editor
Gauri Iyer

Indexer
Hemangini Bari

Editorial Team Leader
Mithun Sehgal

Project Team Leader
Lata Basantani

Project Coordinator
Leena Purkait

Proofreader
Glinert Stevens

Graphics
Nilesh R. Mohite

Production Coordinator
Adline Swetha Jesuthas

Cover Work
Adline Swetha Jesuthas

About the Author

Mariano Iglesias started programming at the early age of 11, moving through a variety of programming languages, and becoming a proficient PHP developer of over 10 years.

Throughout the years, he collaborated on several open source projects, mostly in C++, Java, Python, and PHP. He became a CakePHP and a Lithium contributor, frameworks that are among the most popular web development frameworks.

He divides his time between client work and his current open source projects, which are built with C++, Python, and PHP.

There are no words that can express my gratitude for the CakePHP community, and the CakePHP core team. Their passion and commitment to build one of the best PHP frameworks is to be cherished. Their sincere dedication to sharing knowledge cannot be praised enough.

This book has also benefited from the best team of technical reviewers a CakePHP book could possibly have. Here is my aknowledgement for Jeffrey Smith, John Anderson, Mark Story, Nick Baker, Paul Gardner, and Sam Sherlock. You not only helped me find flaws in my code, but also suggested some impressive improvements. The CakePHP community should be proud to count you as members.

Everyone on the Packt Publishing team has not only accommodated my schedule, but helped me throughout the writing of this book. They are truly a joy to work with, and no writer should walk away from the opportunity of writing for Packt. Thank you guys for your support and trust.

About the Reviewers

Nick Baker, owner of WebTechNick LLC and Senior IT/Developer at healthyhearing. com. Nick is a gifted problem solver who sincerely enjoys all aspects of programming and design, from development to implementation - excelling at programming, testing, documentation, and training in multiple platforms. Nick has worked over 13 years focusing on web development and is an expert in multiple web 2.0 frameworks such as CakePHP and Ruby on Rails. Prior to working with Allied Health LLC, Nick studied Computer Science at the University of New Mexico and helped build the Natural Heritage of New Mexico website - a site used by research scientists to store/retrieve data and map the distribution of endangered plants and animals in the Southwest. UNM holds a patent for multi-layer vector searches in GIS as a direct result of Nick's work.

Sam Sherlock is a web developer who is inspired by the innovations of modern web technology and loves to see them put to use in creative ways that benefit the masses. He has been a keen, early adopter of many popular Open source projects (jQuery, SWFObject. and of course, CakePHP).

He is a co-creator of a CakePHP plugin named BakingPlate, soon to be available via Github. One day he hopes to use modern web technologies to create mathematical teaching guides that are accessible and enjoyable to all.

Jeff Smith grew up in a small town in Indiana named Odon, but has lived in Indianapolis, Indiana (USA) for the last 15 years. Web programming is his hobby, but he plans to make it his career later. He enjoys working with many established frameworks, as well as trying out new ones. He is currently working with Drupal, Joomla!, and Ruby on Rails for various small projects. He is looking forward to learning about Non-SQL databases, Lift, and Scala.

I would like to thank Packt for giving me an opportunity to help out on this book, the Object-oriented PHP book I am working on, and I look forward to helping out on any books I can in the future.

Mark Story graduated from the Ontario College of Art and Design with a degree in Illustration. Art being a difficult industry to break into, he tried his hand at programming. This grew into a skill and passion that allowed him to become the lead developer of the CakePHP framework and secure a position with FreshBooks as a front-end developer. Mark's design background and skills in development produce a unique combination of attention to detail, technical expertise, and, above all, patience. Leading the CakePHP project as the primary contributor for the past two years, Mark contributes to several open-source projects in his spare time.

I'd like to thank my wonderful wife for putting up with all the late nights and my incessant talking about things she doesn't really understand. I'd also like to thank the fantastic CakePHP community CakePHP without you, this book would never have been possible.

www.PacktPub.com

Support files, eBooks, discount offers, and more

You might want to visit www.PacktPub.com for support files and downloads related to your book.

Did you know that Packt offers eBook versions of every book published, with PDF and ePub files available? You can upgrade to the eBook version at www.PacktPub.com and as a print book customer, you are entitled to a discount on the eBook copy. Get in touch with us at service@packtpub.com for more details.

At www.PacktPub.com, you can also read a collection of free technical articles, sign up for a range of free newsletters, and receive exclusive discounts and offers on Packt books and eBooks.

PACKTLiB®

http://PacktLib.PacktPub.com

Do you need instant solutions to your IT questions? PacktLib is Packt's online digital book library. Here, you can access, read and search across Packt's entire library of books.

Why Subscribe?

- Fully searchable across every book published by Packt
- Copy & paste, print and bookmark content
- On demand and accessible via web browser

Free Access for Packt account holders

If you have an account with Packt at www.PacktPub.com, you can use this to access PacktLib today and view nine entirely free books. Simply use your login credentials for immediate access.

I dedicate this book to:

My parents, who have embraced the passion of a restless kid when he decided to become a programmer, and taught him that family is the most important thing.

My brothers (Lorena, Nicolas, Pedro, Ignacio) for accomodating the kid that would not play with them so he could spend countless hours on the computer (or in a notebook when a computer wasn't available). Pedro: thank you for teaching me what life is all about, I miss you every day.

My wife Claudia, who is my soulmate and a partner for life; who has taught me the meaning of love; whose happiness has become my most important objective; and without whom, nothing, nothing at all would be possible. You are the reason why I am, my dear princess.

Table of Contents

Preface

CakePHP is a rapid development framework for PHP that provides an extensible architecture for developing, maintaining, and deploying web applications. While the framework has a lot of documentation and reference guides available for beginners, developing more sophisticated and scalable applications require a deeper knowledge of CakePHP features, a challenge that proves difficult even for well established developers.

The recipes in this cookbook will give you instant results and will help you to develop web applications, leveraging the CakePHP features that allow you to build robust and complex applications. Following the recipes in this book (which show how to work with AJAX, datasources, GEO location, routing, performance optimization, and more), you will be able to understand and use these features in no time.

What this book covers

Chapter 1, Authentication: This chapter explains how to set up authentication on a CakePHP application, starting from the most basic setup and finishing with advanced authorization mechanisms. This is accomplished through the use of tools that are built into the framework core, which allow us to quickly set up secure areas, without losing flexibility to build more complex solutions.

The first two recipes show us how to set up a basic, yet fully working authentication system. The next three recipes allow our users to log in using different information, have their user details saved after a successful login, and show us how to get this user information. The sixth recipe shows a more complex authorization technique that relies on route prefixes. The seventh recipe sets up a complex authentication system through the use of CakePHP's Access Control Layer. Finally, the last recipe shows us how to integrate our application with OpenID.

Chapter 2, Model Bindings: This chapter deals with one of the most important aspects of a CakePHP application: the relationship between models, also known as model bindings or associations. Being an integral part of any application's logic, it is of crucial importance that we master all aspects of how model bindings can be manipulated to get the data we need, when we need it.

In order to do so, we will go through a series of recipes that will show us how to change the way bindings are fetched, what bindings and what information from a binding is returned, how to create new bindings, and how to build hierarchical data structures

Chapter 3, Pushing the Search: Using models to fetch data is one of the most important aspects of any CakePHP application. As such, a good use of the find functions the framework provides can certainly guarantee the success of our application, and as importantly ensure that our code is readable and maintainable.

In this chapter, we have several recipes to resort to manual SQL-based queries when the need arises.

CakePHP also lets us define our custom find types that will extend the basic ones, allowing our code to be even more readable. The last recipes in this chapter show us how to add pagination support to our find type.

Chapter 4, Validation and Behaviors: This chapter deals with two aspects of CakePHP models that are fundamental to most applications: validation and behaviors.

When we are saving information to a data source (such as a database), CakePHP will automatically ensure that the data is quoted in order to prevent attacks, SQL injection being the most common one. If we also need to ensure that the data follows a certain format (for example, that a phone number is valid), we use validation rules.

There are also times where we need to do more than just validate the data we are working with. In some cases, we need to set values for fields that the end user can't specify but are part of our application logic. CakePHP's behaviors allow us to extend the functionality provided by a model, using callbacks to manipulate the data before it's saved, or after it's fetched.

The third recipe shows us how to use model callbacks (such as `beforeFind` and `afterFind`) in behaviors, while the fourth recipe shows how to use behaviors to add additional field values when a `save` operation is being undertaken.

The last two recipes in this chapter give examples on how to use the `Sluggable` behavior (for creating SEO friendly URLs), and the `Geocodable` behavior (to add geocoding support to an `Address` model).

Chapter 5, Datasources: Datasources are the backbone of almost all model operations. They provide an abstraction between model logic and the underlying data layer, allowing a more flexible approach to data manipulation. Through this abstraction, CakePHP applications are able to manipulate data without knowing the specifics of how it's stored, or fetched.

This chapter shows how to get information from existing datasources, use pre-built datasources to deal with non-relational data, and teaches us how to create a full-featured twitter datasource.

Chapter 6, Routing Magic: Almost every web-based application will eventually have to develop a successful strategy to obtain better search engine position through a technique known as search engine optimization.

This chapter starts by introducing some basic concepts of routing through the use of route parameters, and continues to build optimized routes to leverage our search engine placement.

The final section in this chapter shows us how to create highly optimized URLs for our user profiles, and how to build custom `Route` classes to obtain even more flexibility.

Chapter 7, Creating and Consuming Web Services: Web services are essential when looking forward to expose application functionality to third-party applications, or when looking forward to integrate foreign services into our own applications. They offer a broad set of technologies and definitions so systems written in different programming languages can communicate.

This chapter introduces a set of recipes to consume web services and to expose parts of our application as web services.

Chapter 8, Working with Shells: One of the most powerful, yet unknown, features of CakePHP is its shell framework. It provides applications with all that is required for building command line tools, which can be used to perform intensive tasks and any other type of non interactive processing.

This chapter introduces the reader to CakePHP shells by starting with the process of building basic shells, and then moving on to more advanced features, such as sending e-mails, and running controller actions from shells. It finishes by presenting the robot plugin, which offers a fully featured solution for scheduling and running tasks.

Chapter 9, Internationalizing Applications: This chapter includes a set of recipes that allow the reader to internationalize all aspects of their CakePHP applications, including static content (such as those available in views), and dynamic content (such as database records).

The first two recipes show how to allow text that is part of any CakePHP view, or model validation messages, to be ready for translation. The third recipe shows how to translate more complex expressions. The fourth recipe shows how to run CakePHP's built in tools to extract all static content that needs translation, and then translate that content to different languages. The fifth recipe shows how to translate database records. Finally, the last recipe shows how to allow users to change the current application language.

Chapter 10, Testing: This chapter covers one of the most interesting areas of application programming: unit testing through CakePHP's built-in tools, which offers a complete and powerful unit testing framework.

The first recipe shows how to set up the test framework so that we can create our own test cases. The second recipe shows how to create test data (fixtures) and use that data to test model methods. The third and fourth recipes show how to test controller actions, and how to test that our views are showing what we expect. The last recipe shows how to run the test in a non-ordinary fashion.

Chapter 11, Utility Classes and Tools: This chapter introduces a set of utility classes and helpful techniques that improve the architecture of a CakePHP application.

The first recipe shows how to work with a CakePHP class that optimizes the manipulation of arrays. The second recipe shows how to send an e-mail using the `Email` component. The third recipe shows how to use the `MagicDb` class to detect the type of a file, and the last recipe shows how to create application exceptions, and properly handle them when they are thrown.

What you need for this book

We need the following software for the book:

- A web server supported by CakePHP (such as Apache)
- A database engine supported by CakePHP (such as MySQL)
- CakePHP installed, configured, and working properly

Who this book is for

If you are a CakePHP developer who wants to discover quick and easy ways to improve web applications, and to leverage all aspects of the framework, this book is for you. This book assumes that you already have knowledge of CakePHP and general PHP development skills.

Conventions

In this book, you will find a number of styles of text that distinguish between different kinds of information. Here are some examples of these styles, and an explanation of their meaning.

Code words in text are shown as follows: "Create a file named `query_log.php` and place it in your `app/controllers/components` folder with the following contents:"

A block of code is set as follows:

```
CREATE TABLE `accounts`(
  `id` INT UNSIGNED AUTO_INCREMENT NOT NULL,
  `email` VARCHAR(255) NOT NULL,
  PRIMARY KEY(`id`)
);
```

New terms and **important words** are shown in bold. Words that you see on the screen, in menus or dialog boxes for example, appear in the text like this: "In that screen, make sure to grab what is shown as **Consumer key** and **Consumer secret**, as we will need it when going through this recipe."

> Warnings or important notes appear in a box like this.

> Tips and tricks appear like this.

Reader feedback

Feedback from our readers is always welcome. Let us know what you think about this book—what you liked or may have disliked. Reader feedback is important for us to develop titles that you really get the most out of.

To send us general feedback, simply send an e-mail to feedback@packtpub.com, and mention the book title via the subject of your message.

If there is a book that you need and would like to see us publish, please send us a note in the **SUGGEST A TITLE** form on www.packtpub.com or e-mail suggest@packtpub.com.

If there is a topic that you have expertise in and you are interested in either writing or contributing to a book, see our author guide on www.packtpub.com/authors.

Customer support

Now that you are the proud owner of a Packt book, we have a number of things to help you to get the most from your purchase.

> **Downloading the example code for this book**
>
> You can download the example code files for all Packt books you have purchased from your account at http://www.PacktPub.com. If you purchased this book elsewhere, you can visit http://www.PacktPub.com/support and register to have the files e-mailed directly to you.

Errata

Although we have taken every care to ensure the accuracy of our content, mistakes do happen. If you find a mistake in one of our books—maybe a mistake in the text or the code—we would be grateful if you would report this to us. By doing so, you can save other readers from frustration and help us improve subsequent versions of this book. If you find any errata, please report them by visiting `http://www.packtpub.com/support`, selecting your book, clicking on the **errata submission form** link, and entering the details of your errata. Once your errata are verified, your submission will be accepted and the errata will be uploaded on our website, or added to any list of existing errata, under the Errata section of that title. Any existing errata can be viewed by selecting your title from `http://www.packtpub.com/support`.

Piracy

Piracy of copyright material on the Internet is an ongoing problem across all media. At Packt, we take the protection of our copyright and licenses very seriously. If you come across any illegal copies of our works, in any form, on the Internet, please provide us with the location address or website name immediately so that we can pursue a remedy.

Please contact us at `copyright@packtpub.com` with a link to the suspected pirated material.

We appreciate your help in protecting our authors, and our ability to bring you valuable content.

Questions

You can contact us at `questions@packtpub.com` if you are having a problem with any aspect of the book, and we will do our best to address it.

1
Authentication

This chapter will cover the following topics:

- ▸ Setting up a basic authentication system
- ▸ Using and configuring the `Auth` component
- ▸ Allowing logins with e-mail or username
- ▸ Saving the user details after login
- ▸ Getting the current user's information
- ▸ Using prefixes for role-based access control
- ▸ Setting up Access Control Layer based authentication
- ▸ Integrating with OpenID

Introduction

This chapter explains how to set up authentication on a CakePHP application, starting from the most basic setup and finishing with advanced authorization mechanisms. This is accomplished through the use of tools that are built into the framework core, which allow us to quickly set up secure areas without losing flexibility to build more complex solutions.

The first two recipes show us how to set up a basic, yet fully working authentication system. The next three recipes allow our users to log in using different information, have their user details saved after a successful login, and show us how to get this user information. The sixth recipe shows a more complex authorization technique that relies on route prefixes. The seventh recipe sets up a complex authentication system through the use of CakePHP's Access Control Layer. Finally, the last recipe shows us how to integrate our application with OpenID.

Setting up a basic authentication system

The first task to be completed when we are in the process of adding authentication to an application is to identify which controllers will need user access. Normally we would make every controller and action protected by default, and then we would specify which areas of our application allow public access.

Getting ready

We must have a `users` table that should contain, at least, two fields: `username` (to hold the username) and `password` (to hold a hash made out of the user's password).

If you don't have a table for this purpose, you can use the following SQL statement to create it:

```
CREATE TABLE `users`(
    `id` INT UNSIGNED AUTO_INCREMENT NOT NULL,
    `username` VARCHAR(255) NOT NULL,
    `password` CHAR(40) NOT NULL,
    PRIMARY KEY(`id`)
);
```

How to do it...

1. Create a file named `users_controller.php` and place it inside your `app/controllers` folder with the following contents:

    ```php
    <?php
    class UsersController extends AppController {
            public function login() {
            }
            public function logout() {
                    $this->redirect($this->Auth->logout());
            }
    }
    ?>
    ```

2. Create a file named `login.ctp` in your `app/views/users` folder (create the folder if you don't have one already), and add the following contents:

    ```php
    <?php
    echo $this->Form->create(array('action'=>'login'));
    echo $this->Form->inputs(array(
            'legend' => 'Login',
            'username',
            'password'
    ```

```
    ));
    echo $this->Form->end('Login');
    ?>
```

3. Create a file named `app_controller.php` in your `app/` folder with the following contents:

```php
<?php
class AppController extends Controller {
        public $components = array(
                'Auth' => array(
                        'authorize' => 'controller'
                ),
                'Session'
        );
        public function isAuthorized() {
                return true;
        }
}
?>
```

4. Modify the `UsersController`, and add the following code before the `login` method:

```php
public function beforeFilter() {
        parent::beforeFilter();
        $this->Auth->allow('add');
}
public function add() {
        if (!empty($this->data)) {
                $this->User->create();
                if ($this->User->save($this->data)) {
                        $this->Session->setFlash('User created!');
                        $this->redirect(array('action'=>'login'));
                } else {
                        $this->Session->setFlash('Please correct the
errors');
                }
        }
}
```

5. Create a file named `add.ctp` and place it in your `app/views/users` folder with the following contents:

```php
<?php
echo $this->Form->create();
echo $this->Form->inputs(array(
        'legend' => 'Signup',
```

```
            'username',
            'password'
    ));
    echo $this->Form->end('Submit');
    ?>
```

We now have a fully working authentication system. We can add new users by browsing to `http://localhost/users/add`, logging in by browsing to `http://localhost/users/login`, and finally logging out by browsing to `http://localhost/users/logout`.

After creating a user, you should see the login form with a success message, as shown in the following screenshot:

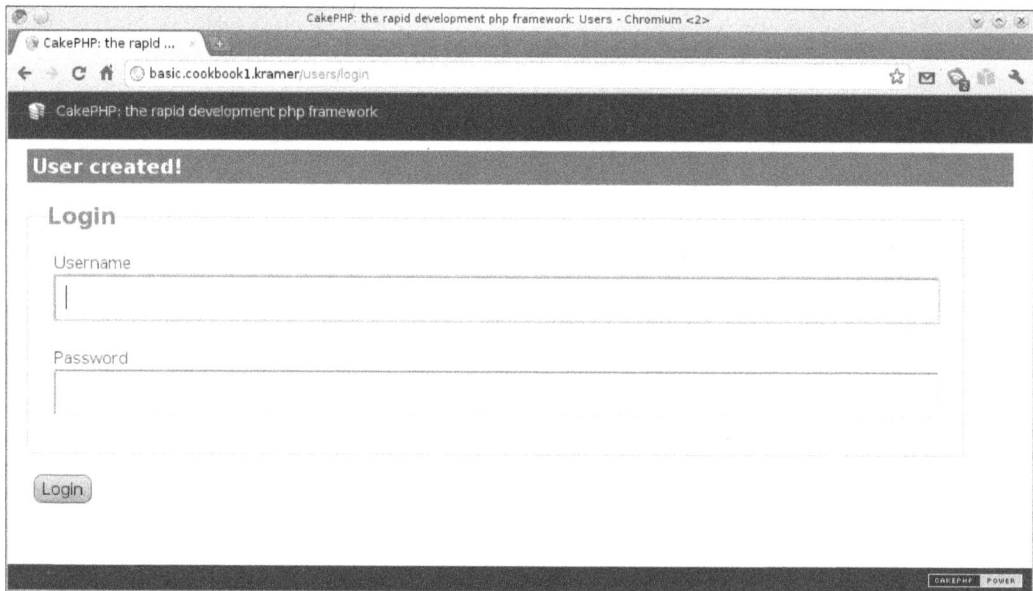

How it works...

We start by creating two actions in the `UsersController` class: `login()`, to show and process submissions of the login form, and `logout()`, to handle users logging out.

You may be surprised that the `login()` method has no logic whatsoever. To display the form, all we need to do is display the action's view. The form submission is taken care of by the `Auth` component, leaving us with no need to implement any controller logic. Therefore, the only implementation we need is to create a view for this action, which includes a simple form with two fields: `username`, and `password`.

> The `inputs` method of CakePHP's `FormHelper` is a shortcut designed to avoid multiple calls to the `input` method. By using it, we can create a full form with elements without the need to call `FormHelper::input()` several times.

The `logout()` controller action simply calls the `Auth` component's `logout()` method. This method removes the logged-in user data from the session, and returns the address to which the user should be redirected after logging out, obtained from the previously configured `logoutRedirect` setting of the component (defaults to the application's home page if the setting was not configured.)

Next, we add two components to the controller: `Session`, and `Auth`. The `Session` component is needed to create the messages (through the use of its `setflash()` method) that informs the user if a login attempt was unsuccessful, or if a user was created.

The `Auth` component operates between your controller's actions and the incoming request by means of the `beforeFilter` callback method. It uses it's `authorize` setting to check what type of authentication scheme is to be used.

> To obtain more information about the `authorize` setting, see the recipe *Using and configuring the Auth component*.

Once the `Auth` component is added to a controller, all actions in that controller are not accessible unless there is a valid user logged in. This means that if we had any actions that should be public (such as the `login()` and `add()` actions in our controller), we would have to tell the `Auth` component about them.

If one wishes to make some actions public, one can add the name of these actions to the `allowedActions` setting of the `Auth` component, or by calling its `allow()` method. We use the later approach to tell the `Auth` component that the `add()` action should be reachable without a logged-in user. The `login()` action is automatically added to the list of public actions by the `Auth` component.

When the user attempts to reach an action that is not within the public actions, the `Auth` component checks the session to see if a user is already logged in. If a valid user is not found, it redirects the browser to the `login` action. If there is a user who is logged in, it uses the controller's `isAuthorized` method to check if the user has access. If its return value is `true`, it allows access, otherwise access is rejected. In our case, we implemented this method in `AppController`, our base controller class. If the attempted action requires a user who is logged in, the `login()` action is executed. After the user submits data using the login form, the component will first hash the password field, and then issue a find operation on the `User` model to find a valid account, using the posted username and password. If a valid record is found, it is saved to the session, marking the user as logged in.

Hashing a password confirmation field

When the `Auth` component is enabled on a controller and the user submits a form with a field named `password` (regardless if it is being rendered in the login form), the component will automatically hash the `password` field before executing the controller's action.

> The `Auth` component uses the salt defined in the configuration setting `Security.salt` (in your `app/config/core.php` file) to calculate the hash. Different salt values will produce different hashes even when using the same password. Therefore, make sure you change the salt on all your CakePHP applications, thus enhancing the security of your authentication system.

This means that the action will never hold the plain password value, and this should be particularly noted when utilizing mechanisms to confirm password validations. When you are implementing such validation, make sure you hash the confirmation field using the proper method:

```
if (!empty($this->data)) {
    $this->data['User']['confirm_password'] = $this->Auth-
>password($this->data['User']['confirm_password']);
    // Continue with processing
}
```

See also

▸ *Using and configuring the Auth component*

▸ *Getting the current user's information*

Using and configuring the Auth component

If there is something that defines the `Auth` component, it is its flexibility that accounts for different types of authentication modes, each of these modes serving different needs. In this recipe, you will learn how to modify the component's default behavior, and how to choose between the different authentications modes.

Getting ready

We should have a fully working authentication system, so follow the entire recipe *Setting up a basic authentication system*.

We will also add support to have disabled user accounts. Add a field named active to your users table with the following SQL statement:

```
ALTER TABLE `users`
ADD COLUMN `active` TINYINT UNSIGNED NOT NULL default 1;
```

How to do it...

1. Modify the definition of the `Auth` component in your `AppController` class, so it looks like the following:

```
public $components = array(
        'Auth' => array(
                'authorize' => 'controller',
                'loginRedirect' => array(
                        'admin' => false,
                        'controller' => 'users',
                        'action' => 'dashboard'
                ),
                'loginError' => 'Invalid account specified',
                'authError' => 'You don\'t have the right permission'
        ),
'Session'
);
```

2. Now while still editing your `app/app_controller.php` file, place the following code right below the `components` property declaration, at the beginning of the `beforeFilter` method in your `AppController` class:

```
public function beforeFilter() {
        if ($this->Auth->getModel()->hasField('active'))
                {$this->Auth->userScope = array('active' => 1);
                }
}
```

3. Copy the default layout from `cake/libs/view/layouts/default.ctp` to your `app/views/layouts` directory, and make sure you place the following line in your layout where you wish to display authentication messages:

```
<?php echo $this->Session->flash('auth'); ?>
```

4. Edit your `app/controllers/users_controller.php` file and place the following method right below the `logout()` method:

```
public function dashboard() {
}
```

5. Finally, create the view for this newly added action in a file named `dashboard.ctp` and place it in your `app/views/users` folder with the following contents:

   `<p>Welcome!</p>`

   If you now browse to `http://localhost/users/login` and enter the wrong credentials (wrong username and/or password), you should see the error message shown in the following screenshot:

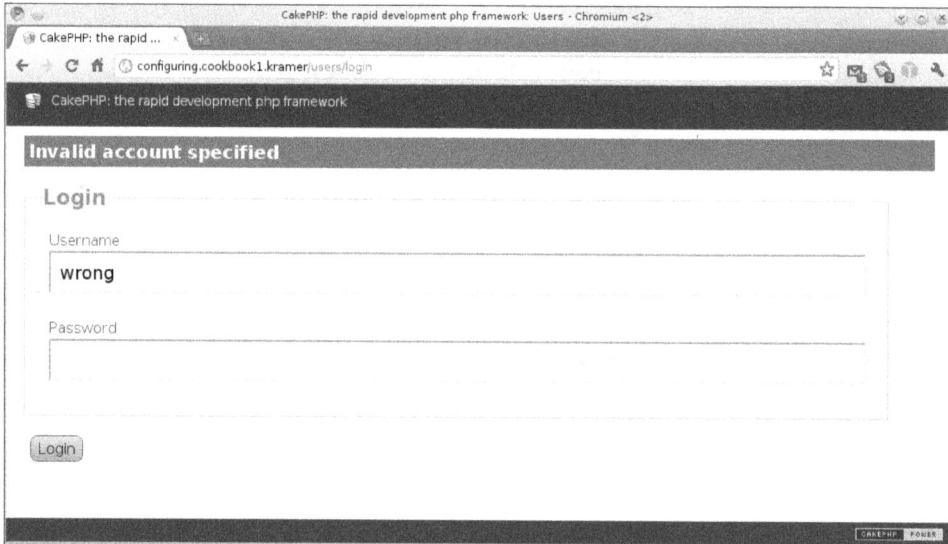

How it works...

As the `Auth` component does its magic right before a controller action is executed, we either need to specify its settings in the `beforeFilter` callback, or pass them in an array when adding the component to the `components` property. A common place to do it is in the `beforeFilter()` method of the `AppController` class, as by doing so we can share the same authentication settings throughout all our controllers.

This recipe changes some `Auth` settings, so that whenever a valid user logs in, they are automatically taken to a `dashboard` action in the `UsersController` (done via the `loginRedirect` setting.) It also adds some default error messages through the component's respective settings: `loginError` for when the given account is invalid, and `authError` for when there is a valid account, but the action is not authorized (which can be achieved by returning `false` from the `isAuthorized()` method implemented in `AppController`.)

It also sets the component's `userScope` setting in `AppController::beforeFilter()`. This setting allows us to define which conditions the `User` find operation need to match to allow a user account to log in. By adding the `userScope` setting, we ensure that only user records that have the `active` field set to `1` are allowed access.

Changing the default user model

As you may have noticed, the role of the User model is crucial, not only to fetch the right user account, but also to check the permissions on some of the authentication schemes. By default, the Auth component will look for a User model, but you can change which model is to be used by setting the userModel property or the userModel key in the settings array.

For example, if your user model is Account, you would add the following setting when adding the Auth component to your controller:

```
'userModel' => 'Account'
```

Or equivalently, you would add the following to the beforeFilter method of your AppController class, in the block of code where you are setting up the component:

```
$this->Auth->userModel = 'Account';
```

There's more...

The $authorize property of the Auth component (or the authorize key in the Auth component settings array) defines which authentication scheme should be used. Possible values are:

- ▶ controller: It makes the component use the controller's isAuthorized method, which returns true to allow access, or false to reject it. This method is particularly useful when obtaining the logged-in user (refer to the *Getting the current user's information* recipe)

- ▶ model: It is similar to controller; instead of using the controller to call the method, it looks for the isAuthorized method in the User model. First, it tries to map the controller's action to a CRUD operation (one of 'create', 'read', 'update', or 'delete'), and then calls the method with three arguments: the user record, the controller that is being accessed, and the CRUD operation (or actual controller action) that is to be executed.

- ▶ object: It is similar to model; instead of using the model to call the method, it looks for the isAuthorized method in a given class. In order to specify which class, set the AuthComponent::$object property to an instance of such a class. It calls the method with three arguments: the user record, the controller that is being accessed, and the action that is to be executed.

- ▶ actions: It uses the Acl component to check for access, which allows a much more grained access control.

- ▶ crud: It is similar to actions; the difference lies in the fact that it first tries to map the controller's action to a CRUD operation (one of 'create', 'read', 'update', or 'delete'.)

▸ *Getting the current user's information*

▸ *Setting up Access Control Layer based authentication*

Allowing logins with username or e-mail

By default the `Auth` component will use the given username posted in the login form to check for a valid user account. However, some applications have two separate fields: one to define the username, and another one to define the user's e-mail. This recipe shows how to allow logins using either a username or an e-mail.

Getting ready

We should have a fully working authentication system, so follow the entire recipe, *Setting up a basic authentication system*.

We also need the field to hold the user's e-mail address. Add a field named `email` to your `users` table with the following SQL statement:

```
ALTER TABLE `users`
    ADD COLUMN `email` VARCHAR(255) NOT NULL;
```

We need to modify the signup page so users can specify their e-mail address. Edit your `app/views/users/add.ctp` file and make the following changes:

```php
<?php
echo $this->Form->create();
echo $this->Form->inputs(array(
    'legend' => 'Signup',
    'email',
    'username',
    'password'
));
echo $this->Form->end('Submit');
?>
```

How to do it...

1. Edit your app/views/users/login.ctp file and make the following changes to it:

```php
<?php
echo $this->Form->create(array('action'=>'login'));
echo $this->Form->inputs(array(
    'legend' => 'Login',
    'username' => array('label'=>'Username / Email'),
    'password'
));
echo $this->Form->end('Login');
?>
```

2. Edit your UsersController class and make sure the login action looks like the following:

```php
public function login() {
    if (
            !empty($this->data) &&
            !empty($this->Auth->data['User']['username']) &&
            !empty($this->Auth->data['User']['password'])
    ) {
    $user = $this->User->find('first', array(
                    'conditions' => array(
                            'User.email' => $this->Auth->data['User']['username'],
                            'User.password' => $this->Auth->data['User']['password']
                    ),
'recursive' => -1
            ));
        if (!empty($user) && $this->Auth->login($user)) {
                    if ($this->Auth->autoRedirect) {
                            $this->redirect($this->Auth->redirect());
                    }
                    } else {
                    $this->Session->setFlash($this->Auth->loginError, $this->Auth->flashElement, array(), 'auth');
            }
        }
}
```

If you now browse to `http://localhost/users/login` and you can enter the user's e-mail and password to log in, as shown in the following screenshot:

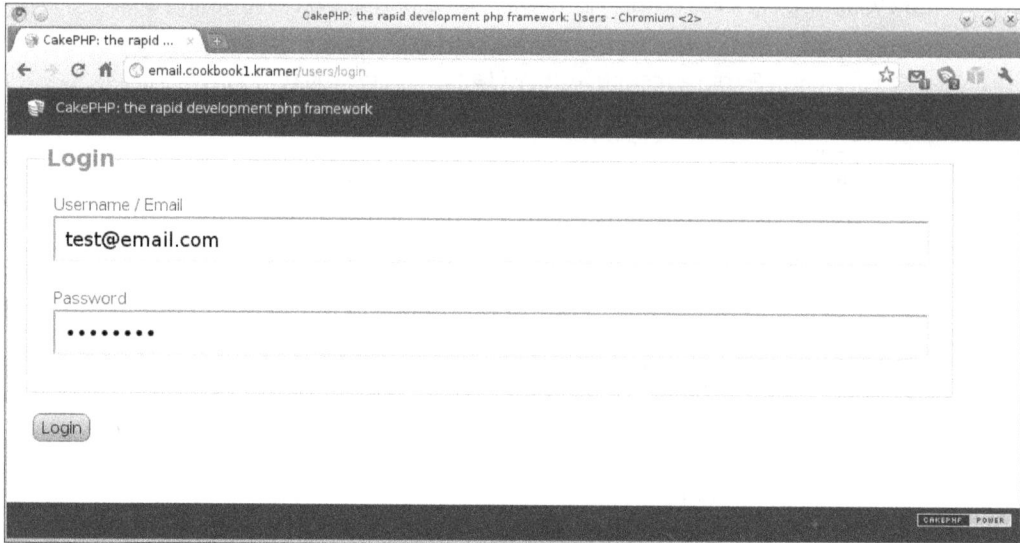

How it works...

When the `Auth` component is unable to find a valid user account using the username and password fields, it gives the control back to the `login` action. Therefore, in the `login` action we can check if there is any submitted data. If that is the case, we know that the `Auth` component was not able to find a valid account.

With this in mind, we can try to find a user account with an e-mail that matches the given username. If there is one, we log the user in and redirect the browser to the default action, similar to what the component would do on a successful attempt.

If we cannot find a valid user account, we simply set the flash message to the default error message specified in the `Auth` component.

There's more...

You may have noticed that when looking for the user record, we used `$this->Auth->data` rather than `$this->data` to use the actual posted values. The reason for this is because the `Auth` component will not only automatically hash the password field, but also remove its value from the controller's `data` property, so if you need to show the login form again, the password field will not be pre-filled for the user.

▸ *Getting the current user's information*

Saving the user details after login

One of the most typical functionalities offered by sites with authentication capabilities is the ability to let the user choose (by clicking on a checkbox) whether they want the system to remember their account after logging in.

Getting ready

We should have a working authentication system, so follow the entire recipe, *Setting up a basic authentication system*.

How to do it...

1. Edit your app/app_controller.php file and add the following Auth component settings to the Auth component. Also add the Cookie component by making the following changes to the components property: AppController (in the $components property) must include the following mandatory setting (if it is not there, add it inside the array of settings for the component):

```php
public $components = array(
        'Auth' => array(
                'authorize' => 'controller',
                'autoRedirect' => false
        ),
        'Cookie',
        'Session'
);
```

2. Edit your app/views/users/login.ctp view file and make the following changes:

```php
<?php
echo $this->Form->create(array('action'=>'login'));
echo $this->Form->inputs(array(
        'legend' => 'Login',
        'username',
        'password',
        'remember' => array('type' => 'checkbox', 'label' =>
'Remember me')
));
```

```
    echo $this->Form->end('Login');
    ?>
```

3. Now, add the following code to the end of the `login` action of your `UsersController` class:

```
if (!empty($this->data)) {
    $userId = $this->Auth->user('id');
    if (!empty($userId)) {
        if (!empty($this->data['User']['remember'])) {
            $user = $this->User->find('first', array(
                'conditions' => array('id' => $userId),
                'recursive' => -1,
                'fields' => array('username', 'password')
            ));
            $this->Cookie->write('User', array_intersect_key(
                $user[$this->Auth->userModel],
                array('username'=>null, 'password'=>null)
            ));
        } elseif ($this->Cookie->read('User') != null) {
            $this->Cookie->delete('User');
        }
        $this->redirect($this->Auth->redirect());
    }
}
```

4. Next, add the following code to the beginning of the `logout()` method of your `UsersController` class:

```
if ($this->Cookie->read('User') != null) {
    $this->Cookie->delete('User');
}
```

5. Finally, add the following method to your `AppController` class, right below the `components` property declaration:

```
public function beforeFilter() {
    if ($this->Auth->user() == null) {
        $user = $this->Cookie->read('User');
        if (!empty($user)) {
            $user = $this->Auth->getModel()->find('first', array(
                'conditions' => array(
                    $this->Auth->fields['username'] =>
$user[$this->Auth->fields['username']],
                    $this->Auth->fields['password'] =>
$user[$this->Auth->fields['password']]
                ),
                'recursive' => -1
```

```
        ));
        if (!empty($user) && $this->Auth->login($user)) {
            $this->redirect($this->Auth->redirect());
        }
      }
    }
  }
```

How it works...

The first task we needed to accomplish was to disable the automatic redirect in the `Auth` component. By doing so, we are able to catch both successful and failed log in attempts, which allows us to check if they **remember me** checkbox is selected. If the checkbox is indeed checked, we create a cookie named `User` that contains the values for the `username` and `password` fields with a value equal to the user ID that logged in. Remember that the `password` value is automatically encrypted by the `Auth` component, so it is safe for storage. The `Cookie` component adds another layer of security by automatically encrypting and decrypting the given values.

In `AppController::beforeFilter()`, when there is no logged-in user, we check to see if the cookie is set. If it is, we use the values for the `username` and `password` fields stored in the cookie to log in a user, and then redirect the browser to the `login` action.

Finally, we delete the cookie when it is appropriate (when a user logs in without the checkbox selected, or when the user manually logs out).

See also

▸ *Getting the current user's information*

Getting the current user's information

CakePHP's authentication system will provide us with the necessary tools to build a strong, flexible `Auth` based application. We can then use it to fetch the current user information and make it available throughout our application.

In this recipe, we will see how to save the current logged-in user's information so it is accessible from any point of our CakePHP application, including its layout, while adding a helpful method to the `User` model to make the job easier.

Getting ready

We should have a working authentication system, so follow the recipe, *Setting up a basic authentication system*.

How to do it...

1. Add the following method to your `AppController` class:

```
public function beforeFilter() {
        $user = $this->Auth->user();
        if (!empty($user)) {
                Configure::write('User', $user[$this->Auth-
>getModel()->alias]);
        }
}
```

2. Also in your `AppController` class, add the following method inside the class definition:

```
public function beforeRender() {
        $user = $this->Auth->user();
        if (!empty($user)) {
                $user = $user[$this->Auth->getModel()->alias];
        }
        $this->set(compact('user'));
}
```

3. Copy the default CakePHP layout file named `default.ctp` from your `cake/libs/view/layouts` folder to your application's `app/views/layouts` folder. Place the following code in the `app/views/layouts/default.ctp` folder. While editing this layout, add the following code right where you want login / logout links to appear:

```
<?php if (!empty($user)) { ?>
Welcome back <?php echo $user['username']; ?>!
        <?php
        echo $this->Html->link('Log out', array('plugin'=>null,
'admin'=>false, 'controller'=>'users', 'action'=>'logout'));
} else {
        echo $this->Html->link('Log in', array('plugin'=>null,
'admin'=>false, 'controller'=>'users', 'action'=>'login'));
}
?>
```

4. Add the following method to the `User` model. If you do not have a model created for the `users` table, proceed to create a file named `user.php` and place it in your `app/models` directory. If you do have one already, make sure you add the `get` method to it:

```php
<?php
class User extends AppModel {
        public static function get($field = null) {
                $user = Configure::read('User');
                if (empty($user) || (!empty($field) && !array_key_
exists($field, $user))) {
                        return false;
                }
        return !empty($field) ? $user[$field] : $user;
        }
}
?>
```

How it works...

By storing the user record in an application-wide configuration variable, we are able to obtain the current user information from anywhere in our application, whether it is controllers, components, models, and so on. This gives us the power to know if there's a logged-in user at any point.

We also need to make sure that views are able to learn whether there is a logged-in user. Even though a view could, technically speaking, still have access to the configure variable, it is normally more elegant to set a view variable to avoid any interaction with PHP classes from the view (except for the view helpers).

> When you set variables for the view in `AppController`, it is very important to make sure no controller action will overwrite the variable. Choose a unique name wisely, and make sure you don't set a view variable with the same name in your controllers.

Finally, we add a handy method to the `User` model, so we can obtain the current user from our controllers without having to deal with the `Configure` variable. We can also use the `get` method to collect a particular bit of user information. For example, to fetch the current user's username from a controller, we would do something like the following:

```php
$userName = User::get('username');
```

You should not have to load the `User` model class yourself, as the `Auth` component does it for you.

See also

▸ *Allowing logins with e-mail or username.*

Using prefixes for role-based access control

Even though CakePHP provides a very powerful access control layer, sometimes we just need to implement user roles without having to go into the details of specifying which role is allowed access to which action.

This recipe shows how to limit access to certain actions by role-using routing prefixes, which constitutes a perfect solution for simple role-based authentication. In order to accomplish this recipe, we will assume the need to add three user roles in our application: administrators, managers, and users.

Getting ready

We should have a working authentication system, so follow the recipe, *Setting up a basic authentication system*. The `users` table should also contain a field to hold the user's role (named `role`.) Add this field with the following SQL statement:

```
ALTER TABLE `users`
    ADD COLUMN `role` VARCHAR(255) DEFAULT NULL AFTER `password`;
```

How to do it...

1. Edit your `app/config/core.php` file and look for the line that defines the `Routing.prefixes` setting. If it is commented out, uncomment it. Then change it to:

   ```
   Configure::write('Routing.prefixes', array('admin', 'manager'));
   ```

2. Add the following code at the end of your `UsersController` class definition:

   ```
   public function dashboard() {
               $role = $this->Auth->user('role');
               if (!empty($role)) {
                       $this->redirect(array($role => true, 'action'
   => 'dashboard'));
               }
   }
   public function admin_dashboard() {
   }
   public function manager_dashboard() {
   }
   ```

3. Create a view for each of these actions, and put content into it to reflect which view is being rendered. Therefore, you would have to create three files:

- ❑ `app/views/users/admin_dashboard.ctp`
- ❑ `app/views/users/manager_dashboard.ctp`
- ❑ `app/views/users/dashboard.ctp`

For example, the contents for `dashboard.ctp` could simply be:

`<h1>Dashboard (User)</h1>`

4. Edit your `app/controllers/app_controller.php` file and change the `components` property declaration to include the following setting for the `Auth` component:

```
public $components = array(
        'Auth' => array(
                'authorize' => 'controller',
                'loginRedirect' => array(
                        'admin' => false,
                        'controller' => 'users',
                        'action' => 'dashboard'
                )
        ),
        'Session'
);
```

5. While still editing your `AppController` class, change the `isAuthorized` method and replace it entirely with the following:

```
public function isAuthorized() {
        $role = $this->Auth->user('role');
        $neededRole = null;
        $prefix = !empty($this->params['prefix']) ?
                $this->params['prefix'] :
                null;
        if (
                !empty($prefix) &&
                in_array($prefix, Configure::read('Routing.
prefixes'))
        ) {
        $neededRole = $prefix;
        }
        return (
                empty($neededRole) ||
                strcasecmp($role, 'admin') == 0 ||
                strcasecmp($role, $neededRole) == 0
        );
}
```

6. Copy the default CakePHP layout file named `default.ctp` from your `cake/libs/view/layouts` folder to your application's `app/views/layouts` folder. While editing this layout, place the following code in the `app/views/layouts/default.ctp` layout file, right where you want the link to the dashboard to appear.

```php
<?php
$dashboardUrl = array('controller'=>'users',
'action'=>'dashboard');
if (!empty($user['role'])) {
        $dashboardUrl[$user['role']] = true;
}
echo $this->Html->link('My Dashboard', $dashboardUrl);
?>
```

How it works...

CakePHP will recognize prefixes defined in the `Routing.prefixes` setting as part of the URL, when they are preceding a normal route. For example, if `admin` is a defined prefix, the route `/admin/articles/index` will translate to the `admin_index` action in `ArticlesController`.

Since we are utilizing the controller authentication scheme in the `Auth` configuration, we know that every time a user is trying to access a non-public action, `AppController::isAuthorized()` is executed, and inside the method we set `true` if the user has access, or `false` otherwise.

Knowing that, we can check to see if a prefix is being used when a controller action is about to be executed. If the current route being accessed includes a prefix, we can match that prefix against the user's role to make sure they have access to the requested resource.

We are able to link to a role-only resource just by prefixing it with the appropriate prefix in the route. For example, to link to the manager's dashboard, the URL would be:

```php
array(
        'manager' => true,
        'controller' => 'users',
        'action' => 'dashboard'
);
```

See also

▶ *Setting up Access Control Layer based authentication.*

Setting up Access Control Layer-based authentication

The more roles an application has, the more complex its Access Control Layer becomes. Luckily, one of the authentication schemes provided by the `Auth` component allows us to easily define which actions are accessible by certain roles (known as groups), using command-line tools. In this recipe, you will learn how to set up ACL on your application.

Getting ready

We should have a table to hold the roles, named `groups`.

If you do not have one already, create it using the following statement:

```
CREATE TABLE `groups`(
    `id` INT NOT NULL AUTO_INCREMENT,
    `name` VARCHAR(255) NOT NULL,
    PRIMARY KEY(`id`)
);
```

If you do not have any records in your `groups` table, create some by running the following SQL statement:

```
INSERT INTO `groups`(`id`, `name`) VALUES
    (1, 'Administrator'),
    (2, 'Manager'),
    (3, 'User');
```

We must also have a `users` table to hold the users, which should contain a field (named `group_id`) to contain a reference to the group a user belongs to. If you do not have such a table, create it using the following statement:

```
CREATE TABLE `users`(
    `id` INT NOT NULL AUTO_INCREMENT,
    `group_id` INT NOT NULL,
    `username` VARCHAR(255) NOT NULL,
`password` CHAR(40) NOT NULL,
    PRIMARY KEY(`id`),
    KEY `group_id`(`group_id`),
    CONSTRAINT `users__groups` FOREIGN KEY(`group_id`) REFERENCES
`groups`(`id`)
);
```

We also need to have the ARO / ACO tables initialized. Using your operating system console, switch to your application directory, and run:

- ❑ If you are on a GNU Linux / Mac / Unix system:

  ```
  ../cake/console/cake schema create DbAcl
  ```

- ❑ If you are on Microsoft Windows:

  ```
  ..\cake\console\cake.bat schema create DbAcl
  ```

How to do it...

> The following initial steps are very similar to what is shown in *Setting up a basic authentication system*. However, there are some differences between the two that are crucial, so make sure you go through these instructions carefully.

1. Create a controller for the User model (in a file named users_controller.php placed inside your app/controllers folder), which should contain the following:

   ```php
   <?php
   class UsersController extends AppController {
           public function login() {
           }
           public function logout() {
                   $this->redirect($this->Auth->logout());
           }
   }
   ?>
   ```

2. Create a file named login.ctp in your app/views/users folder (create the folder if you do not have one already), with the following contents:

   ```php
   <?php
   echo $this->Form->create(array('action'=>'login'));
   echo $this->Form->inputs(array(
           'legend' => 'Login',
           'username',
           'password'
   ));
   echo $this->Form->end('Login');
   ?>
   ```

3. Create a file named `app_controller.php` in your app/ folder. Make sure it contains the following:

```php
<?php
class AppController extends Controller {
        public $components = array(
                'Acl',
                'Auth' => array(
                        'authorize' => 'actions',
                        'loginRedirect' => array(
                                'admin' => false,
                                'controller' => 'users',
                                'action' => 'dashboard'
                        )
                ),
        'Session'
        );
}
?>
```

4. Modify the `UsersController` class and add the following code before its `login()` method:

```php
public function beforeFilter() {
        parent::beforeFilter();
        $this->Auth->allow('add');
}
public function add() {
        if (!empty($this->data)) {
                $this->User->create();
                if ($this->User->save($this->data)) {
                        $this->Session->setFlash('User created!');
                        $this->redirect(array('action'=>'login'));
                } else {
                        $this->Session->setFlash('Please correct the
errors');
                }
        }
        $this->set('groups', $this->User->Group->find('list'));
}
```

5. Add the view for the action in the folder app/views/users by creating a file named add.ctp with the following contents:

```php
<?php
echo $this->Form->create();
echo $this->Form->inputs(array(
```

```
              'legend' => 'Signup',
              'username',
              'password',
              'group_id'
      ));
      echo $this->Form->end('Submit');
      ?>
```

6. Create a file named `group.php` and place it in your `app/models` folder with the following contents:

```php
<?php
class Group extends AppModel {
        public $actsAs = array('Acl' => 'requester');
        public function parentNode() {
                if (empty($this->id) && empty($this->data)) {
                        return null;
                }
        $data = $this->data;
                if (empty($data)) {
                        $data = $this->find('first', array(
                                'conditions' => array('id' => $this-
>id),
                                'fields' => array('parent_id'),
                                'recursive' => -1
                        ));
                }
                if (!empty($data[$this->alias]['parent_id'])) {
                        return $data[$this->alias]['parent_id'];
                }
                return null;
        }
}
?>
```

7. Create a file named `user.php` and place it in your `app/models` folder with the following contents:

```php
<?php
class User extends AppModel {
        public $belongsTo = array('Group');
        public $actsAs = array('Acl' => 'requester');
        public function parentNode() {
        }
        public function bindNode($object) {
                if (!empty($object[$this->alias]['group_id'])) {
```

```
                              return array(
                                      'model' => 'Group',
                                      'foreign_key' => $object[$this->alias]
        ['group_id']
                              );
                    }
                }
        }
        ?>
```

> Take note of the IDs for all the records in your `groups` table, as they are needed to link each group to an *ARO* record.

8. Run the following commands in your console (change the references to 1, 2, 3 to meet your own group IDs, if they are different).

   ❑ If you are on a GNU Linux / Mac / Unix system, the commands are:

```
../cake/console/cake acl create aro root Groups
../cake/console/cake acl create aro Groups Group.1
../cake/console/cake acl create aro Groups Group.2
../cake/console/cake acl create aro Groups Group.3
```

   ❑ If you are on Microsoft Windows, the commands are:

```
..\cake\console\cake.bat acl create aro root Groups
..\cake\console\cake.bat acl create aro Groups Group.1
..\cake\console\cake.bat acl create aro Groups Group.2
..\cake\console\cake.bat acl create aro Groups Group.3
```

9. Add the following code at the end of your `UsersController` class definition:

```
public function dashboard() {
        $groupName = $this->User->Group->field('name',
                array('Group.id'=>$this->Auth->user('group_id'))
        );
        $this->redirect(array('action'=>strtolower($groupName)));
}
public function user() {
}
public function manager() {
}
public function administrator() {
}
```

10. Create a view for each of these actions, and put some distinctive content on each one of them to reflect which view is being rendered. Therefore, you have to create three files:

    ❑ `app/views/users/user.ctp`

    ❑ `app/views/users/manager.ctp`

    ❑ `app/views/users/administrator.ctp`.

    For example the contents for `user.ctp` could simply be:

    ```
    <h1>Dashboard (User)</h1>
    ```

11. We have to tell ACL about these restricted actions. Run the following commands in your console.

    ❑ If you are on a GNU Linux / Mac / Unix system, the commands are:

    ```
    ../cake/console/cake acl create aco root controllers
    ../cake/console/cake acl create aco controllers Users
    ../cake/console/cake acl create aco controllers/Users
    logout
    ../cake/console/cake acl create aco controllers/Users user
    ../cake/console/cake acl create aco controllers/Users
    manager
    ../cake/console/cake acl create aco controllers/Users
    administrator
    ```

    ❑ If you are on Microsoft Windows, the commands are:

    ```
    ..\cake\console\cake.bat acl create aco root controllers
    ..\cake\console\cake.bat acl create aco controllers Users
    ..\cake\console\cake.bat acl create aco controllers/Users
    logout
    ..\cake\console\cake.bat acl create aco controllers/Users
    user
    ..\cake\console\cake.bat acl create aco controllers/Users
    manager
    ..\cake\console\cake.bat acl create aco controllers/Users
    administrator
    ```

12. Finally, we have to grant permissions by linking each ARO (groups) to each ACO (controller's actions). Run the following commands in your console.

    ❑ If you are on a GNU Linux / Mac / Unix system, the commands are:

    ```
    ../cake/console/cake acl grant Group.1 controllers/Users
    all
    ../cake/console/cake acl grant Group.2 controllers/Users/
    logout all
    ../cake/console/cake acl grant Group.2 controllers/Users/
    manager all
    ```

```
../cake/console/cake acl grant Group.3 controllers/Users/
logout all
../cake/console/cake acl grant Group.3 controllers/Users/
user all
```

❑ If you are on Microsoft Windows, the commands are:

```
..\cake\console\cake.bat acl grant Group.1 controllers/
Users all
..\cake\console\cake.bat acl grant Group.2 controllers/
Users/logout all
..\cake\console\cake.bat acl grant Group.2 controllers/
Users/manager all
..\cake\console\cake.bat acl grant Group.3 controllers/
Users/logout all
..\cake\console\cake.bat acl grant Group.3 controllers/
Users/user all
```

We now have a fully working ACL based authentication system. We can add new users by browsing to `http://localhost/users/add`, logging in with `http://localhost/users/login`, and finally logging out with `http://localhost/users/logout`.

Users should only have access to `http://localhost/users/user`, managers to `http://localhost/users/manager`, and administrators should be able to access all those actions, including `http://localhost/users/administrator`.

How it works...

When setting the `authorize` configuration option of the `Auth` component to `actions`, and after adding `Acl` to the list of controller-wide components, CakePHP will check to see if the current action being accessed is a public action. If this is not the case, it will check for a logged-in user with a matching ACO record. If there is no such record, it will deny access.

Once there is a matching ACO for the controller action, it will use the `bindNode` method in the `User` model to see how a user record is matched to an ARO. The method implementation we added specifies that a user record should be looked up in the `aros` table by means of the group that the user belongs to.

After having both the matching ACO and ARO, it lastly checks to see whether there is a valid permission set up (in the `aros_acos` table) for the given ARO and ACO records. If it finds one, it allows access, otherwise it will reject authorization.

It is of vital importance that each record in the groups table has a matching ARO record. We set that association by issuing `aro create` commands to link each group ID to an ARO record of the form `Group.ID`, where ID is the actual ID.

Similarly, all controller actions that are not within the defined public actions should have a matching ACO record. Just as with AROs, we create the association between controller's actions and ACOs issuing `aco create` commands, setting the ACO name to be the action name, and making them child of an ACO which name is the controller name.

Finally, to grant the permission of an ARO (group) to an ACO (controller's actions), we issue `acl grant` commands, specifying as the first argument the ARO (`Group.ID`) and the second argument either a whole controller (such as `controllers/Users`), or a specific controller action (such as `controllers/Users/logout`). The last argument to the grant command (`all`) simply gives a further control of the type of access, and makes more sense when using ACL to control access to custom objects, or when using the `crud` authentication scheme.

There's more...

While developing an application, the task of matching each controller action to an ACO may be somewhat troublesome. Fortunately, several people in the CakePHP community felt the need for an easier solution. One of the solutions that I'd recommend is adopting `acl_extras`, a plugin developed by Mark Story, the lead developer of the CakePHP 1.3 release. By using this plugin, you will be able to continuously synchronize your controllers with the `acos` table. Find more about it, including its installation instructions, at `http://github.com/markstory/acl_extras`.

See also

▶ *Using prefixes for role-based access control.*

Integrating with OpenID

OpenID (`http://openid.net`) is a great way to allow users to log in without having to have an actual username in your application. It is a solution that is widely adopted, and has proven itself on many popular sites (such as Google, Yahoo, MySpace, and AOL).

This recipe shows how to add support for OpenID logins in a transparent way, while still working with a valid `Auth` implementation.

Getting ready

We should have a working authentication system, so follow the recipe, *Setting up a basic authentication system*.

We will also need the PHP OpenID Library. Download the latest release from `https://github.com/openid/php-openid/downloads` and extract the folder named `Auth` from the downloaded file into your `app/vendors` folder. You should now have a directory named `Auth` inside your `vendors` folder.

Finally, we need to download the OpenID plugin for CakePHP. Go to `http://github.com/mariano/openid/downloads` and download the latest release. Uncompress the downloaded file into your `app/plugins` folder. You should now have a directory named `openid` inside `app/plugins`.

How to do it...

1. Edit your `AppController` class and change the reference for the `Auth` component from `Auth` to `Openid.OpenAuth`. The `components` property should now look like this:

```
public $components = array(
        'Openid.OpenAuth' => array(
                'authorize' => 'controller'
        ),
        'Session'
);
```

2. Next, edit the login view (in `app/views/users/login.ctp`) and add a field to allow the user to specify their OpenID URL. The view should now look like this:

```php
<?php
echo $this->Form->create(array('action'=>'login'));
echo $this->Form->inputs(array(
        'legend' => 'Login',
        'openid' => array('label' => 'OpenID URL'),
        'username',
        'password'
));
echo $this->Form->end('Login');
?>
```

You should now be able to log in using either a valid username and password combination, or an OpenID URL, as shown in the following screenshot:

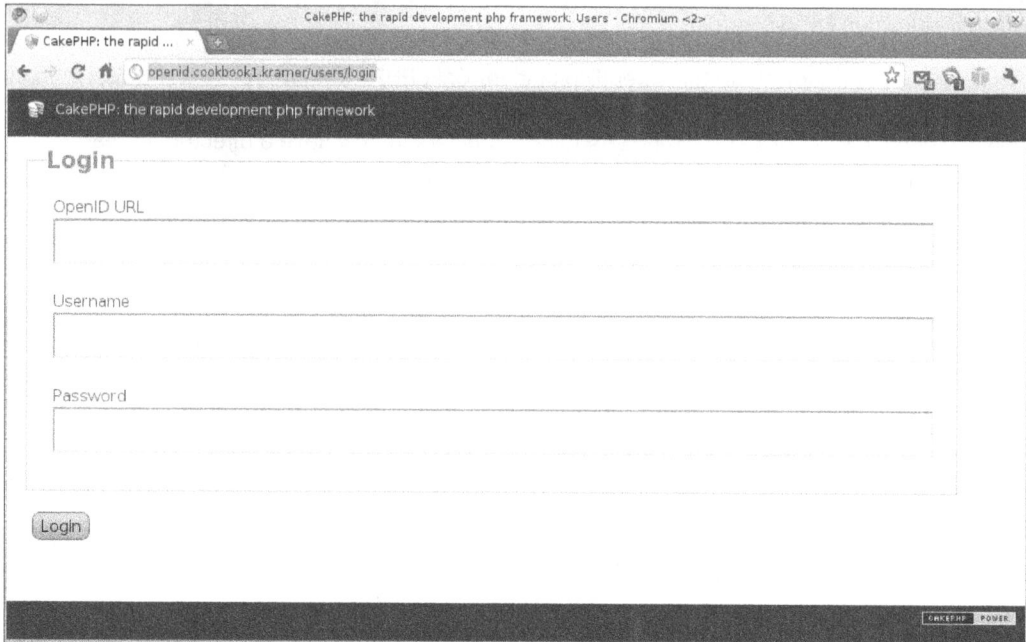

How it works...

As the `OpenAuth` component (a part of the `openid` plugin) extends the CakePHP built-in `Auth` component, it works in a similar fashion. When the component cannot seem to find a way to log in the user with a username and password, it will check whether the OpenID URL is specified.

If this is the case, it will attempt to authenticate the URL against the OpenID server. When it does, the user is taken to the OpenID server so the application can be granted permission to access the OpenID credentials. When permission is given, the user is taken back to the application, at a point on which the `OpenAuth` component is able to mark the user as logged in, and resume the normal application work flow.

There's more...

The `openid` plugin has further options to customize its behavior; including the ability to specify which user information should be given back. Check the documentation in `http://github.com/mariano/openid`.

Being a standard `Auth` implementation, this integration can be combined with any of the other recipes we have seen in this chapter, which allows for a flexible open authentication solution. If you do, make sure to note that the user given back by the `OpenAuth` component does not contain a valid user record, so you should create one upon log in.

Even when you are using the `OpenAuth` component which clearly has a different name than `Auth`, you can still use `$this->Auth` to set properties or call, for example, the `allow` method. This is possible because the component creates an alias.

See also

▶   *Getting the current user's information.*

2
Model Bindings

In this chapter, we will cover:

- Adding `Containable` to all models
- Limiting the bindings returned in a find
- Modifying binding parameters for a find
- Modifying binding conditions for a find
- Changing the JOIN type of one-to-one associations
- Defining multiple associations to the same model
- Adding bindings on the fly

Introduction

This chapter deals with one of the most important aspects of a CakePHP application: the relationship between models, also known as **model bindings** or **associations**.

Being an integral part of any application's logic, it is of crucial importance that we master all aspects of how model bindings can be manipulated to get the data we need, when we need it.

In order to do so, we will go through a series of recipes that will show us how to change the way bindings are fetched, what bindings and what information from a binding is returned, how to create new bindings, and how to build hierarchical data structures.

Adding Containable to all models

The `Containable` behavior is a part of the CakePHP core, and is probably one of the most important behaviors we have to help us deal with model bindings.

Almost all CakePHP applications will benefit from its functionalities, so in this recipe we see how to enable it for all models.

How to do it...

Create a file named `app_model.php` and place it in your `app/` folder, with the following contents. If you already have one, make sure that either you add the `actsAs` property shown as follows, or that your `actsAs` property includes `Containable`.

```php
<?php
class AppModel extends Model {
    public $actsAs = array('Containable');
}
?>
```

How it works...

The `Containable` behavior is nothing more and nothing less than a wrapper around the `bindModel()` and `unbindModel()` methods, defined in the CakePHP's `Model` class. It is there to help us deal with the management of associations without having to go through a lengthy process of redefining all the associations when calling one of these methods, thus making our code much more readable and maintainable.

This is a very important point, because a common mistake CakePHP users make is to think that `Containable` is involved in the query-making process, that is, during the stage where CakePHP creates actual SQL queries to fetch data.

`Containable` saves us some unneeded queries, and optimizes the information that is fetched for each related model, but it will not serve as a way to change how queries are built in CakePHP.

See also

- *Limiting the bindings returned in a find*
- *Modifying binding parameters for a find*
- *Modifying binding conditions for a find*

Limiting the bindings returned in a find

This recipe shows how to use `Containable` to specify what related models are returned as a result of a `find` operation. It also shows us how to limit which fields are obtained for each association.

Getting ready

To go through this recipe we need some sample tables to work with.

1. Create a table named `families`, using the following SQL statement:

```
CREATE TABLE `families`(
        `id` INT UNSIGNED AUTO_INCREMENT NOT NULL,
        `name` VARCHAR(255) NOT NULL,
        PRIMARY KEY(`id`)
);
```

2. Create a table named `people`, using the following SQL statement:

```
CREATE TABLE `people`(
        `id` INT UNSIGNED AUTO_INCREMENT NOT NULL,
        `family_id` INT UNSIGNED NOT NULL,
        `name` VARCHAR(255) NOT NULL,
        `email` VARCHAR(255) NOT NULL,
        PRIMARY KEY(`id`),
        KEY `family_id`(`family_id`),
        CONSTRAINT `people__families` FOREIGN KEY(`family_id`)
REFERENCES `families`(`id`)
);
```

3. Create a table named `profiles`, using the following SQL statement:

```
CREATE TABLE `profiles`(
        `id` INT UNSIGNED AUTO_INCREMENT NOT NULL,
        `person_id` INT UNSIGNED NOT NULL,
        `website` VARCHAR(255) default NULL,
        `birthdate` DATE default NULL,
        PRIMARY KEY(`id`),
        KEY `person_id`(`person_id`),
        CONSTRAINT `profiles__people` FOREIGN KEY(`person_id`)
REFERENCES `people`(`id`)
);
```

4. Create a table named `posts`, using the following SQL statement:

```
CREATE TABLE `posts`(
        `id` INT UNSIGNED AUTO_INCREMENT NOT NULL,
        `person_id` INT UNSIGNED NOT NULL,
        `title` VARCHAR(255) NOT NULL,
        `body` TEXT NOT NULL,
        `created` DATETIME NOT NULL,
        `modified` DATETIME NOT NULL,
        PRIMARY KEY(`id`),
        KEY `person_id`(`person_id`),
        CONSTRAINT `posts__people` FOREIGN KEY(`person_id`)
REFERENCES `people`(`id`)
);
```

> Even if you do not want to add foreign key constraints to your tables, make sure you use KEYs for each field that is a reference to a record in another table. By doing so, you will significantly improve the speed of your SQL queries when the referenced tables are joined.

5. Add some sample data, using the following SQL statements:

```
INSERT INTO `families`(`id`, `name`) VALUES
        (1, 'The Does');
```

```
INSERT INTO `people`(`id`, `family_id`, `name`, `email`) VALUES
        (1, 1, 'John Doe', 'john.doe@example.com'),
        (2, 1, 'Jane Doe', 'jane.doe@example.com');
```

```
INSERT INTO `profiles`(`person_id`, `website`, `birthdate`) VALUES
        (1, 'http://john.example.com', '1978-07-13'),
        (2, NULL, '1981-09-18');
```

```
INSERT INTO `posts`(`person_id`, `title`, `body`, `created`,
`modified`) VALUES
        (1, 'John\'s Post 1', 'Body for John\'s Post 1', NOW(),
NOW()),
        (1, 'John\'s Post 2', 'Body for John\'s Post 2', NOW(),
NOW());
```

6. We need `Containable` added to all our models, so follow the recipe *Adding Containable to all models*.

7. We proceed now to create the main model. Create a file named `person.php` and place it in your `app/models` folder with the following contents:

```php
<?php
class Person extends AppModel {
        public $belongsTo = array('Family');
```

```
        public $hasOne = array('Profile');
        public $hasMany = array('Post');
}
?>
```

8. Create the model `Family` in a file named `family.php` and place it in your `app/models` folder with the following contents:

```
<?php
class Family extends AppModel {
        public $hasMany = array('Person');
}
?>
```

How to do it...

When `Containable` is available for our models, we can add a setting to the `find` operation called `contain`. In that setting we specify, in an array-based hierarchy, the associated data we want returned. A special value `contain` can receive is `false`, or an empty array, which tells `Containable` not to return any associated data.

For example, to get the first `Person` record without associated data, we simply do:

```
$person = $this->Person->find('first', array(
    'contain' => false
));
```

> Another way to tell CakePHP not to obtain related data is through the use of the `recursive` find setting. Setting `recursive` to `-1` will have exactly the same effect as setting `contain` to `false`.

If we want to obtain the first `Person` record together with the `Family` they belong to, we do:

```
$person = $this->Person->find('first', array(
    'contain' => array('Family')
));
```

Using our sample data, the above query will result in the following array structure:

```
array(
    'Person' => array(
            'id' => '1',
            'family_id' => '1',
            'name' => 'John Doe',
            'email' => 'john.doe@example.com'
```

```
    ),
    'Family' => array(
            'id' => '1',
            'name' => 'The Does'
    )
)
```

Let's say that now we also want to obtain all `Post` records for the person and all members in the family that `Person` belongs to. We would then have to do:

```
$person = $this->Person->find('first', array(
    'contain' => array(
            'Family.Person'
            'Post'
    )
));
```

The above would result in the following array structure (the `created` and `modified` fields have been removed for readability):

```
array(
    'Person' => array(
            'id' => '1',
            'family_id' => '1',
            'name' => 'John Doe',
            'email' => 'john.doe@example.com'
    ),
    'Family' => array(
            'id' => '1',
            'name' => 'The Does',
            'Person' => array(
                    array(
                            'id' => '1',
                            'family_id' => '1',
                            'name' => 'John Doe',
                            'email' => 'john.doe@example.com'
                    ),
                    array(
                            'id' => '2',
                            'family_id' => '1',
                            'name' => 'Jane Doe',
                            'email' => 'jane.doe@example.com'
                    )
            )
    ),
    'Post' => array(
```

```
       array(
              'id' => '1',
              'person_id' => '1',
              'title' => 'John\'s Post 1',
              'body' => 'Body for John\'s Post 1'
       ),
       array(
              'id' => '2',
              'person_id' => '1',
              'title' => 'John\'s Post 2',
              'body' => 'Body for John\'s Post 2'

       )
   )
)
```

We can also use `Containable` to specify which fields from a related model we want to fetch. Using the preceding sample, let's limit the `Post` fields so we only return the `title` and the `Person` records for the person's `Family`, so we only return the `name` field. We do so by adding the name of the field to the associated model hierarchy:

```
$person = $this->Person->find('first', array(
    'contain' => array(
           'Family.Person.name',
           'Post.title'
    )
));
```

The returned data structure will then look like this:

```
array(
    'Person' => array(
           'id' => '1',
           'family_id' => '1',
           'name' => 'John Doe',
           'email' => 'john.doe@example.com'
    ),
    'Family' => array(
           'id' => '1',
           'name' => 'The Does',
           'Person' => array(
                  array(
                         'name' => 'John Doe',
                         'family_id' => '1',
                         'id' => '1'
                  ),
                  array(
```

```
                                'name' => 'Jane Doe',
                                'family_id' => '1',
                                'id' => '2'
                        )
                )
        ),
        'Post' => array(
                array(
                        'title' => 'John\'s Post 1',
                        'id' => '1',
                        'person_id' => '1'
                ),
                array(
                        'title' => 'John\'s Post 2',
                        'id' => '2',
                        'person_id' => '1'
                )
        )
)
```

You may notice that even when we indicated specific fields for the `Family => Person` binding, and for the `Post` binding, there are some extra fields being returned. Those fields (such as `family_id`) are needed by CakePHP, and known as foreign key fields, to fetch the associated data, so `Containable` is smart enough to include them in the query.

Let us say that we also want a person's e-mail. As there is more than a field needed, we will need to use the array notation, using the `fields` setting to specify the list of fields:

```
$person = $this->Person->find('first', array(
    'contain' => array(
            'Family' => array(
                    'Person' => array(
                            'fields' => array('email', 'name')
                    )
            ),
            'Post.title'
    )
));
```

How it works...

We use the `contain` find setting to specify what type of containment we want to use for the find operation. That containment is given as an array, where the array hierarchy mimics that of the model relationships. As the hierarchy can get deep enough to make array notation complex to deal with, the dot notation used throughout this recipe serves as an useful and more readable alternative.

If we want to refer to the model `Person` that belongs to the model `Family`, the proper `contain` syntax for that is `Person => Family` (we can also use `Person.Family`, which is more concise.)

We also use the `fields` setting to specify which fields we want fetched for a binding. We do that by specifying an array of field names as part of the binding `Containable` setting.

`Containable` looks for the `contain` find setting right before we issue a find operation on a model. If it finds one, it alters the model bindings to be returned by issuing `unbindModel()` calls on the appropriate models to unbind those relationships that are not specified in the `contain` find setting. It then sets the `recursive` find setting to the minimum value required to fetch the associated data.

Let us use a practical example to further understand this wrapping process. Using our `Person` model (which has a `belongsTo` relationship to `Family`, a `hasOne` relationship to `Profile`, and a `hasMany` relationship to `Post`), the following `Containable` based query:

```
$person = $this->Person->find('first', array(
    'contain' => array('Family.Person')
));
```

or the same query using array notation:

```
$person = $this->Person->find('first', array(
    'contain' => array('Family' => 'Person')
));
```

is equivalent to the following set of instructions, which do not use `Containable`, but the built in `unbindModel()` method available in CakePHP's `Model` class:

```
$this->Person->unbindModel(array(
    'hasOne' => array('Profile'),
    'hasMany' => array('Post')
));
$person = $this->Person->find('first', array(
    'recursive' => 2
));
```

Not using `Containable` is not only much more complicated, but can also pose a problem if we decide to alter some of our relationships. In the preceding example, if we decide to remove the `Profile` binding, or change its relationship type, we would have to modify the `unbindModel()` call. However, if we are using `Containable`, the same code applies, without us having to worry about such changes.

Format of the contain find parameter

We have seen how to use the `contain` find parameter to limit which bindings are returned after a `find` operation. Even when its format seems self-explanatory, let us go through another example to have a deeper understanding of `Containable`'s array notation. Assume that we have the models and relationships shown in the following diagram:

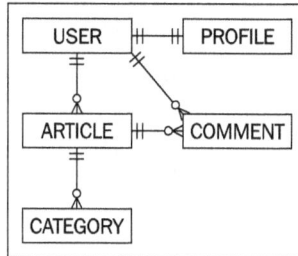

Transforming that diagram to something the `Containable` behavior understands is as simple as writing it using an array structure. For example, if we are issuing a `find` operation on the `User` model and we want to refer to the `Profile` relationship, a simple `array('Profile')` expression would suffice, as the `Profile` model is directly related to the `User` model.

If we want to refer to the `Comment` relationship for the `Article` records the `User` is an owner of, which belongs to an `Article` that itself belongs to our `User` model, then we add another dimension to the structure, which is now represented as `array('Article' => 'Comment')`.

We can already deduce how the next example will look like. Assume we want to obtain the `Comment` together with the `Profile` of the `User` that commented on each `Article`. The structure will then look like: `array('Article' => array('Comment' => array('User' => 'Profile')))`.

Sometimes we want to simplify the readability, and fortunately the `Containable` behavior allows the above expression to be rewritten as `array('Article.Comment.User.Profile')`, which is known as dot notation. However, if you want to change other parameters to the binding, then this syntax would have to be changed to the full array-based expression (see section *See also* in this recipe).

Reset of binding changes

When you issue a find operation that uses the `Containable` behavior to change some of its bindings, CakePHP will reset all bindings' changes to their original states, once the find is completed. This is what is normally wanted on most cases, but there are some scenarios where you want to keep your changes until you manually reset them, such as when you need to issue more than one find operation and have all those finds use the modified bindings.

To force our binding changes to be kept, we use the `reset` option in the `contain` find parameter, setting it to `false`. When we are ready to reset them, we issue a call to the `resetBindings()` method added by the `Containable` behavior to our model. The following sample code shows this procedure:

```
$person = $this->Person->find('first', array(
    'contain' => array(
            'reset' => false,
            'Family'
    )
));
// ...
$this->Person->resetBindings();
```

Another way to achieve the same result is by calling the `contain()` method (setting its first argument to the contained bindings, and its second argument to `false` to indicate that we wish to keep these containments), available to all models that use `Containable`, issue the find (without, need to use the `contain` setting), and then reset the bindings:

```
$this->Person->contain(array('Family'), false);
$person = $this->Person->find('first');

// ...
$this->Person->resetBindings();
```

See also

▶ *Modifying binding parameters for a find*
▶ *Modifying binding conditions for a find*

Modifying binding parameters for a find

This recipe shows how to use `Containable` to change some of the parameters that affect model bindings.

Getting ready

To go through this recipe, we need some sample tables to work with.

1. Create a table named `users`, using the following SQL statement:

```
CREATE TABLE `users`(
        `id` INT UNSIGNED AUTO_INCREMENT NOT NULL,
        `name` VARCHAR(255) NOT NULL,
        `email` VARCHAR(255) NOT NULL,
        PRIMARY KEY(`id`)
);
```

2. Create a table named `profiles`, using the following SQL statement:

```
CREATE TABLE `profiles`(
        `id` INT UNSIGNED AUTO_INCREMENT NOT NULL,
        `user_id` INT UNSIGNED NOT NULL,
        `website` VARCHAR(255) default NULL,
        `birthdate` DATE default NULL,
        PRIMARY KEY(`id`),
        KEY `user_id`(`user_id`),
        CONSTRAINT `profiles__users` FOREIGN KEY(`user_id`)
REFERENCES `users`(`id`)
);
```

3. Create a table named `articles`, using the following SQL statement:

```
CREATE TABLE `articles`(
        `id` INT UNSIGNED AUTO_INCREMENT NOT NULL,
        `user_id` INT UNSIGNED NOT NULL,
        `title` VARCHAR(255) NOT NULL,
        `body` TEXT NOT NULL,
        `published` TINYINT NOT NULL default 1,
        `created` DATETIME NOT NULL,
        `modified` DATETIME NOT NULL,
        PRIMARY KEY(`id`),
        KEY `user_id`(`user_id`),
        CONSTRAINT `articles__users` FOREIGN KEY(`user_id`)
REFERENCES `users`(`id`)
);
```

4. Add some sample data, using the following SQL statements:

```sql
INSERT INTO `users`(`id`, `name`, `email`) VALUES
        (1, 'John Doe', 'john.doe@example.com'),
        (2, 'Jane Doe', 'jane.doe@example.com');

INSERT INTO `profiles`(`user_id`, `website`, `birthdate`) VALUES
        (1, 'http://john.example.com', '1978-07-13'),
        (2, NULL, '1981-09-18');

INSERT INTO `articles`(`user_id`, `title`, `body`, `published`,
`created`, `modified`) VALUES
        (1, 'John\'s Post 1', 'Body for John\'s Post 1', 1, NOW(),
NOW()),
        (1, 'John\'s Post 2', 'Body for John\'s Post 2', 1, NOW(),
NOW()),
        (1, 'John\'s Post 3', 'Body for John\'s Post 3', 0, NOW(),
NOW()),
        (1, 'John\'s Post 4', 'Body for John\'s Post 4', 1, NOW(),
NOW()),
        (2, 'Jane\'s Post 1', 'Body for Jane\'s Post 1', 1, NOW(),
NOW());
```

5. Add the `Containable` behavior to all your models by following the recipe *Adding Containable to all models*.

6. Now we need to create the main model. Create a file named `user.php` and place it in your `app/models` folder with the following contents:

```php
<?php
class User extends AppModel {
        public $hasOne = array('Profile');
        public $hasMany = array('Article');
}
?>
```

How to do it...

If we want to obtain the first `User` record together with the `Article` records that the `User` owns, but ordered by latest articles first, we use the `order` binding setting (we also use the `fields` setting to limit the fields returned for each `Article`):

```php
$user = $this->User->find('first', array(
    'contain' => array(
        'Article' => array(
            'fields' => array('Article.title'),
            'order' => array(
```

```
                        'Article.created' => 'desc',
                        'Article.id' => 'desc'
                )
        )
    )
));
```

Using our sample data, the above query will result in the following array structure:

```
array(
    'User' => array(
            'id' => '1',
            'name' => 'John Doe',
            'email' => 'john.doe@example.com',
    ),
    'Article' => array(
            array(
                    'title' => 'John\'s Post 4',
                    'user_id' => '1'
            ),
            array(
                    'title' => 'John\'s Post 3',
                    'user_id' => '1'
            ),
            array(
                    'title' => 'John\'s Post 2',
                    'user_id' => '1'
            ),
            array(
                    'title' => 'John\'s Post 1',
                    'user_id' => '1'
            )
    )
)
```

If we want to get the same data, but make sure we only obtain the latest `Article` a `User` has written, we use the `limit` binding setting:

```
$user = $this->User->find('first', array(
    'contain' => array(
            'Article' => array(
                    'fields' => array('Article.title'),
                    'order' => array(
                            'Article.created' => 'desc',
                            'Article.id' => 'desc'
```

```
        ),
        'limit' => 1
      )
    )
));
```

Using our sample data, the above query will result in the following array structure:

```
array(
    'User' => array(
        'id' => '1',
        'name' => 'John Doe',
        'email' => 'john.doe@example.com',
    ),
    'Article' => array(
        array(
            'title' => 'John\'s Post 4',
            'user_id' => '1'
        )
    )
)
```

Another option that is useful on some scenarios is `offset`, applicable to the `hasMany` and `hasAndBelongsToMany` bindings. Using the example above, we now want to obtain the two most recent articles a `User` created, after the latest `Article`.

```
$user = $this->User->find('first', array(
    'contain' => array(
        'Article' => array(
            'fields' => array('Article.title'),
            'order' => array(
                'Article.created' => 'desc',
                'Article.id' => 'desc'
            ),
            'limit' => 2,
            'offset' => 1
        )
    )
));
```

The returned data structure now looks like this:

```
array(
    'User' => array(
        'id' => '1',
        'name' => 'John Doe',
```

```
                   'email' => 'john.doe@example.com',
           ),
           'Article' => array(
                   array(
                           'title' => 'John\'s Post 3',
                           'user_id' => '1'
                   ),
                   array(
                           'title' => 'John\'s Post 2',
                           'user_id' => '1'
                   )
           )
    )
```

How it works...

The `Containable` behavior uses the built-in `bindModel()` method defined in CakePHP's `Model` class to alter the binding settings defined in the `contain` find setting.

It goes through the defined bindings and checks to see whether there are defined binding settings. If there are, it passes them to the `bindModel()` method for each of the specified bindings.

Some binding settings make sense only on some relationship types. For example, the `limit` setting used previously would not be useful on `belongsTo` or `hasOne` relationships.

The following list includes which settings can be specified for each relationship type:

- belongsTo: `className, conditions, foreignKey, order`.
- hasOne: `className, conditions, foreignKey, order`.
- hasMany: `className, conditions, finderQuery, foreignKey, limit, offset, order`.
- hasAndBelongsToMany: `associationForeignKey, className, conditions, deleteQuery, finderQuery, foreignKey, insertQuery, joinTable, limit, offset, order, unique, with`.

See also

- *Modifying binding conditions for a find*

Modifying binding conditions for a find

This recipe shows how to use `Containable` to change the conditions used to fetch data related to a model through a binding.

Getting ready

We need to have `Containable` added to our models, and we also need some sample models and data to work with. Follow the recipe, *Adding Containable to all models*, and the *Getting ready* section of the recipe, *Modifying binding parameters for a find*.

How to do it...

If we want to obtain the first `User` record together with the published `Article` records that user owns, but ordered by latest articles first, and limiting some of the returned fields, we use the `conditions` binding setting:

```
$user = $this->User->find('first', array(
    'contain' => array(
            'Article' => array(
                    'fields' => array('Article.title'),
                    'conditions' => array(
                            'Article.published' => 1
                    )
            )
    )
));
```

Using our sample data, the preceding query will result in the following array structure:

```
array(
    'User' => array(
            'id' => '1',
            'name' => 'John Doe',
            'email' => 'john.doe@example.com',
    ),
    'Article' => array(
            array(
                    'title' => 'John\'s Post 1',
                    'user_id' => '1'
            ),
            array(
                    'title' => 'John\'s Post 2',
                    'user_id' => '1'
            ),
```

```
        array(
                'title' => 'John\'s Post 4',
                'user_id' => '1'
        )
    )
)
```

How it works...

The conditions binding setting is another binding parameter, such as those shown in the recipe, *Modifying binding parameters for a find*. As such, the `Containable` behavior uses the built-in `bindModel()` method defined in CakePHP's `Model` class to alter the binding conditions defined in the `contain` find operation.

Changing the JOIN type of one-to-one associations

When we are querying a model that has other associated models, CakePHP will issue a new query to fetch the associated data, or use a `LEFT JOIN` SQL statement if the associated model has a one-to-one relationship with the main model (through a binding defined with `belongsTo` or `hasOne`.)

However there are times where we need to change the join type for one-to-one associations, to use either a `RIGHT JOIN` or an `INNER JOIN`. This recipe shows us how to change the join type for `belongsTo` and `hasOne` associations.

Getting ready

Follow the *Getting ready* section of the recipe, *Limiting the bindings returned in a find*.

How to do it...

1. Edit the `Person` model, and change the binding definitions for `belongsTo` and `hasOne` associations, as shown below:

```php
<?php
class Person extends AppModel {
        public $belongsTo = array('Family' => array('type' =>
'INNER'));
        public $hasOne = array('Profile' => array('type' =>
'RIGHT'));
        public $hasMany = array('Post');
}
?>
```

How it works...

When we add bindings to a model, we can pass an array of settings to the binding definition to configure different aspects of the binding. One of those settings is `type`, only applicable to `belongsTo` and `hasOne` bindings.

The `type` setting allows us to define what type of `JOIN` CakePHP will use when fetching the associated model (only when querying the main model.) The available `JOIN` types are:

- ► `INNER JOIN`: Joins and only returns records from associated models that match the default join condition. When a binding is set to use this join type, only records that have a record for the binding will be returned. In the example above, only `Person` records that belong to a `Family` will be returned.

- ► `LEFT JOIN`: This is the default join type used by CakePHP. All records are returned even if there is no record for the binding. In the example above, if the `Family` binding type is set to `LEFT`, then `Person` records will be returned even if they don't belong to a `Family`.

- ► `RIGHT JOIN`: The opposite of `LEFT JOIN`, shows all records from the related model even if they are not related to the main model, and shows only records in the main model that are linked to the related model.

Defining multiple associations to the same model

This recipe shows how to set up more than one association from one model to the same model, a need that normally arises on most applications.

Getting ready

To go through this recipe we need some sample tables to work with.

1. Create a table named `addresses`, using the following SQL statement:

```
CREATE TABLE `addresses`(
        `id` INT UNSIGNED AUTO_INCREMENT NOT NULL,
        `address` TEXT NOT NULL,
        `city` VARCHAR(255) default NULL,
        `state` VARCHAR(255) NOT NULL,
        `zip` VARCHAR(10) NOT NULL,
        `country` CHAR(3) NOT NULL,
        PRIMARY KEY (`id`)
);
```

2. Create a table named `users`, using the following SQL statement:

```
CREATE TABLE `users`(
        `id` INT UNSIGNED AUTO_INCREMENT NOT NULL,
        `billing_address_id` INT UNSIGNED default NULL,
        `home_address_id` INT UNSIGNED default NULL,
        `name` VARCHAR(255) NOT NULL,
        `email` VARCHAR(255) NOT NULL,
        PRIMARY KEY(`id`),
        KEY `billing_address_id`(`billing_address_id`),
        KEY `home_address_id`(`home_address_id`),
        CONSTRAINT `addresses__billing_address_id` FOREIGN
KEY(`billing_address_id`) REFERENCES `addresses`(`id`),
        CONSTRAINT `addresses__home_address_id` FOREIGN KEY(`home_
address_id`) REFERENCES `addresses`(`id`)
);
```

3. Add some sample data, using the following SQL statements:

```
INSERT INTO `addresses`(`id`, `address`, `city`, `state`, `zip`,
`country`) VALUES
        (1, '123 Street', 'Palo Alto', 'CA', '94310', 'USA'),
        (2, '123 Street', 'London', 'London', 'SE10AA', 'GBR');

INSERT INTO `users`(`billing_address_id`, `home_address_id`,
`name`, `email`) VALUES
        (1, 2, 'John Doe', 'john.doe@example.com');
```

4. Now we need to create the main model. Create a file named `user.php` and place it in your `app/models` folder with the following contents:

```php
<?php
class User extends AppModel {
}
?>
```

How to do it...

Edit the `User` model, and add the binding definitions to include both references to the `Address` model:

```php
<?php
class User extends AppModel {
    public $belongsTo = array(
        'BillingAddress' => array(
                'className' => 'Address'
        ),
        'HomeAddress' => array(
```

```
                        'className' => 'Address'
                )
        );
    }
?>
```

If we issue a find operation to fetch the `User`, we would obtain the following data structure:

```
array(
    'User' => array(
            'id' => '1',
            'billing_address_id' => '1',
            'home_address_id' => '2',
            'name' => 'John Doe',
            'email' => 'john.doe@example.com',
    ),
    'BillingAddress' => array(
            'id' => '1',
            'address' => '123 Street',
            'city' => 'Palo Alto',
            'state' => 'CA',
            'zip' => '94310',
            'country' => 'USA'
    ),
    'HomeAddress' => array(
            'id' => '2',
            'address' => '123 Street',
            'city' => 'London',
            'state' => 'London',
            'zip' => 'SE10AA',
            'country' => 'GBR'
    )
)
```

There's more...

In this example, the naming convention we used for the bindings is the standard CakePHP uses for field names, where each uppercase letter is prefixed by an underscore sign, everything is converted to lowercase, and the suffix `_id` is added. Thus, the standard field name the binding named `BillingAddress` is `billing_address_id`.

However there are times where we need to use a field name that does not comply with this standard. In that case, we can use the `foreignKey` binding setting to specify the field name. For example, we could change the `User` model definition so the name of the `HomeAddress` becomes `Address`, which would make the `User` model look like this:

```php
<?php
class User extends AppModel {
    public $belongsTo = array(
            'BillingAddress' => array(
                    'className' => 'Address'
            ),
            'Address' => array(
                    'className' => 'Address',
                    'foreignKey' => 'home_address_id'
            )
    );
}
?>
```

> When we use different aliases to refer to the same model, certain model callback implementations, such as `beforeSave`, will need to be changed to avoid using the name of the model directly, and instead use the property `alias`, available in all models. More information about this can be obtained from Nick Baker's article available at `http://www.webtechnick.com/blogs/view/230/The_Power_of_CakePHP_aliases`.

Adding bindings on the fly

This recipe shows how to set up new bindings right before a find operation, including bindings that are automatically removed after the operation is executed, and bindings that are permanently added.

Getting ready

We need some sample models and data to work with. Follow the *Getting ready* section of the recipe, *Modifying binding parameters for a find*.

How to do it...

If we want to obtain the latest published `Article` when we are fetching a `User`, we could add a permanent binding to the `User` model. However, if we want to do this on a need-by-need basis, it is smarter to add the binding before the find operation that needs it, thus avoiding the unneeded overhead for other operations.

We can add the needed binding and then issue the `find` operation:

```
$this->User->bindModel(array(
    'hasOne' => array(
        'LastArticle' => array(
            'className' => 'Article',
            'conditions' => array(
                'LastArticle.published' => 1
            ),
            'order' => array(
                'LastArticle.created' => 'desc',
                'LastArticle.id' => 'desc'
            )
        )
    )
));
$user = $this->User->find('first', array(
    'conditions' => array(
        'User.id' => 1
    ),
    'contain' => array(
        'LastArticle' => array('fields' => array('title'))
    )
));
```

The preceding code would give us the following data structure:

```
array(
    'User' => array(
        'id' => '1',
        'name' => 'John Doe',
        'email' => 'john.doe@example.com',
    ),
    'LastArticle' => array(
        'title' => 'John\'s Post 4'
    )
)
```

If we want to make the binding permanent until the request ends, but without adding the binding to the User model, we simply add the value false as a second parameter to the bindModel() call (this is needed if the operation is a paginate () call, as this call will issue two find operations):

```
$this->User->bindModel(array(
    'hasOne' => array(
        'LastArticle' => array(
            'className' => 'Article',
            'conditions' => array(
                'LastArticle.published' => 1
            ),
            'order' => array(
                'LastArticle.created' => 'desc',
                'LastArticle.id' => 'desc'
            )
        )
    )
), false);
```

How it works...

When you issue a bindModel() call, CakePHP will add the binding as if you specified it on the model itself. If you did not set the second parameter to the method as false, that binding will be automatically removed after the find operation is completed. If you did set it in order to avoid the reset, then it will be kept until the script instance of your application is finished.

The format to specify bindings through bindModel() is an array, indexed by the binding type (one of belongsTo, hasOne, hasMany, and hasAndBelongsToMany), whose value for each binding type is an array of associations.

You define each association (as you would normally do) in the model, indexing it by association name (if it is different than the model's name it is pointing to or if you have binding parameters to define), or, optionally, simply referring to the related model.

3
Pushing the Search

In this chapter, we will cover:

- ▶ Performing GROUP and COUNT queries
- ▶ Using virtual fields
- ▶ Building queries with ad-hoc JOINs
- ▶ Searching for all items that match search terms
- ▶ Implementing a custom find type
- ▶ Paginating a custom find type
- ▶ Implementing AJAX-based pagination

Introduction

Using models to fetch data is one of the most important aspects of any CakePHP application. As such, a good use of the find functions the framework provides can certainly guarantee the success of our application, and as importantly ensure that our code is readable and maintainable.

CakePHP provides the following basic find types:

- ▶ `all`: To find all records that match the given find options.
- ▶ `count`: To count how many records match the given options.
- ▶ `first`: To find the first record that matches the given find options.
- ▶ `list`: To find all records that match the given find options, and formats them as a list, using the format provided.

- ▶ `neighbors`: To find the previous and after records of a matching record, based on the value of a particular field.

- ▶ `threaded`: To finds a set of results, and return them in a hierarchy, based on the value of a field named `parent_id`.

Mastering these types is as easy as understanding the available find options all types deal with. In this chapter, we have several recipes to make the most out of these options, and to resort to manual SQL based queries when the need arises.

CakePHP also lets us define our custom find types that will extend the three basic ones, allowing our code to be even more readable. The last recipes in this chapter show us how to create our own find type, with pagination support.

Performing GROUP and COUNT queries

This recipe shows how to use CakePHP's built-in find types to perform relatively complex GROUP and COUNT queries, including the combination of both.

Getting ready

To go through this recipe we need some sample tables to work with.

1. Create a table named `users`, using the following SQL statement:

```
CREATE TABLE `users`(
        `id` INT UNSIGNED AUTO_INCREMENT NOT NULL,
        `name` VARCHAR(255) NOT NULL,
        `email` VARCHAR(255) NOT NULL,
        PRIMARY KEY(`id`)
);
```

2. Create a table named `blogs`, using the following SQL statement:

```
CREATE TABLE `blogs`(
        `id` INT UNSIGNED AUTO_INCREMENT NOT NULL,
        `user_id` INT UNSIGNED NOT NULL,
        `name` VARCHAR(255) NOT NULL,
        PRIMARY KEY(`id`),
        KEY `user_id`(`user_id`),
        CONSTRAINT `blogs__users` FOREIGN KEY(`user_id`) REFERENCES `users`(`id`)
);
```

3. Create a table named `posts`, using the following SQL statement:

```
CREATE TABLE `posts`(
        `id` INT UNSIGNED AUTO_INCREMENT NOT NULL,
        `blog_id` INT UNSIGNED NOT NULL,
        `title` VARCHAR(255) NOT NULL,
        `body` TEXT NOT NULL,
        `created` DATETIME NOT NULL,
        `modified` DATETIME NOT NULL,
        PRIMARY KEY(`id`),
        KEY `blog_id`(`blog_id`),
        CONSTRAINT `posts_blogs` FOREIGN KEY(`blog_id`) REFERENCES
`blogs`(`id`)
);
```

4. Add some sample data, using the following SQL statements:

```
INSERT INTO `users`(`id`, `name`, `email`) VALUES
        (1, 'John Doe', 'john.doe@example.com'),
        (2, 'Jane Doe', 'jane.doe@example.com');

INSERT INTO `blogs`(`user_id`, `name`) VALUES
        (1, 'John Doe\'s Blog'),
        (2, 'Jane Doe\'s Blog');

INSERT INTO `posts`(`blog_id`, `title`, `body`, `created`,
`modified`) VALUES
        (1, 'John\'s Post 1', 'Body for John\'s Post 1', '2010-04-19
14:00:00', '2010-04-19 14:00:00'),
        (1, 'John\'s Post 2', 'Body for John\'s Post 2', '2010-04-19
14:30:00', '2010-04-19 14:30:00'),
        (1, 'John\'s Post 3', 'Body for John\'s Post 3', '2010-04-20
14:00:00', '2010-04-20 14:00:00'),
        (1, 'John\'s Post 4', 'Body for John\'s Post 4', '2010-05-03
14:00:00', '2010-05-03 14:00:00'),
        (2, 'Jane\'s Post 1', 'Body for Jane\'s Post 1', '2010-04-19
15:00:00', '2010-04-19 15:00:00'),
        (2, 'Jane\'s Post 2', 'Body for Jane\'s Post 2', '2010-06-18
15:00:00', '2010-06-18 15:00:00'),
        (2, 'Jane\'s Post 3', 'Body for Jane\'s Post 3', '2010-10-06
15:00:00', '2010-10-06 15:00:00');
```

5. We proceed now to create the required model. Create the model `Post` in a file named `post.php` and place it in your `app/models` folder with the following contents:

```
<?php
class Post extends AppModel {
```

```
            public $belongsTo = array('Blog');
    }
    ?>
```

6. We will put all our example code in the `index()` method of a controller. Create a file named `posts_controller.php` and place it in your `app/controllers` folder with the following contents:

```php
<?php
class PostsController extends AppController {
        public function index() {
                $this->set(compact('data'));
        }
}
?>
```

7. Now, create a folder named `posts` and place it in your `app/views` folder. Inside this newly created folder, create a file named `index.ctp`, with the following contents:

```php
<?php debug($data); ?>
```

How to do it...

Grouping rows by a certain field is as simple as specifying the group setting when issuing a `find` operation. For example, the following statement, while not exactly practical by itself, shows how to use the setting:

```php
$data = $this->Post->find('all', array(
    'group' => array('Blog.id')
));
```

If we also want to obtain the number of rows for each grouped set, which in our case means the number of posts per blog, we would do:

```php
$data = $this->Post->find('all', array(
    'fields' => array('COUNT(Post.id) AS total', 'Blog.*'),
    'group' => array('Blog.id')
));
```

The preceding query will return the following data structure:

```php
array(
    array(
            0 => array(
                    'total' => 4
            ),
            'Blog' => array(
```

```
                'id' => 1,
                'user_id' => 1,
                'name' => 'John Doe\'s Blog'
        )
    ),
    array(
            0 => array(
                'total' => 3
            ),
            'Blog' => array(
                'id' => 2,
                'user_id' => 2,
                'name' => 'Jane Doe\'s Blog'
            )
        )
    )
)
```

Let us now make sure that every time we have a calculated field (which come in the index 0 of each resulting row), they become part of the resulting model, for easier readability. To do so, we override the afterFind() method. If you don't have one already, create a file named app_model.php in your app/ folder. Make sure your AppModel class includes the following contents:

```php
<?php
class AppModel extends Model {
    public function afterFind($results, $primary = false) {
        if (!empty($results)) {
            foreach($results as $i => $row) {
                if (!empty($row[0])) {
                    foreach($row[0] as $field => $value) {
                        if (!empty($row[$this->alias][$field])) {
                            $field = 'total_' . $field;
                        }
                        $results[$i][$this->alias][$field] = $value;
                    }
                    unset($results[$i][0]);
                }
            }
        }
        return parent::afterFind($results, $primary);
    }
}
?>
```

> Whenever you override a model method, such as `beforeFind()` or `afterFind()`, make sure you call the parent implementation by using the `parent` keyword.

As a result, the previous query, which uses GROUP and COUNT, will now look like a much more readable result set:

```
array(
    array(
        'Blog' => array(
            'id' => 1,
            'user_id' => 1,
            'name' => 'John Doe\'s Blog'
        ),
        'Post' => array(
            'total' => 4
        )
    ),
    array(
        'Blog' => array(
            'id' => 2,
            'user_id' => 2,
            'name' => 'Jane Doe\'s Blog'
        ),
        'Post' => array(
            'total' => 3
        )
    )
)
```

If we want to subdivide the post counts for each blog according to the month they were created on, we would have to add another level of grouping:

```
$data = $this->Post->find('all', array(
    'fields' => array(
        'CONCAT(YEAR(Post.created), \'-\', MONTH(Post.created)) AS
period',
        'COUNT(Post.id) AS total',
        'Blog.*'
    ),
    'group' => array('Blog.id', 'period')
));
```

Considering our `afterFind` implementation, the preceding query would produce the following results:

```
array(
    array(
        'Blog' => array(
            'id' => 1,
            'user_id' => 1,
            'name' => 'John Doe\'s Blog'
        ),
        'Post' => array(
            'period' => '2010-4',
            'total' => 4
        )
    ),
    array(
        'Blog' => array(
            'id' => 1,
            'user_id' => 1,
            'name' => 'John Doe\'s Blog'
        ),
        'Post' => array(
            'period' => '2010-5',
            'total' => 1
        )
    ),
    array(
        'Blog' => array(
            'id' => 2,
            'user_id' => 2,
            'name' => 'Jane Doe\'s Blog'
        ),
        'Post' => array(
            'period' => '2010-10',
            'total' => 1
        )
    ),
    array(
        'Blog' => array(
            'id' => 2,
            'user_id' => 2,
            'name' => 'Jane Doe\'s Blog'
        ),
        'Post' => array(
```

```
                            'period' => '2010-4',
                            'total' => 1
                )
        )
        array(
                'Blog' => array(
                        'id' => 2,
                        'user_id' => 2,
                        'name' => 'Jane Doe\'s Blog'
                ),
                'Post' => array(
                        'period' => '2010-6',
                        'total' => 1
                )
        )
    )
```

How it works...

We use the `group` find setting to specify what fields will be used for grouping the resulting rows. That setting is given as an array, where each element is a field to group in. When we specify more than one field, such as the last example in the recipe, grouping of rows occurs in the given order of grouping fields.

Calculated fields, that is, expressions that result in a value (such as the `COUNT(*) AS total` expression used throughout the recipe) are placed in the index 0 of each resulting row, because they are not real fields defined in the model. Because of that, we overrode the `afterFind()` method, executed after a result for a find operation is obtained, and with some basic logic we make sure those calculated fields get included in the resulting row within a much more readable index: the model name.

The last example in the recipe shows not only how to group on more than one field, but how to properly use some SQL methods (such as `MONTH` and `YEAR`) with an alias, so we can easily return the value of that expression and also use it to group or optionally order the rows.

See also

▶   *Using virtual fields*

Using virtual fields

In the recipe, *Performing GROUP and COUNT queries,* we learnt how to add computed SQL expressions to a `find` operation. Some of these expressions may be needed regularly for a model, introducing the need for virtual fields.

Using virtual fields, we get the resulting values of our SQL expressions as if they were real fields of our models. They allow us to get the same results shown in the previous recipe in a much more transparent way, without needing the override of `afterFind`.

Getting ready

We need some sample models and data to work with. Follow the *Getting ready* section of the recipe, *Performing GROUP and COUNT queries.*

How to do it...

Open the `Post` model and add the `virtualfields` definition shown as follows:

```php
<?php
class Post extends AppModel {
    public $belongsTo = array('Blog');
    public $virtualFields = array(
            'period' => 'CONCAT(YEAR(Post.created), \'-\', MONTH(Post.
created))',
            'total' => 'COUNT(*)'
    );
}
?>
```

To obtain a count of all the posts per blog, grouped by the period they were created, we do:

```php
$data = $this->Post->find('all', array(
    'fields' => array(
            'period',
            'total',
            'Blog.*'
    ),
    'group' => array('Blog.id', 'period')
));
```

Using our sample data, the preceding query will result in the following array structure, which is exactly the same result as the one obtained in the last example shown in the recipe *Performing GROUP and COUNT queries*:

```
array(
    array(
            'Blog' => array(
                    'id' => 1,
                    'user_id' => 1,
                    'name' => 'John Doe\'s Blog'
            ),
            'Post' => array(
                    'period' => '2010-4',
                    'total' => 4
            )
    ),
    array(
            'Blog' => array(
                    'id' => 1,
                    'user_id' => 1,
                    'name' => 'John Doe\'s Blog'
            ),
            'Post' => array(
                    'period' => '2010-5',
                    'total' => 1
            )
    ),
    array(
            'Blog' => array(
                    'id' => 2,
                    'user_id' => 2,
                    'name' => 'Jane Doe\'s Blog'
            ),
            'Post' => array(
                    'period' => '2010-10',
                    'total' => 1
            )
    ),
    array(
            'Blog' => array(
                    'id' => 2,
                    'user_id' => 2,
```

```
                        'name' => 'Jane Doe\'s Blog'
                ),
                'Post' => array(
                        'period' => '2010-4',
                        'total' => 1
                )
        )
    array(
                'Blog' => array(
                        'id' => 2,
                        'user_id' => 2,
                        'name' => 'Jane Doe\'s Blog'
                ),
                'Post' => array(
                        'period' => '2010-6',
                        'total' => 1
                )
        )
    )
```

Virtual fields are always obtained when issuing a `find` operation on the model. The only real way to avoid including them is specifying a list of fields to obtain in the find, and omitting the virtual fields:

```
$data = $this->Post->find('all', array(
    'fields' => array_keys($this->Post->schema())
));
```

> The `schema()` model function returns the list of real fields in the model, with information about each field, such as data type, and length.

We will now add a way for us to manage which virtual fields, if any, are returned. To do so, we override the `beforeFind()` and `afterFind()` model methods. If you don't have one already, create a file named `app_model.php` in your `app/` folder. Make sure your `AppModel` class includes the following contents:

```
<?php
class AppModel extends Model {
    public function beforeFind($query) {
            if (!empty($this->virtualFields)) {
                    $virtualFields = isset($query['virtualFields']) ?
                            $query['virtualFields'] :
```

```
                        array_keys($this->virtualFields);
                if ($virtualFields !== true) {
                        $this->_backVirtualFields = $this-
        >virtualFields;

                        $this->virtualFields = !empty($virtualFields)
        ?
                                array_intersect_key($this-
        >virtualFields, array_flip((array) $virtualFields)) :
                                array();
                }
        }
        return parent::beforeFind($query);
    }

    public function afterFind($results, $primary = false) {
        if (!empty($this->_backVirtualFields)) {
                $this->virtualFields = $this->_backVirtualFields;
        }
        return parent::afterFind($results, $primary);
    }
}
?>
```

If we want to disable virtual fields when issuing a `find` operation, we can easily do so by specifying the `virtualFields` find setting to `false`. We can also set it to the list of virtual fields we want to include. For example, to only include the `period` virtual field, we do:

```
$person = $this->Post->find('all', array(
    'virtualFields' => array('period')
));
```

How it works...

CakePHP treats virtual fields almost as if they were real model fields. They are not exactly like real fields because we cannot specify a value for a virtual field when creating / editing a model record. However, in regards to `find` operations, they are treated like any other field.

Virtual fields are included on every `find` operation performed against the model to which they belong. However, there are times were we don't want or need certain virtual fields. This is particularly important when we include virtual fields that depend on grouping expressions, such as COUNT, as they affect the number of rows returned. In these cases, we want to be able to specify what, or even if, virtual fields should be returned.

To allow us to control virtual fields returned from a `find` operation, we add a new find setting by overriding the `beforeFind` and `afterFind` model callbacks. In the `beforeFind` callback, executed before a `find` operation is executed, we check for the existence of a `virtualFields` setting. If such setting is defined, we use its value to check if virtual fields should be returned or not.

Based on these setting values, we alter the real value of the model `virtualFields` property. We backup its original value, and then restore it after the `find` operation is completed, that is, in the `afterFind` callback.

See also

▶ *Performing GROUP and COUNT queries*

Building queries with ad-hoc JOINs

CakePHP has a very easy way to handle bindings, and through the use of the `Containable` behavior, as shown in several recipes in *Chapter 2, Model Bindings*, we have a lot of flexibility when dealing with bindings.

However, there are times where we need to fall outside of a normal find operation and perform queries that join several models, without using normal binding operations, to save us some valuable queries. In this recipe, we will see how to specify `JOIN` operations when performing a find on a model.

Getting ready

We need some sample models and data to work with. Follow the *Getting ready* section of the recipe, *Performing GROUP and COUNT queries*.

To illustrate the difference between normal binding operations and what is shown in this recipe, we need the `Containable` behavior. Create a file named `app_model.php` and place it in your `app/` folder, with the following contents. If you already have one, make sure that, either you add the `actsAs` property shown as follows, or your `actsAs` property includes `Containable`.

```php
<?php
class AppModel extends Model {
    public $actsAs = array('Containable');
}
?>
```

We also need the `Blog` model. Create a file named `blog.php` and place it in your `app/ models` folder with the following contents:

```php
<?php
class Blog extends AppModel {
    public $belongsTo = array('User');
}
?>
```

How to do it...

We want to obtain the first post with the `Blog` it belongs to, and the `User` information that owns the `Blog`. Using `Containable` (refer to the recipe *Limiting the bindings returned in a find* in *Chapter 2, Model Bindings* for more information), we do:

```php
$post = $this->Post->find('first', array(
    'contain' => array(
            'Blog' => array(
                    'fields' => array('name'),
                    'User' => array('fields' => array('name'))
            )
    )
));
```

This operation is performed by CakePHP using three SQL queries:

```sql
SELECT `Post`.`id`, `Post`.`blog_id`, `Post`.`title`, `Post`.`body`,
`Post`.`created`, `Post`.`modified`, `Blog`.`name`, `Blog`.`user_id`
FROM `posts` AS `Post` LEFT JOIN `blogs` AS `Blog` ON (`Post`.`blog_
id` = `Blog`.`id`) WHERE 1 = 1 LIMIT 1;

SELECT `Blog`.`name`, `Blog`.`user_id` FROM `blogs` AS `Blog` WHERE
`Blog`.`id` = 1;

SELECT `User`.`name` FROM `users` AS `User` WHERE `User`.`id` = 1;
```

We can save some of these queries if we JOIN the relevant tables into one single operation. We specify these JOIN statements using the appropriate join find setting:

```php
$post = $this->Post->find('first', array(
    'fields' => array(
            'Post.id',
            'Post.title',
            'Blog.name',
            'User.name'
    ),
    'joins' => array(
            array(
                    'type' => 'inner',
```

```
                    'alias' => 'Blog',
                    'table' => $this->Post->Blog->table,
                    'conditions' => array(
                            'Blog.id = Post.blog_id'
                    )
            ),
            array(
                    'type' => 'inner',
                    'alias' => 'User',
                    'table' => $this->Post->Blog->User->table,
                    'conditions' => array(
                            'User.id = Blog.user_id'
                    )
            )
    ),
    'recursive' => -1
));
```

The preceding statement will produce the following SQL query:

```
SELECT `Post`.`id`, `Post`.`blog_id`, `Post`.`title`, `Post`.`body`,
`Post`.`created`, `Post`.`modified` FROM `posts` AS `Post` inner JOIN
blogs AS `Blog` ON (`Blog`.`id` = `Post`.`blog_id`) inner JOIN users
AS `User` ON (`User`.`id` = `Blog`.`user_id`) WHERE 1 = 1 LIMIT 1
And would generate the following data structure:
array(
    'Post' => array(
            'id' => 1,
            'title' => 'John\'s Post 1'
    ),
    'Blog' => array(
            'name' => 'John Doe\'s Blog'
    ),
    'User' => array(
            'name' => 'John Doe'
    )
)
```

How it works...

The `joins` find setting allows us to define which `JOIN` statements to add to the generated SQL query. We have full control when defining the operation, being able to change the `type` (one of `left`, `right`, and `inner`), the `table` to which to join, the `alias` to use, and the `conditions` used when joining.

We used this setting to join the `Post` model with two models: `Blog`, by means of its table and required condition, and `User`, using its appropriate table and condition. As the `Post` model `belongsTo` the `Blog` model, CakePHP will automatically try to do a `LEFT JOIN` with it, unless we tell it not to.

We therefore set `recursive` to `-1`, forcing CakePHP to only use our defined `JOIN`. If the recursive statement is removed, we would have to choose a different `alias` for our `Blog` `JOIN` definition, as it would conflict with CakePHP's built-in binding.

See also

 ▶   *Adding Containable* in *Chapter 2, Model Bindings*

Searching for all items that match search terms

Finding records that match a set of search terms is almost a must-have on most web applications. Even when there is a good number of more in-depth, complex search solutions, sometimes a simple search is all we need.

This recipe shows how to implement a `LIKE`-based search to find records that match some terms.

Getting ready

We need some sample models and data to work with. Follow the *Getting ready* section of the recipe, *Performing GROUP and COUNT queries*.

How to do it...

If we want to find all posts that have the word `Post 1` or the word `Post 2`, either in its title, or post, we do:

```
$posts = $this->Post->find('all', array(
    'fields' => array('Post.id', 'Post.title'),
    'conditions' => array('or' => array(
```

```
            array('Post.title LIKE ?' => '%Post 1%'),
            array('Post.body LIKE ?' => '%Post 1%'),
            array('Post.title LIKE ?' => '%Post 2%'),
            array('Post.body LIKE ?' => '%Post 2%'),
        )),
        'recursive' => -1
    ));
```

The preceding statement will produce the following result:

```
array(
    'Post' => array(
            'id' => 1,
            'title' => 'John\'s Post 1'
    ),
    'Post' => array(
            'id' => 2,
            'title' => 'John\'s Post 2'
    ),
    'Post' => array(
            'id' => 5,
            'title' => 'Jane\'s Post 1'
    ),
    'Post' => array(
            'id' => 6,
            'title' => 'Jane\'s Post 2'
    )
)
```

How it works...

LIKE-based conditions are like any other model find condition, except that they are specified in a special form: they become part of the key of the condition and use the character ? to tell where the actual value will be inserted, the value being an actual LIKE expression. Therefore, the following condition:

```
array('Post.title LIKE ?' => '%term%')
```

will be evaluated to SQL like so:

```
`Post`.`title` LIKE '%term%'
```

As the LIKE expression is specified as an array index, it's important to note that we need to wrap each expression in an array of its own, avoiding the override of a previous expression. To illustrate this, let us add another condition for the Post.title field.

```
array(

    'Post.title LIKE ?' => '%term%',

    'Post.title LIKE ?' => '%anotherTerm%'

)
```

This would be translated to the following SQL expression:

```
`Post`.`title` LIKE '%anotherTerm%'
```

Naturally, the second index is overriding the first, because they are both the same. We therefore have to wrap both expressions in an array, to avoid overriding the already used indexes:

```
array(

    array('Post.title LIKE ?' => '%term%'),

    array('Post.title LIKE ?' => '%anotherTerm%')

)
```

which would be translated to the following SQL statement:

```
`Post`.`title` LIKE '%term%' OR `Post`.`title` LIKE '%anotherTerm%'
```

See also

▶   *Implementing a custom find type*

Implementing a custom find type

The recipe, *Searching for all items that match search terms*, gives us a great starting point to create a custom find type. Custom find types allow us to extend the basic find types any model has, allowing our code to become more readable and extensible.

This recipe shows how to create a custom find type to allow the Post model to be searched against a set of terms, thus extending the functionality shown in the previous recipe.

Getting ready

We need some sample models and data to work with. Follow the *Getting ready* section of the recipe, *Performing GROUP and COUNT queries*.

How to do it...

1. Open the `post.php` file and add the `search` find type to the list of find methods using the `_findMethods` property, together with the actual implementation of the `_findSearch()` method.

```php
<?php
class Post extends AppModel {
        public $belongsTo = array('Blog');
        public $_findMethods = array('search' => true);

        protected function _findSearch($state, $query, $results =
array()) {
                if ($state == 'before') {
                        if (!empty($query['terms'])) {
                                $fields = array('title', 'body');
                                $conditions = array();
                                foreach ((array) $query['terms'] as
$term) {
                                        foreach ($fields as $field) {
                                                $model = $this->alias;
                                                if (strpos($field, '.')
!== false) {
                                                        list($model, $field)
= explode('.', $field);
                                                }
                                                $conditions[] = array(
                                                        $model . '.' .
$field . ' LIKE ?' => '%'.$term.'%'
                                                );
                                        }
                                }
                                if (empty($query['fields'])) {
                                        $query['fields'] = array('Post.
title', 'Post.body');
                                }
                                $query['conditions'][] = array('or' =>
$conditions);
                        }
                        return array_diff_key($query,
array('terms'=>null));
                }
```

```
                    return $results;
        }
    }
?>
```

2. We can now use these custom find types by specifying the list of terms to search with using the `search` find setting:

```
$posts = $this->Post->find('search', array(
        'terms' => array(
                'Post 1',
                'Post 2'
        ),
        'recursive' => -1
));
```

3. If we now browse to `http://localhost/posts`, we get the `id` and `title` fields for four posts, as it is partially shown in the following screenshot:

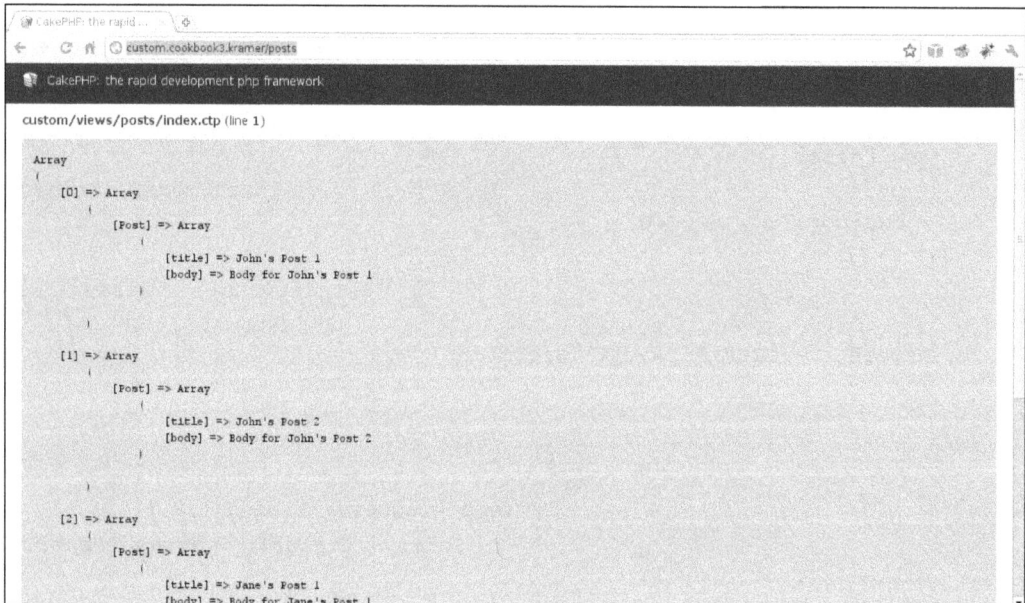

4. Let us now also allow the execution of count operations for custom find types. Because we want a generic solution, we will add this to `AppModel`. Open the file `app_model.php` in your `app/` folder (create it if you don't have one), and override the `find()` method as shown below:

```
<?php
class AppModel extends Model {
```

```
       public function find($conditions=null, $fields=array(),
$order=null, $recursive=null) {
              if (

                     is_string($conditions) && $conditions=='count'
&&
                     is_array($fields) && !empty($fields['type'])
&&
                     array_key_exists($fields['type'],$this->_
findMethods)
              ) {
                     $fields['operation'] = 'count';
                     return parent::find($fields['type'], array_
diff_key(
                            $fields,
                            array('type'=>null)
                     ));
              }

              return parent::find($conditions, $fields, $order,
$recursive);
       }
}
?>
```

5. Now edit your app/models/post.php file and make the following changes to the
   _findSearch() method:

```
protected function _findSearch($state, $query, $results = array())
{
       if ($state == 'before') {
              if (!empty($query['terms'])) {
                     $fields = array('title', 'body');
                     $conditions = array();
                     foreach ((array) $query['terms'] as $term) {
                            foreach ($fields as $field) {
                                   $model = $this->alias;
                                   if (strpos($field, '.') !==
false) {
                                          list($model, $field) =
explode('.', $field);
                                   }
                                   $conditions[] = array(
                                          $model . '.' . $field . '
LIKE ?' => '%'.$term.'%'
                                   );
```

```
                              }
                      }
                      if (empty($query['fields'])) {
                              $query['fields'] = array('Post.title',
'Post.body');
                      }
                      if (!empty($query['operation']) &&
$query['operation'] == 'count') {
                              $query['fields'] = 'COUNT(*) AS total';
                      }
                      $query['conditions'][] = array('or' =>
$conditions);
                  }
              return array_diff_key($query, array('terms'=>null));
          } elseif (
                  $state == 'after' &&
!empty($query['operation']) &&
                  $query['operation'] == 'count'
          ) {
              return (!empty($results[0][0]['total']) ? $results[0]
[0]['total'] : 0);
          }
      return $results;
}
```

6. If we wanted to obtain the number of posts that match a set of terms, we would do:

```
$count = $this->Post->find('count', array(
      'type' => 'search',
      'terms' => array(
              'Post 1',
              'Post 2'
      )
));
```

Which would correctly return 4.

How it works...

Custom find types are defined in the model `_findMethods` property. We add types by adding the name of the find type to the property as its index, and setting `true` as its value in the model that contains the find type.

The method responsible for dealing with the actual find type is named using the following syntax: `_findType()`, where `Type` is the find type name, with its first case in uppercase. For a find type of name popular, the method would be named `_findPopular()`.

Every find type method receives three arguments:

- ▶ `state`: The state at which the `find` operation is currently on. This can be `before` (used right before the find operation is to be executed), or `after` (executed after the find operation is finished, and the perfect place to modify the obtained results.) The `before` state is where we change the query parameters to meet our needs.

- ▶ `query`: The data for the query, containing typical find settings (such as `fields` or `conditions`), and any extra settings specified in the `find` operation (in our case, `terms`).

- ▶ `results`: Only applicable when the state is set to `after`, and includes the result of the `find` operation.

When the state of the find is set to `before`, the custom find type implementation needs to return the query, as an array of find settings. Therefore, in our implementation, we look for a custom find setting named `terms`. If there are terms specified, we use them to add `LIKE`-based conditions to a fixed list of fields. Once we are done, we return the modified query.

When the state is set to `after`, the implementation needs to return the results. This is the opportunity to modify the resulting rows, if needed, before returning them. In our implementation, we simply return them as they were sent to us.

The last part of the recipe shows us how to add count support for our custom find types. This is something that CakePHP does not offer out of the box, so we implement our own solution. We do so by overriding the `find()` method and checking to make sure a set of conditions are met:

1. The `find` operation being executed is set to `count`
2. There's a `type` setting specified in the query
3. The `type` setting is in fact a valid custom find type

When these conditions are met, we add a new query parameter named `operation`, setting it to `count`, and we then call the parent `find()` implementation using the custom find type. This way, our find implementation can check for the `operation` find setting, and when it is set to `count`, it forces the `fields` find setting to `COUNT(*)` in the `before` state, and correctly gets the result of the count operation in the `after` state.

See also

▸ *Paginating a custom find type*

▸ *Searching for all items that match search terms*

Paginating a custom find type

The recipe, *Implementing a custom find type*, showed us the power of extending the built-in model find types, including support to use the implemented custom types for fetching records or counting them.

Now that we know how to fetch and count custom find types, we can easily paginate a set of resulting rows. This recipe shows how to use CakePHP's built-in pagination support to paginate a set of rows that come as a result of a custom find type.

Getting ready

We need some sample models and data to work with, and we need the override of the `find()` method in `AppModel` to allow `count` operations on custom find types. Therefore, make sure you follow the entire recipe, *Implementing a custom find type*, including its *Getting ready* section.

How to do it...

1. Create a file named `posts_controller.php` in your `app/controllers` folder. If you already have one, make sure its `index()` method is as follows:

```php
<?php
class PostsController extends AppController {
    public function index() {
        $this->paginate['Post'] = array(
            'search',
            'fields' => array(
                'Post.id',
                'Post.title'
            ),
            'terms' => array(
                'Post 1',
                'Post 2'
            ),
            'limit' => 3
        );
```

```
            $posts = $this->paginate('Post');
            $this->set(compact('posts'));
        }
    }
?>
```

2. Create the view for the `index` action. If you don't have a folder named `posts` in your `app/views` folder, create it. Next, create a file named `index.ctp` in your `app/views` folder with the following contents:

```
<p>
<?php echo $this->Paginator->prev(); ?>
 
<?php echo $this->Paginator->numbers(); ?>
 
<?php echo $this->Paginator->next(); ?>
</p>
<ul>
<?php foreach($posts as $post) { ?>
        <li>#<?php echo $post['Post']['id']; ?>: <?php echo
$post['Post']['title']; ?></li>
<?php } ?>
</ul>
```

3. If we now browse to `http://localhost/posts`, we see a paginated list of matching posts, showing the first three posts out of two pages, as shown in the following screenshot:

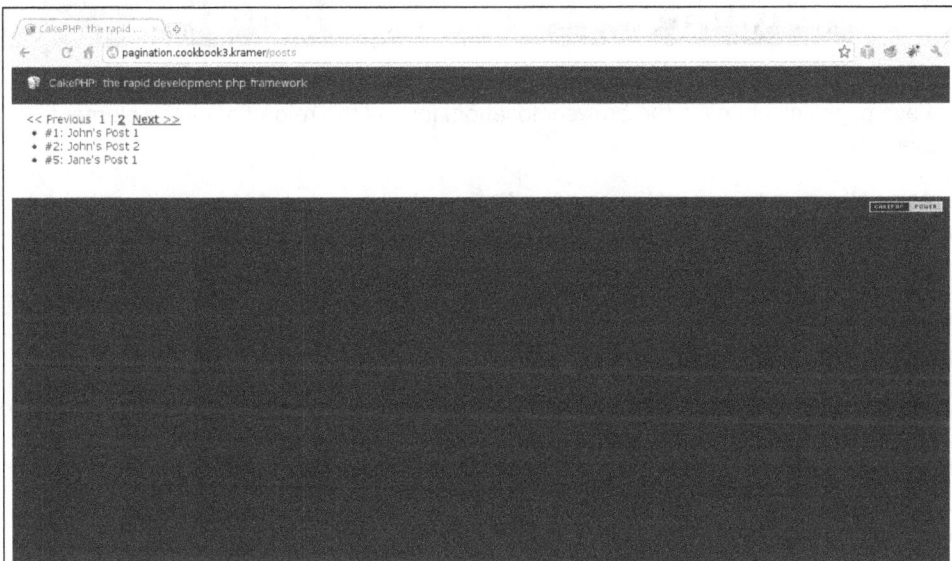

How it works...

To paginate a custom find type, we need to specify the name of the find type as the value for index 0 of the pagination settings (or the first value if no index is defined). We can then pass any custom find settings as part of the pagination settings, as shown in the following code snippet:

```
$this->paginate['Post'] = array(
    'search',
    'terms' => array(
            'Post 1',
            'Post 2'
    ),
    'limit' => 3
);
```

CakePHP's `paginate()` method will first issue a `count` (specifying the find type name in the `type` find setting) to get the total number of rows, and then a `find` operation using the custom find type to get the rows for the current page.

See also

▸ *Implementing AJAX based pagination*

Implementing AJAX based pagination

The previous recipe, *Paginating a custom find type*, showed us how to paginate a custom find type. Each page link changes the browser location, forcing the reload of all the elements in the page.

This recipe allows us to use AJAX (using the `jQuery javascript library`) to only load what is really needed, so that every time a page is changed, only the set of rows is changed without having to load a whole new page.

Getting ready

We need some sample models and data to work with, and we need a fully working pagination of a custom find type. Follow the entire recipe, *Paginating a custom find type*, including its *Getting ready* section.

How to do it...

1. We start by adding the jQuery javascript library to our layout. If you don't have one already, create a file named default.ctp in your app/views/layouts directory. Make sure you add the link to the jQuery library (here we are using the Google-hosted one), the place holder for a loading message (to be shown when an AJAX connection is in progress), and that you wrap the view content with a DIV with an ID set to content.

```
<head>
        <title><?php echo $title_for_layout; ?></title>
        <?php echo $this->Html->script('http://ajax.googleapis.com/
ajax/libs/jquery/1.4.2/jquery.min.js'); ?>
</head>
<body>
<div id="main">
        <div id="loading" style="display: none; float:
right;">Loading...</div>
        <div id="content">
                <?php echo $content_for_layout; ?>
        </div>
</div>
</body>
</html>
```

2. Open the PostsController and add the RequestHandler component, and the Jquery helper engine (the rest of the controller remains unmodified:

```
<?php
class PostsController extends AppController {
        public $components = array('RequestHandler');
        public $helpers = array('Js' => 'Jquery');
        public function index() {
                $this->paginate['Post'] = array(
                        'search',
                        'terms' => array(
                                'Post 1',
                                'Post 2'
                        ),
                        'limit' => 3
                );
                $posts = $this->paginate('Post');
                $this->set(compact('posts'));
        }
```

```
        }
    ?>
```

3. Now let the `Paginator` helper know that we are using AJAX-based pagination. Edit the view file `app/views/posts/index.ctp` and add the highlighted lines:

```php
<?php
$this->Paginator->options(array(
        'evalScripts' => true,
        'update' => '#content',
        'before' => $this->Js->get('#loading')->effect('fadeIn',
array('speed'=>'fast')),
        'complete' => $this->Js->get('#loading')->effect('fadeOut',
array('speed'=>'fast')),
));
?>
<p>
<?php echo $this->Paginator->prev(); ?>
 
<?php echo $this->Paginator->numbers(); ?>
 
<?php echo $this->Paginator->next(); ?>
</p>
<ul>
<?php foreach($posts as $post) { ?>
        <li>#<?php echo $post['Post']['id']; ?>: <?php echo
$post['Post']['title']; ?></li>
<?php } ?>
</ul>
<?php echo $this->Js->writeBuffer(); ?>
```

How it works...

When the update setting is specified to the `options()` method of the `Paginator` helper, the `Paginator` knows it is dealing with an AJAX-based pagination. The update setting points to the ID of the DOM element holding the content that changes when each pagination link is clicked. In our case, that DOM element is a DIV with an ID set to `content`, defined in the layout.

The other option we specify to the `Paginator` helper is `evalScripts`, which tells the helper to evaluate any Javascript code that is being obtained as a result of an AJAX request. That way, when a page with results is being obtained through AJAX, the Javascript code that is automatically added by the JQuery engine will be executed. Similarly, we need to print out this generated code, and we do so by calling the `writeBuffer()` method at the end of the `index.ctp` view.

The other two options we use are `before`, and `complete`, which are sent directly to the AJAX operation. The `before` option, executed before an AJAX request is made, is an ideal place for us to show the loading DIV. The `complete` option, executed after an AJAX operation is completed, is utilized to hide the loading DIV.

We could also specify Javascript code to the `before` and `complete` options, rather than utilizing the helper methods provided by the jQuery engine. The same effect could be achieved by changing the options as follows:

```php
<?php
$this->Paginator->options(array(
    'evalScripts' => true,
    'update' => '#content',
    'before' => '$("#loading").fadeIn("fast");',
    'complete' => '$("#loading").fadeOut("fast");'
));
?>
```

4
Validation and Behaviors

In this chapter, we will cover:

- ▶ Adding multiple validation rules
- ▶ Creating a custom validation rule
- ▶ Using callbacks in behaviors
- ▶ Using behaviors to add new fields for saving
- ▶ Using the Sluggable behavior
- ▶ Geocoding addresses with the Geocodable behavior

Introduction

This chapter deals with two aspects of CakePHP models that are fundamental to most applications: validation, and behaviors.

When we are saving information to a data source, such as a database, CakePHP will automatically ensure that the data is quoted in order to prevent attacks, SQL injection being the most common one. If we also need to ensure that the data follows a certain format, for example, that a phone number is valid, we use validation rules.

There are also times where we need to do more than just validate the data we are working with. In some cases, we need to set values for fields that the end user can't specify but are part of our application logic. CakePHP's behaviors allow us to extend the functionality provided by a model, using callbacks to manipulate the data before it's saved, or after it's fetched.

The third recipe shows us how to use model callbacks (such as `beforeFind` and `afterFind`) in behaviors, while the fourth recipe shows how to use behaviors to add additional field values when a `save` operation is being undertaken.

The last two recipes in this chapter give examples on how to use the `Sluggable` behavior for creating SEO friendly URLs, and the `Geocodable` behavior to add geocoding support to an `Address` model.

Adding multiple validation rules

This recipe shows how to not only use some basic validation rules provided by CakePHP, but also how to use more than one of these rules per field.

Getting ready

To go through this recipe we need a sample table to work with. Create a table named `profiles` using the following SQL statement:

```sql
CREATE TABLE `profiles`(
    `id` INT UNSIGNED AUTO_INCREMENT NOT NULL,
    `email` VARCHAR(255) NOT NULL,
    `name` VARCHAR(255) default NULL,
    `twitter` VARCHAR(255) default NULL,
    PRIMARY KEY(`id`)
);
```

We proceed now to create the required model. Create the model `Profile` in a file named `profile.php` and place it in your `app/models` folder with the following contents:

```php
<?php
class Profile extends AppModel {
    public $validate = array(
        'email' => array('rule' => 'notEmpty'),
        'name' => array('rule' => 'notEmpty')
    );
}
?>
```

Create its appropriate controller `ProfilesController` in a file named `profiles_controller.php` and place it in your `app/controllers` folder with the following contents:

```php
<?php
class ProfilesController extends AppController {
    public function add() {
        if (!empty($this->data)) {
```

```php
        $this->Profile->create();
        if ($this->Profile->save($this->data)) {
            $this->Session->setFlash('Profile created');
            $this->redirect('/');
        } else {
            $this->Session->setFlash('Please correct the errors');
        }
      }
    }
  }
?>
```

Create a folder named `profiles` in your `app/views` folder. Create the view to hold the form in a file named `add.ctp`, and place it in your `app/views/profiles` folder, with the following contents:

```php
<?php
echo $this->Form->create();
echo $this->Form->inputs(array(
    'email',
    'name',
    'twitter'
));
echo $this->Form->end('Create');
?>
```

How to do it...

We already have basic validation rules set for the `email` and `name` fields, which guarantee that none of these fields can be empty. We now want to add another validation rule to ensure that the email entered is always a valid e-mail address. Edit the `Profile` model and change the defined validation rule as follows:

```php
class Profile extends AppModel {
    public $validate = array(
        'email' => array(
            'valid' => array(
                'rule' => 'email',
                'message' => 'The email entered is not a valid email
address'
            ),
            'required' => array(
                'rule' => 'notEmpty',
                'message' => 'Please enter an email'
            )
```

```
        ),
        'name' => array('rule' => 'notEmpty')
    );
}
```

If we now browse to `http://localhost/profiles/add` and click the **Create** button without entering any information, we should see the customized error message for the `email` field and the default error message for the `name` field as shown in the following screenshot:

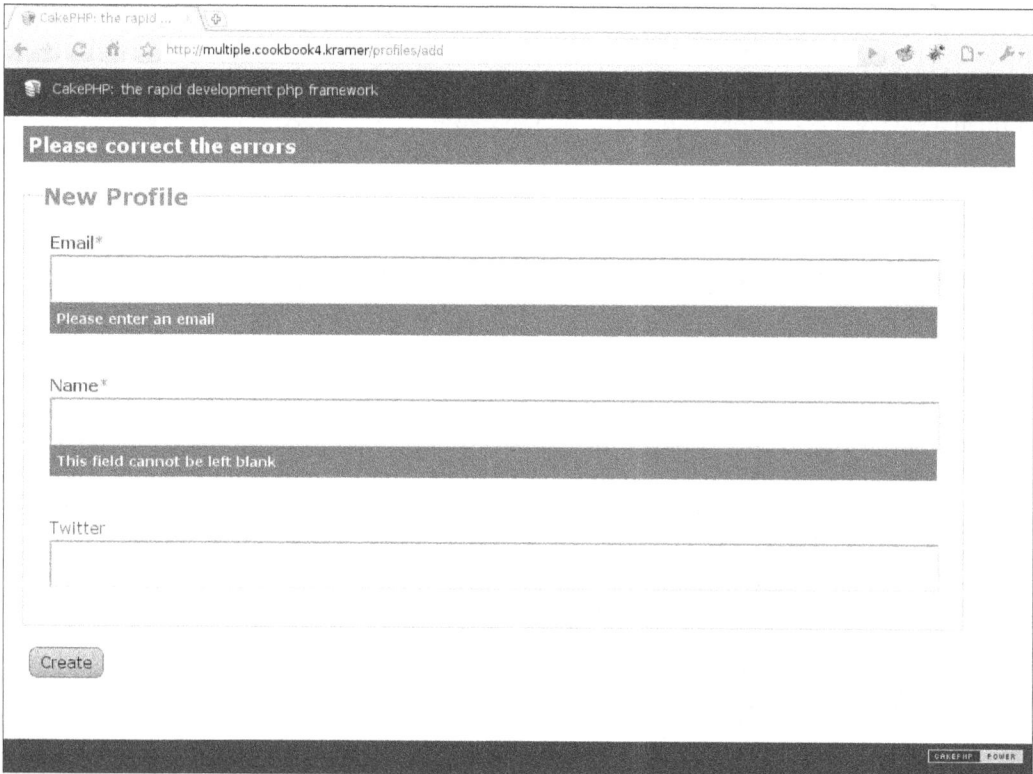

If we instead specify an invalid e-mail address, the validation message should change to the one specified in the view.

How it works...

Each field specified in the model's `validate` property can contain any number of validation rules. When we specify more than one rule, we wrap them in an array, indexing it with a descriptive key to help us identify which rule failed. Therefore, we chose to index the `notEmpty` rule with a `required` key, and the `email` rule with a `valid` key.

When we specify more than one validation rule, CakePHP will evaluate each rule in the order we used when adding them to the `validate` property. If more than one validation rule fails for a field, the last rule that failed is the one that is used to trigger the error message. In our case, the first rule is `valid`, and the second one `required`. Therefore if both rules fail, the field is set to have failed the `required` rule.

If we wanted to ensure that a particular rule is executed after all others have, we use the `last` rule setting. Setting it to `true` will ensure that a particular rule is executed after all others. In our example, we could have defined the `required` validation first in the list of rules for the `email` field and set its `last` setting to `true`, which would have the same result as defining the `required` rule after all others.

There's more...

In this recipe, we used the model to specify what error message is shown for each failing rule. We could instead choose to do it in the view.

Using the indexes that identify each rule, we can specify which error message should be shown whenever one of these rules fails validation. We do so by setting the `error` option in the field definition to an array of error messages, each indexed by a matching validation rule key (in our case, one of `required` and `valid` for the `email` field).

Edit the `app/views/profiles/add.ctp` file and change the `email` field definition as follows:

```php
<?php
echo $this->Form->create();
echo $this->Form->inputs(array(
  'email' => array(
    'error' => array(
      'required' => 'Please enter an email',
      'valid' => 'The email entered is not a valid email address'
    )
  ),
  'name',
  'twitter'
));
echo $this->Form->end('Create');
?>
```

See also

▸ *Internationalizing model validation messages* in the *Internationalizing applications* chapter.

Creating a custom validation rule

CakePHP provides a handful of validation rules out of the box, which together covers the need for most applications. The following table lists the built-in validation rules (found in CakePHP's `Validation` class.)

Rule	Purpose
_alphaNumeric	Checks that the value contains only integers or letters.
_between	Checks that the string length of the value is within the specified range.
_blank	Succeeds if the value is empty, or consists of only spaces (whitespaces, tabs, newlines, and so on).
_boolean	Checks if value can be interpreted as a Boolean.
_cc	Validates a credit card number.
_comparison	Compares the value to a given value, using the specified operator.
_custom	Validates the value using a custom regular expression.
_date	Validates the value as a date, using the given format or regular expression.
_decimal	Succeeds if value is a valid decimal number.
_email	Validates an e-mail address.
_equalTo	Succeeds if the value is equal to the given value.
_extension	Interprets the value as a file name and checks for the given extension.
_inList	Checks that the value is within a list of allowed values.
_ip	Validates an IP address.
_maxLength	Checks that the length of the string value does not exceed a certain number of characters.
_minLength	Similar to maxLength, but ensures that the string value has at least the given number of characters.
_money	Checks that the value is a valid monetary amount.
_multiple	Validates a multiple select against a set of options.
_numeric	Succeeds if the value is numeric.
_phone	Checks a phone number.
_postal	Validates a postal code.
_range	Succeeds if the value is within a numeric range.
_ssn	Checks a social security/national identity number.
_time	Validates the value as a time (24 hours format).
_uuid	Validates the value as a UUID.
_url	Succeeds if the value is a valid URL.

However, there are times where we require a custom validation, or where we need to change the way an existing validation works.

In this recipe, we will learn how to create our custom validation rule to check the validity of a given twitter user name.

Getting ready

We need some sample models to work with. Follow the *Getting ready* section of the recipe *Adding multiple validation rules*.

How to do it...

Edit the `Profile` model by opening your `app/models/profile.php` file and make the following changes:

```
class Profile extends AppModel {
    public $validate = array(
        'email' => array('rule' => 'notEmpty'),
        'name' => array('rule' => 'notEmpty'),
        'twitter' => array(
        'rule' => 'validateTwitter',
        'allowEmpty' => true,
        'message' => 'This twitter account is not valid'
        )
    );
    protected static $httpSocket;

    protected function validateTwitter($data) {
        if (!isset(self::$httpSocket)) {
            App::import('Core', 'HttpSocket');
            self::$httpSocket = new HttpSocket();
        }

        $value = current($data);
        self::$httpSocket->get('http://twitter.com/status/user_
timeline/' . $value . '.json?count=1');
        return (self::$httpSocket->response['status']['code'] != 404);
    }
}
```

If we now browse to `http://localhost/profiles/add` and click the `Create` button after entering a Nonexistent Twitter account, we should see the error message for the `twitter` field shown in the following screenshot:

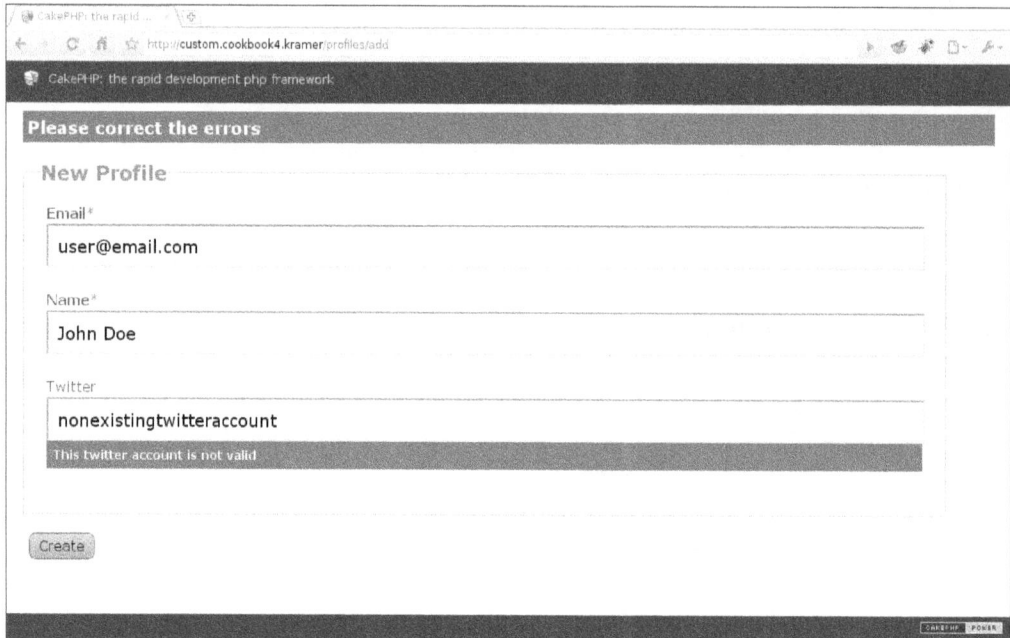

If we instead specify a valid account, or leave it empty, there will be no error message displayed for the `twitter` field.

How it works...

When we set the `rule` validate option to the name of a method that is available in the model (validateTwitter() in our example), CakePHP calls that method when the field needs to be validated.

The method `validateTwitter()`, like any custom validation method, receives an array in its first argument. This array is indexed by the field name, and the value is set to the value entered by the user. In the example shown in the previous screenshot, the `data` argument comes in as:

```
array('twitter' => 'nonexistingtwitteraccount')
```

The validation method needs to return a Boolean value to indicate success: `true` if the validation succeeded, `false` if it failed. If we don't set the `allowEmpty` option to `true`, then the validation method will also be called when the field value is empty.

[If the custom validation method returns a string, the field is marked to have failed validation, and the returned string is used as the error message.]

The method `validateTwitter()` first checks to see if an instance of the CakePHP `HttpSocket` class is already set. We use a static instance to make sure the class is initialized only once, thus avoiding unnecessary processing if the method is called several times for the same process.

Once we have the `HttpSocket` instance, we get the value to be validated (first value set in the array, as shown above), and we use it to fetch the contents of a twitter URL.

[We could have used an `http://twitter.com/$account` URL, which returns the HTML containing the user latest tweets. However we chose to use a JSON request, and limit the number of tweets to 1, to reduce bandwidth usage from our server]

This publicly available Twitter URL is used to get the timeline for a Twitter account, which returns an HTTP status of `404` when the account is not registered with Twitter. If the status is indeed `404`, we consider the Twitter account to be nonexistent, thus failing validation. Any other status code will result in a successful validation.

There's more...

Some custom validation methods need more than just the value to be validated to be able to tell if validation succeeded. Fortunately, CakePHP not only sends us an array of options utilized to perform the validation in the second argument, but also provides an easy way to add parameters to our validation methods. Using our example, we now want to be able to provide a different URL to use when checking the Twitter account.

To utilize the array of options, edit the `Profile` model by opening your `app/models/profile.php` file and make the following changes:

```
class Profile extends AppModel {
    public $validate = array(
        'email' => array('rule' => 'notEmpty'),
        'name' => array('rule' => 'notEmpty'),
        'twitter' => array(
            'rule' => 'validateTwitter',
            'allowEmpty' => true,
            'url' => 'http://twitter.com/%TWITTER%'
        )
    );
```

```
    protected function validateTwitter($data, $options) {
        static $httpSocket;
        if (!isset($httpSocket)) {
            App::import('Core', 'HttpSocket');
            $httpSocket = new HttpSocket();
        }

        $options = array_merge(array(
            'url' => 'http://twitter.com/status/user_timeline/%TWITTER%.
json?count=1'
        ), $options);
        $value = current($data);
        $httpSocket->get(str_ireplace('%TWITTER%', $value,
$options['url']));
        return ($httpSocket->response['status']['code'] != 404);
    }
}
```

If instead of utilizing the array of options, we want to utilize the ability to use extra parameters, we simply add arguments to our validation method, and pass those argument values as elements of the `validate` definition. To do so, edit the `Profile` model by opening your `app/models/profile.php` file and make the following changes:

```
class Profile extends AppModel {
    public $validate = array(
        'email' => array('rule' => 'notEmpty'),
        'name' => array('rule' => 'notEmpty'),
        'twitter' => array(
            'rule' => array(
                'validateTwitter',
                'http://twitter.com/%TWITTER%'
            ),
            'allowEmpty' => true
        )
    );
    protected static $httpSocket;

    protected function validateTwitter($data, $url = 'http://twitter.
com/status/user_timeline/%TWITTER%.json?count=1') {
        if (!isset(self::$httpSocket)) {
            App::import('Core', 'HttpSocket');
            self::$httpSocket = new HttpSocket();
        }

        $value = current($data);
        self::$httpSocket->get(str_ireplace('%TWITTER%', $value, $url));
        return (self::$httpSocket->response['status']['code'] != 404);
    }
}
```

See also

> ▸ *Adding multiple validation rules*

Using callbacks in behaviors

CakePHP behaviors are a great way to not only extend model functionality, but also share that functionality across different models, and applications. Using behaviors, we can keep our model code concise and to the point, extracting code that may not be directly related to our business logic, but still affect how our models behave.

In this recipe we will learn how to use model callbacks to automatically retrieve each profile's latest tweets, and how to add a custom validation method to the behavior.

Getting ready

We need some sample models to work with. Follow the *Getting ready* section of the recipe *Adding multiple validation rules*.

We will also need a method to list all profiles. Edit your `app/controllers/profiles_controller.php` file and add the following `index()` method to the `ProfilesController` class:

```php
public function index() {
    $profiles = $this->Profile->find('all');
    $this->set(compact('profiles'));
}
```

Create the respective view in a file named `app/views/profiles/index.ctp`, with the following contents:

```php
<?php foreach($profiles as $profile) { ?>
<p>
    <?php echo $this->Html->link(
        $profile['Profile']['twitter'],
        'http://twitter.com/' . $profile['Profile']['twitter'],
        array('title' => $profile['Profile']['twitter'])
    ); ?>
</p>
<?php } ?>
```

How to do it...

1. Create a class named `TwitterAccountBehavior` in a file named `twitter_account.php` and place it in your `app/models/behaviors` folder, with the following contents:

```php
<?php
App::import('Core', 'HttpSocket');

class TwitterAccountBehavior extends ModelBehavior {
    protected static $httpSocket;

    public function setup($model, $config = array()) {
        parent::setup($model, $config);
        $this->settings[$model->alias] = array_merge(array(
            'field' => 'twitter'
        ), $config);
    }

    protected function timeline($twitter, $count = 10,
$returnStatus = false) {
        if (!isset(self::$httpSocket)) {
            self::$httpSocket = new HttpSocket();
        }

        $content = self::$httpSocket->get('http://twitter.com/
status/user_timeline/' . $twitter . '.json?count=' . $count);
        $status = self::$httpSocket->response['status']['code'];
        if (!empty($content)) {
            $content = json_decode($content);
        }

        if ($returnStatus) {
            return compact('status', 'content');
        }
        return $content;
    }
}
?>
```

2. Now that we have created the behavior with its `setup()` method implemented and a helper `timeline()` method to obtain tweets from a Twitter account, we can proceed to add the required validation.

   Add the following custom validation method to the `TwitterAccountBehavior` class:

```php
public function validateTwitter($model, $data) {
  $field = $this->settings[$model->alias]['field'];
  if (!empty($data[$field])) {
    $value = $data[$field];
    $result = $this->timeline($value, 1, true);
    if ($result['status'] == 404) {
      $result = false;
    }
  }
  return $result;
}
```

3. Let us now attach the behavior to the `Profile` model, and add the validation for the `twitter` field. Open your `app/models/profile.php` file and add the following `actsAs` property and the `twitter` field validation:

```php
<?php
class Profile extends AppModel {
public $actsAs = array('TwitterAccount');
    public $validate = array(
        'email' => array('rule' => 'notEmpty'),
        'name' => array('rule' => 'notEmpty'),
        'twitter' => array(
        'rule' => 'validateTwitter',
        'allowEmpty' => true,
        'message' => 'This twitter account is not valid'
        )
    );
}
?>
```

4. Just like the recipe *Creating a custom validation rule,* entering a nonexistant Twitter account should display the error message for the `twitter` field shown in the following screenshot:

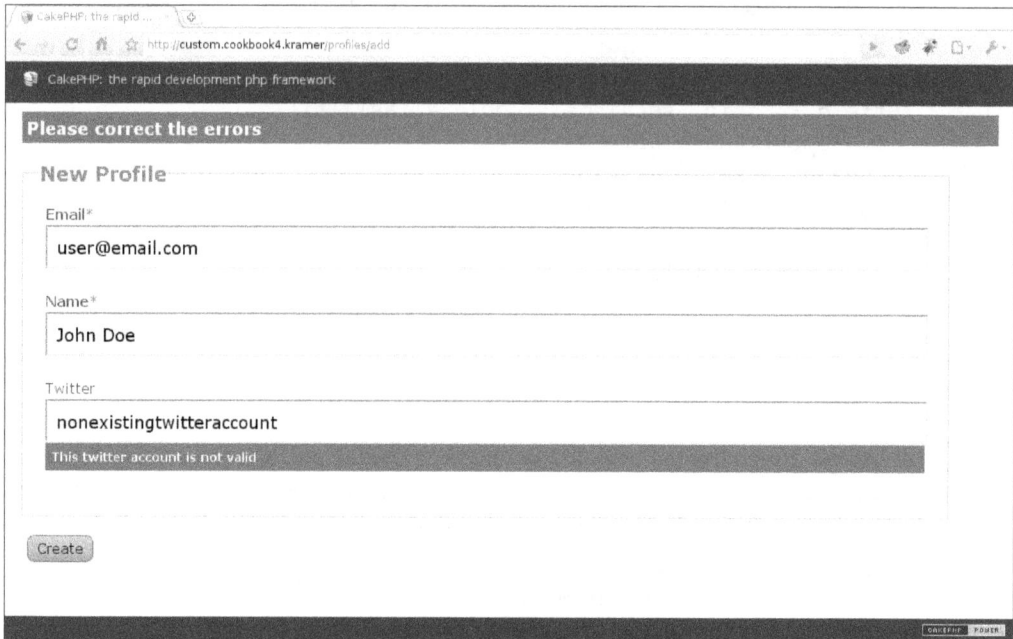

5. Let us now use other callbacks to get a certain number of tweets for each profile after a find operation is performed. Add the following `beforeFind()` and `afterFind()` methods to the `TwitterAccountBehavior` class:

```php
public function beforeFind($model, $query) {
    $this->settings[$model->alias]['tweets'] =
!isset($query['tweets']) ? true : $query['tweets'];
    return parent::beforeFind($model, $query);
}

public function afterFind($model, $results, $primary) {
    $rows = parent::afterFind($model, $results, $primary);
    if (!is_null($rows)) {
        $results = $rows;
    }
    if (!empty($this->settings[$model->alias]['tweets'])) {
        $field = $this->settings[$model->alias]['field'];
        $count = is_int($this->settings[$model->alias]['tweets']) ?
            $this->settings[$model->alias]['tweets'] :
            10;
        foreach($results as $i => $result) {
```

```php
        $twitter = $result[$model->alias][$field];
        $tweets = array();
        if (!empty($result[$model->alias][$field])) {
            $result = $this->timeline($twitter, $count);
            if (!empty($result) && is_array($result)) {
                foreach($result as $tweet) {
                    $tweets[] = array(
                        'created' => date('Y-m-d H:i:s',
strtotime($tweet->created_at)),
                        'source' => $tweet->source,
                        'user' => $tweet->user->screen_name,
                        'text' => $tweet->text
                    );
                }
            }
        }
        $results[$i]['Tweet'] = $tweets;
    }
}
return $results;
}
```

6. Edit the `app/views/profiles/index.ctp` view and make the following changes:

```php
<?php foreach($profiles as $profile) { ?>
<p>
    <?php echo $this->Html->link(
        $profile['Profile']['twitter'],
        'http://twitter.com/' . $profile['Profile']['twitter'],
        array('title' => $profile['Profile']['twitter'])
    ); ?>
<?php if (!empty($profile['Tweet'])) { ?>
<ul>
    <?php foreach($profile['Tweet'] as $tweet) { ?>
        <li>
            <code><?php echo $tweet['text']; ?></code>
            from <?php echo $tweet['source']; ?>
                on <?php echo $tweet['created']; ?>
        </li>
    <?php } ?>
</ul>
<?php } ?>
</p>
<?php } ?>
```

After adding a valid Twitter account, browsing to `http://localhost/profiles` would generate a listing, such as the one shown in the following screenshot:

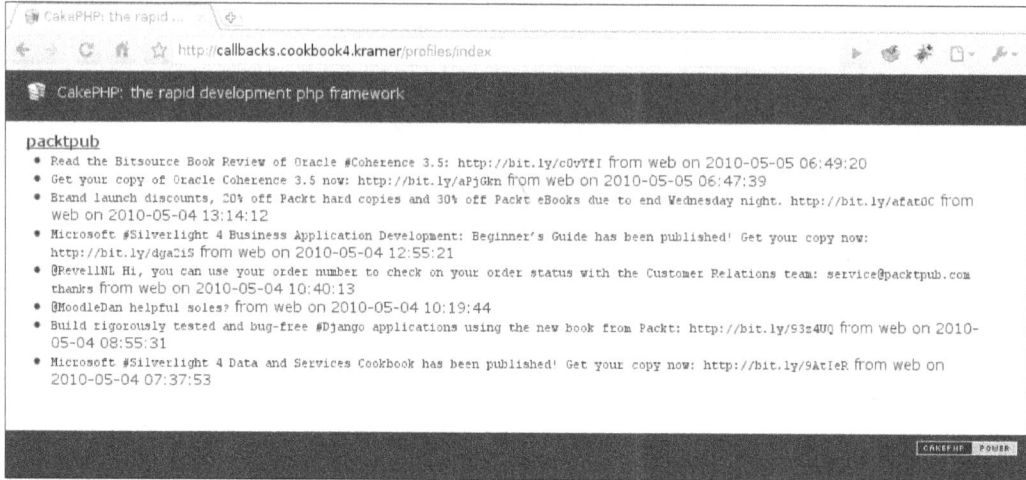

How it works...

We started with the skeleton for our `TwitterAccountBehavior`, implementing the `setup()` method, called automatically by CakePHP whenever the behavior is attached to a model, and the `timeline()` method, which is nothing more than the `validateTwitter()` method shown in the recipe *Create a custom validation rule* optimized for reutilization.

The `beforeFind` callback is triggered by CakePHP whenever a find operation is about to be executed, and we used it to check the existence of the custom `tweets` find setting. We use this setting to allow the developer to either disable the fetch of tweets, by setting it to `false`:

```
$this->Profile->find('all', array('tweets' => false));
```

or specify how many tweets should be obtained. For example, if we wanted to obtain only the latest tweet, we would do:

```
$this->Profile->find('all', array('tweets' => 1));
```

The `afterFind` callback is executed after a find operation is executed, and gives us an opportunity to modify the results. Therefore we check to make sure we are told to obtain the tweets, and if so we use the `timeline()` method to obtain the specified number of tweets. We then append each tweet's basic information into the index `Tweet` for each profile.

There's more...

One thing that is clear in our implementation is that, unless we set the `tweets` find option to `false`; we are obtaining tweets for each profile record on every `find` operation performed against the `Profile` model. Adding caching support would greatly improve the performance of our `find` operations, since we would only obtain the tweets when the cached information is no longer valid.

> More information about caching through CakePHP's Cache class can be obtained at `http://book.cakephp.org/view/1511/Cache`.

We will allow the developer to specify what cache configuration to use when caching tweets. Open the `TwitterAccountBehavior` class and make the following modifications to its `setup()` method:

```php
public function setup($model, $config = array()) {
    parent::setup($model, $config);
    $this->settings[$model->alias] = array_merge(array(
        'field' => 'twitter',
        'cache' => 'default'
    ), $config);
}
```

While editing the `TwitterAccountBehavior` class, make the following modifications to its `afterFind()` method:

```php
public function afterFind($model, $results, $primary) {
    $rows = parent::afterFind($model, $results, $primary);
    if (!is_null($rows)) {
        $results = $rows;
    }
    if (!empty($this->settings[$model->alias]['tweets'])) {
        $field = $this->settings[$model->alias]['field'];
        $count = is_int($this->settings[$model->alias]['tweets']) ?
            $this->settings[$model->alias]['tweets'] :
            10;
        $cacheConfig = $this->settings[$model->alias]['cache'];
        foreach($results as $i => $result) {
            $twitter = $result[$model->alias][$field];
            $tweets = array();
            if (!empty($cacheConfig)) {
                $tweets = Cache::read('tweets_' . $twitter, $cacheConfig);
            }
            if (empty($tweets) && !empty($result[$model->alias][$field]))
            {
```

```
                $result = $this->timeline($twitter, $count);
                if (!empty($result) && is_array($result)) {
                    foreach($result as $tweet) {
                        $tweets[] = array(
                            'created' => date('Y-m-d H:i:s',
strtotime($tweet->created_at)),
                            'source' => $tweet->source,
                            'user' => $tweet->user->screen_name,
                            'text' => $tweet->text
                        );
                    }
                }
                Cache::write('tweets_' . $twitter, $tweets, $cacheConfig);
            }
            $results[$i]['Tweet'] = $tweets;
        }
    }
    return $results;
}
```

Finally, add the following `beforeDelete` and `afterDelete` callback implementations:

```
public function beforeDelete($model, $cascade = true) {
    $field = $this->settings[$model->alias]['field'];
    $this->settings[$model->alias]['delete'] = $model->field($field,
array(
        $model->primaryKey => $model->id
    ));
    return parent::beforeDelete($cascade);
}

public function afterDelete($model) {
    if (!empty($this->settings[$model->alias]['delete'])) {
        $cacheConfig = $this->settings[$model->alias]['cache'];
        $twitter = $this->settings[$model->alias]['delete'];
        Cache::delete('tweets_' . $twitter, $cacheConfig);
    }
    return parent::afterDelete($model);
}
```

Using `beforeDelete()` we are storing the tweet that is to be deleted. If indeed the profile was deleted, the `afterDelete()` method will remove its cached tweets.

See also

▸ *Adding multiple validation rules*

▸ *Create a custom validation rule*

▸ *Using behaviors to add new fields for saving*

Using behaviors to add new fields for saving

In the recipe *Using callbacks in behaviors* we learnt how to implement different model callbacks to perform some tasks automatically. In this recipe we will continue that process and we will learn how to automatically save data that may not be provided in a `save` operation.

We will use the Twitter example we have been using in this chapter, so that when a profile is saved, its Twitter URL and its last tweet are saved when creating a new record, or when updating an existing one.

Getting ready

We need a working `TwitterAccountBehavior` together with its controllers, models, and views. Follow the recipe *Using callbacks in behaviors* (there's no need to enable caching in the behavior, so you can omit the *There's more* section).

Add two fields to the profiles table, `url` and `last_tweet`, by issuing the following SQL command:

```
ALTER TABLE `profiles`
    ADD COLUMN `url` VARCHAR(255) default NULL,
    ADD COLUMN `last_tweet` VARCHAR(140) default NULL;
```

How to do it...

1. Edit your `app/models/behaviors/twitter_account.php` file and add the following `beforeSave` implementation to the `TwitterAccountBehavior` class:

```
public function beforeSave($model) {
    $field = $this->settings[$model->alias]['field'];
    $twitter = null;
    if (!array_key_exists($field, $model->data[$model->alias]) &&
$model->exists()) {
        $twitter = $model->field($field, array(
            $model->primaryKey => $model->id
        ));
```

```
    } elseif (array_key_exists($field, $model->data[$model-
>alias])) {
        $twitter = $model->data[$model->alias][$field];
    }
    $data = array(
        'url' => !empty($twitter) ? 'http://twitter.com/' . $twitter
: null,
        'last_tweet' => null
    );
    if (!empty($twitter)) {
        $tweets = $this->timeline($twitter, 1);
        if (!empty($tweets) && is_array($tweets)) {
            $data['last_tweet'] = $tweets[0]->text;
        }
    }

    $model->data[$model->alias] = array_merge(
        $model->data[$model->alias],
        $data
    );
    $this->_addToWhitelist($model, array_keys($data));

    return parent::beforeSave($model);
}
```

2. Whenever we create a new profile with a valid Twitter account, both the `url` and `last_tweet` fields will be automatically populated. If we are instead modifying a profile, the `last_tweet` field will be updated to reflect the latest tweet from the relevant account.

How it works...

The `beforeSave` callback is triggered before a save operation is performed on a model, giving us the chance to add new fields to the set of fields that are about to be saved, or modify other field values.

We started by determining which Twitter account is linked to the profile being saved. If no Twitter account is specified in the data that is about to be saved, and if we are modifying an existing record (we use `$model->exists()` for this check), we obtain the account specified in its `twitter` field. If instead there's an account specified in the data to be saved, we use that instead.

Regardless of the type of save operation that is about to be performed (creating or updating a record), we set the `last_tweet` field to the last tweet published by the specific Twitter account. However, we set the `url` field to the appropriate URL-based, on the Twitter account only when we are creating a new record.

Once we have set the data to be saved in the $data array, we append that data to the $model->data property that contains all the information that will be saved. We then use the behavior's _addToWhitelist() method, defined in CakePHP's ModelBehavior class from which our behavior extends, so that if the developer has chosen to limit the save operation to only a specific set of fields, then our fields are guaranteed to be saved regardless of this restriction.

See also

▸ *Using callbacks in behaviors*

Using the Sluggable behavior

One of the main concerns most applications have is optimizing their content for search engines, so that their sites rank as high as possible on most engines. Among several recommendations found in most SEO (Search Engine Optimization) guides, building URLs that include relevant keywords is one of the most effective ones.

If we are building a content-based site, this is achievable by making sure that permanent links to each item include most of the words that are part of the item title. As an example, if we have a post whose title is *Top 10 CakePHP Behaviors*, an SEO-friendly URL could be:

`http://localhost/articles/view/top-10-cakephp-behaviors.`

The top-10-cakephp-behaviors part is commonly known as a *slug*, a part of the URL that uses relevant keywords. In this recipe, we will learn how to use the publicly available Sluggable behavior to automatically add slugs to our application.

> The Sluggable behavior is one of the many classes I released as open source to help fellow CakePHP developers. Feel free to send me any feedback.

Getting ready

To go through this recipe, we need a sample table to work with. Create a table named posts, using the following SQL statement:

```
CREATE TABLE `posts`(
    `id` INT UNSIGNED AUTO_INCREMENT NOT NULL,
    `slug` VARCHAR(255) NOT NULL,
    `title` VARCHAR(255) NOT NULL,
    `text` TEXT NOT NULL,
    PRIMARY KEY(`id`),
    UNIQUE KEY `slug`(`slug`)
);
```

We proceed now to create the required model. Create the model Post in a file named post.php and place it in your app/models folder, with the following contents:

```php
<?php
class Post extends AppModel {
    public $validate = array(
        'title' => array('rule' => 'notEmpty'),
        'text' => array('rule' => 'notEmpty')
    );
}
?>
```

Create its appropriate controller PostsController in a file named posts_controller.php and place it in your app/controllers folder, with the following contents:

```php
<?php
class PostsController extends AppController {
    public function add() {
        if (!empty($this->data)) {
            $this->Post->create();
            if ($this->Post->save($this->data)) {
                $this->Session->setFlash('Post created');
                $this->redirect('/');
            } else {
                $this->Session->setFlash('Please correct the errors');
            }
        }
    }
}
?>
```

Create a folder named posts in your app/views folder, then create the view to hold the form in a file named add.ctp and place it in your app/views/posts folder, with the following contents:

```php
<?php
echo $this->Form->create();
echo $this->Form->inputs(array(
    'title',
    'text'
));
echo $this->Form->end('Create');
?>
```

Finally, we need to download the Syrup plugin for CakePHP. Go to `http://github.com/mariano/syrup/downloads` and download the latest release. Uncompress the downloaded file into your `app/plugins` folder. You should now have a directory named `syrup` inside `app/plugins`.

How to do it...

1. We start by attaching the `Sluggable` behavior to the `Post` model. Edit your `app/models/post.php` file and add the `$actsAs` property:

```php
<?php
class Post extends AppModel {
    public $actsAs = array('Syrup.Sluggable');
    public $validate = array(
        'title' => array('rule' => 'notEmpty'),
        'text' => array('rule' => 'notEmpty')
    );
}
?>
```

2. Let's create an action to list posts. Add the following method to the `PostsController` class:

```php
public function index() {
    $this->paginate['limit'] = 10;
    $posts = $this->paginate();
    $this->set(compact('posts'));
}
```

3. Create the view `views/posts/index.ctp` with the following contents:

```php
<div class="paging">
<?php echo $this->Paginator->prev(); ?>
 
<?php echo $this->Paginator->numbers(); ?>
 
<?php echo $this->Paginator->next(); ?>
</div>
<br />
<ul>
<?php foreach($posts as $post) { ?>
    <li><?php echo $this->Html->link($post['Post']['title'],
array('action'=>'view', $post['Post']['slug'])); ?></li>
<?php } ?>
</ul>
```

Next, create the action to view a post by slug. Add the following method to the `PostsController` class:

```
public function view($slug) {
    $post = $this->Post->find('first', array(
        'conditions' => array('Post.slug' => $slug),
        'recursive' => -1
    ));
    $this->set(compact('post'));
}
```

Create the view `views/posts/view.ctp` with the following contents:

```
<h1><?php echo $post['Post']['title']; ?></h1>
<p><?php echo $post['Post']['text']; ?></p>
<?php echo $this->Html->link('Posts', array('action'=>'index'));
?>
```

After creating some posts using the form at `http://localhost/posts`, the list of posts could look like the following screenshot:

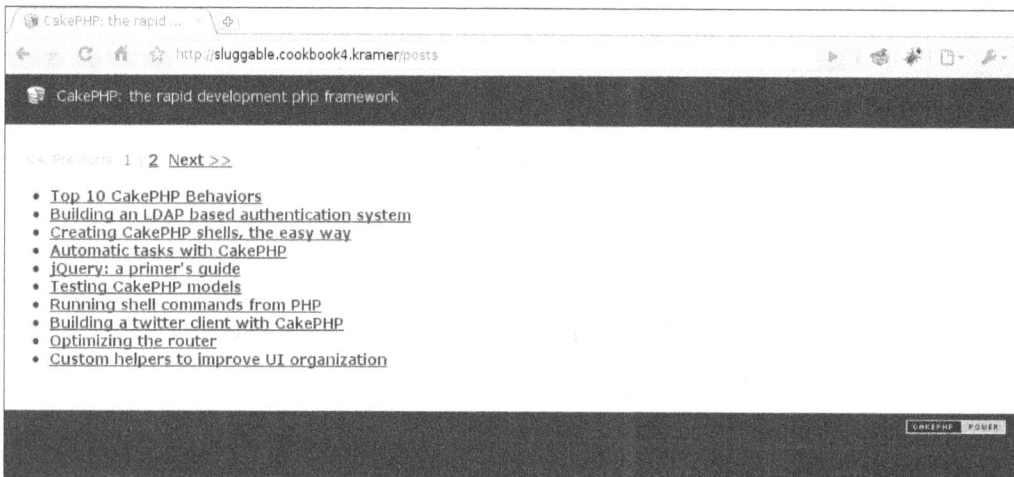

4. If you hover over the links, you should see SEO-friendly links. For example, for the post entitled *Automatic tasks with CakePHP*, its URL would be:

   `http://localhost/posts/view/automatic-tasks-with-cakephp`

5. Clicking on this URL would show the details for the post.

How it works...

The `Sluggable` behavior implements the `beforeSave` callback to automatically add the generated slug on the specified field. It ensures that all generated slugs are unique, and provides a full set of options to modify how a slug is generated. The following options can be specified when attaching the behavior to a model:

Option	Purpose
ignore	List of words that should not be part of a slug. Optional, and defaults to: and, for, is, of, and the.
label	Field name (string), or list of field names (in an array) that are used to create the slug. Defaults to a single field named title.
length	Maximum length of the generated slug. Defaults to 100.
overwrite	If set to true, the slug is generated even when modifying a record that already has a slug. Defaults to false
real	If set to true, it will ensure that the field names defined in the label option exists in the table. Defaults to true.
separator	Character to use when separating words in the slug. Defaults to -.
slug	Name of the field where the slug is stored. Defaults to slug.

Geocoding addresses with the Geocodable behavior

Since the introduction of Google Maps and other location services, a broad set of possibilities are open to web applications, allowing geographical information to be used for building services.

This recipe shows how to use the Geocode plugin to add location information to our own `Address` model, allowing us to search address records by proximity.

> The Geocode plugin is another open source project I released. More information about it can be obtained at `http://github.com/mariano/geocode`.

Getting ready

To go through this recipe we need a sample table to work with. Create a table named `addresses`, using the following SQL statement:

```sql
CREATE TABLE `addresses`(
    `id` INT UNSIGNED AUTO_INCREMENT NOT NULL,
    `address_1` VARCHAR(255) NOT NULL,
    `city` VARCHAR(255) default NULL,
    `state` VARCHAR(255) NOT NULL,
    `zip` VARCHAR(10) default NULL,
    `latitude` FLOAT(10,7) NOT NULL,
    `longitude` FLOAT(10,7) NOT NULL,
    PRIMARY KEY(`id`)
);
```

We proceed now to create the required model. Create the model `Address` in a file named `address.php` and place it in your `app/models` folder with the following contents (we are only specifying a few states for readability):

```php
<?php
class Address extends AppModel {
    public $validate = array(
        'address_1' => array('rule' => 'notEmpty'),
        'state' => array('rule' => 'notEmpty')
    );
    public static $states = array(
        'CA' => 'California',
        'FL' => 'Florida',
        'NY' => 'New York'
    );
}
?>
```

Create its appropriate controller `AddressesController` in a file named `addresses_controller.php` and place it in your `app/controllers` folder. With the following contents:

```php
<?php
class AddressesController extends AppController {
    public function add() {
        if (!empty($this->data)) {
            $this->Address->create();
            if ($this->Address->save($this->data)) {
                $this->Session->setFlash('Address created');
                $this->redirect('/');
            } else {
```

```
            $this->Session->setFlash('Please correct the errors');
        }
    }
    $states = $this->Address->states;
    $this->set(compact('states'));
    }
}
?>
```

Create a folder named `addresses` in your `app/views` folder, then create the view to hold the form in a file named `add.ctp` and place it in your `app/views/addresses` folder, with the following contents:

```php
<?php
echo $this->Form->create();
echo $this->Form->inputs(array(
    'address_1' => array('label' => 'Address'),
    'city',
    'state' => array('options'=>$states),
    'zip'
));
echo $this->Form->end('Create');
?>
```

We need to download the Geocode plugin for CakePHP. Go to `http://github.com/mariano/geocode/downloads` and download the latest release. Uncompress the downloaded file into your `app/plugins` folder. You should now have a directory named `geocode` inside `app/plugins`.

Finally, we need to sign up for a Google Maps API key. To do so, go to `http://code.google.com/apis/maps/signup.html` and follow the instructions given.

> The Geocode plugin also supports Yahoo maps. If you wish to use Yahoo Maps instead, follow the instructions shown on the plugin homepage.

How to do it...

1. Edit your `app/config/bootstrap.php` file and place the following statement right before the closing PHP statement, replacing the string `APIKEY` with your own Google Maps API key:

   ```php
   Configure::write('Geocode.key', 'APIKEY');
   ```

2. We will now make our `Address` model extend the skeleton model provided by the plugin. Edit your `app/models/address.php` file and make the following changes:

```php
<?php
App::import('Model', 'Geocode.GeoAddress');
class Address extends GeoAddress {
    public $validate = array(
        'address_1' => array('rule' => 'notEmpty'),
        'state' => array('rule' => 'notEmpty')
    );
    public static $states = array(
        'CA' => 'California',
        'FL' => 'Florida',
        'NY' => 'New York'
    );
}
?>
```

3. By extending `GeoAddress`, the `Geocodable` behavior is automatically attached to our model. We can now use the form at `http://localhost/addresses/add` to add new addresses. After adding quite a few, we are ready to implement a paginated listing with support to finding addresses that are near a certain location.

4. To simplify this operation, we will force the point of origin in our controller action, instead of letting the user specify the address. With this in mind, add the following action to the `AddressesController` class:

```php
public function index() {
    $address = '1211 La Brad Lane, Tampa, FL';
    $this->paginate = array(
        'near',
        'address' => $address
    );
    $addresses = $this->paginate();
    $this->set(compact('address', 'addresses'));
}
```

5. Now create the view `app/views/addresses/index.ctp`, with the following contents:

```php
<h1>Addresses near <strong><?php echo $address; ?></strong></h1>
<div class="paging">
<?php echo $this->Paginator->prev(); ?>
 
<?php echo $this->Paginator->numbers(); ?>
 
<?php echo $this->Paginator->next(); ?>
</div>
```

```
<br />
<ul>
<?php foreach($addresses as $currentAddress) { ?>
    <li>
        <?php echo $currentAddress['Address']['address_1']; ?>
        at
        <strong><?php echo number_format($currentAddress['Address']
['distance'], 2) . ' km.'; ?></strong>
    </li>
<?php } ?>
</ul>
```

If you inserted sample addresses that are near the specified address, the output could be similar to that shown in the following screenshot:

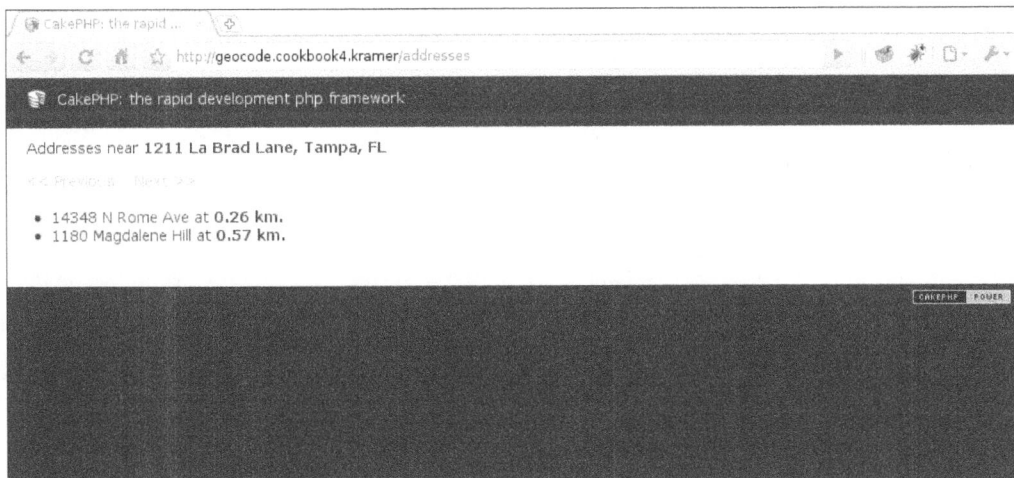

How it works...

We started by downloading the plugin and configuring it by setting our own Google Maps API key in the `bootstrap.php` configuration file. We then made our `Address` model inherit from the `GeoAddress` model provided by the plugin, which makes our model use the `Geocodable` behavior, and implements the `near` custom find type.

Since our `Address` model is now attached to the `Geocodable` behavior, every time we create new address records the plugin will use the Google Maps API to save the appropriate location in the `latitude` and `longitude` fields.

Using the `near` custom find type, we can easily find addresses that are near a certain address, and we can also see what distance separates each of those addresses from the point of origin.

There's more...

The Geocode plugin is quite flexible, and even includes a helper to show addresses in a visual map. To find out all it has to offer, go to its website at `http://github.com/mariano/geocode`.

5
Datasources

In this chapter, we will cover:

- ► Improving the SQL datasource query log
- ► Parsing CSV files with a datasource
- ► Consuming RSS feeds with a datasource
- ► Building a Twitter datasource
- ► Adding transaction and locking support to the MySQL datasource

Introduction

Datasources are the backbone of almost all model operations. They provide an abstraction between model logic and the underlying data layer, allowing a more flexible approach to data manipulation. Through this abstraction, CakePHP applications are able to manipulate data without knowing the specifics of how it's stored or fetched.

This chapter shows how to get information from existing datasources, use pre-built datasources to deal with non-relational data, and teaches us how to create a full-featured Twitter datasource.

Improving the SQL datasource query log

This recipe shows how to create a component that will offer extended logging of all queries executed on any SQL-based datasource that supports the EXPLAIN command (this recipe is designed to work with MySQL, but can be adapted to other SQL based datasources), and show that information when the appropriate debug setting is set.

Getting ready

To go through this recipe we need a sample table to work with. Create a table named accounts, using the following SQL statement:

```sql
CREATE TABLE `accounts`(
  `id` INT UNSIGNED AUTO_INCREMENT NOT NULL,
  `email` VARCHAR(255) NOT NULL,
  PRIMARY KEY(`id`)
);
```

Create a table named profiles, using the following SQL statement:

```sql
CREATE TABLE `profiles`(
  `id` INT UNSIGNED AUTO_INCREMENT NOT NULL,
  `account_id` INT UNSIGNED NOT NULL,
  `name` VARCHAR(255) default NULL,
  PRIMARY KEY(`id`),
  KEY `account_id`(`account_id`),
  FOREIGN KEY `profiles__accounts`(`account_id`) REFERENCES
`accounts`(`id`)
);
```

Add some sample data, using the following SQL statements:

```sql
INSERT INTO `accounts`(`id`, `email`) VALUES
  (1, 'john.doe@example.com'),
  (2, 'jane.doe@example.com');
INSERT INTO `profiles`(`id`, `account_id`, `name`) VALUES
  (1, 1, 'John Doe'),
  (2, 2, 'Jane Doe');
```

We proceed now to create the required model. Create the model Profile in a file named profile.php and place it in your app/models folder with the following contents:

```php
<?php
class Profile extends AppModel {
  public $belongsTo = array(
    'Account' => array('type' => 'INNER')
  );
}
?>
```

Create its appropriate controller `ProfilesController` in a file named `profiles_controller.php` and place it in your `app/controllers` folder with the following contents:

```php
<?php
class ProfilesController extends AppController {
    public function index() {
        $profiles = $this->Profile->find('all');
        $this->set(compact('profiles'));
    }
}
?>
```

Create a folder named `profiles` in your `app/views` folder, and then create the view in a file named `index.ctp` and place it in your `app/views/profiles` folder with the following contents:

```php
<ul>
<?php foreach($profiles as $profile) { ?>
    <li>#<?php echo $profile['Profile']['id']; ?>:
    <?php echo $this->Html->link($profile['Profile']['name'], 'mailto:'
. $profile['Account']['email']); ?></li>
<?php } ?>
</ul>
```

If you don't have a layout, copy the layout file named `default.ctp` from your `cake/libs/view/layouts` folder to your application `app/views/layouts` folder. If you do have a layout, make sure it includes the standard SQL view element where you want the SQL logging placed:

```php
<?php echo $this->element('sql_dump'); ?>
```

Finally, set your debug level to 2 by editing your `app/config/core.php` file and changing the `Configure::write('debug')` line to:

```php
Configure::write('debug', 2);
```

How to do it...

1. Create a file named `query_log.php` and place it in your `app/controllers/components` folder with the following contents:

```php
<?php
class QueryLogComponent extends Object {
    public $minimumTime = 10;
    public $explain = 'EXPLAIN %s';
    public function initialize($controller, $settings = array()) {
        $this->_set($settings);
        if (!is_bool($this->enabled)) {
```

```
                    $this->enabled = Configure::read('debug') >= 2;
            }
        }
    }
    ?>
```

2. While still editing the `query_log.php` file, add the following method to the QueryLogComponent:

```
class:public function beforeRender($controller)
    {
        if ($this->enabled)
        {
            $queryLog = array();
            $datasources = ConnectionManager::sourceList();
            foreach($datasources as $name)
            {
                $datasource = ConnectionManager::getDataSource($name);
                if ($datasource->isInterfaceSupported('getLog'))
                {
                    $log = $datasource->getLog();
                    foreach($log['log'] as $i => $line)
                    {
                        if (empty($line['error']) && $line['took'] >=
                            $this->minimumTime &&
                            stripos(trim($line['query']), 'SELECT')
                            === 0)
                        {
                            $explain = $datasource->query(sprint
                            ($this->explain, $line['query']
                            ));
                        if (!empty($explain))
                        {
                            foreach($explain as $j => $explainLine)
                            {
                                $explain[$j] = array_combine
                                (array_map('strtolower',
                                array_keys($explainLine[0])),
                                $explainLine[0]);
                            }
                            $log['log'][$i]['explain'] = $explain;
                        }
                    }
                }
                if (!empty($log['log']))
                {
```

```php
                    $queryLog[$name] = $log;
                }
            }
        }
        if (!empty($queryLog))
        {
            $controller->set(compact('queryLog'));
        }
    }
}
```

3. Add the `QueryLog` component to all your controllers. Create a file named `app_controller.php` and place it in your `app/` folder with the following contents:

```php
<?php
class AppController extends Controller
    {
        public $components = array(
            'QueryLog' => array(
                'minimumTime' => 0
            )
        );
    }
?>
```

If you already have an `app_controller.php` file, make sure your `components` property includes the `QueryLog` component as shown previously.

4. Create a file named `query_log.ctp` and place it in your `app/views/elements` folder with the following contents:

```php
<?php
if (empty($queryLog))
    {
        echo $this->element('sql_dump');
        return;
    }
foreach($queryLog as $datasource => $log)
    {
?>
    <table class="cake-sql-log">
    <caption>
        Datasource <strong><?php echo $datasource; ?></strong>:
        <?php echo number_format($log['count']) . ' queries (' .
$log['time'] . ' ms. total time)'; ?>
    </caption>
    <thead><tr>
        <th>Query</th>
```

```
<th>Error</th>
<th>Affected</th>
<th>Num. rows</th>
<th>Took</th>
    </tr></thead>
    <tbody>
        <?php foreach($log['log'] as $line) { ?>
        <tr>
            <td>
<?php echo $line['query']; ?>
        <?php if (!empty($line['explain'])) { ?>
            <br /><br />
            <table class="cake-sql-log-explain">
            <thead><tr>
                <th>ID</th>
<th>Select Type</th>
<th>Table</th>
<th>Type</th>
<th>Possible Keys</th>
<th>Key</th>
<th>Ref</th>
<th>Rows</th>
<th>Extra</th>
            </tr></thead>
            <tbody>
            <?php foreach($line['explain'] as $explainLine) { ?>
              <tr>
              <td><?php echo $explainLine['id']; ?></td>
              <td><?php echo $explainLine['select_type']; ?></td>
              <td><?php echo $explainLine['table']; ?></td>
              <td><?php echo $explainLine['type']; ?></td>
             <td><?php echo $explainLine['possible_keys']; ?></td>
              <td><?php
              echo $explainLine['key'];
              if (!empty($explainLine['key_len'])) {
                  echo ' (' . number_format($explainLine['key_
len']) . ' )';
              }
              ?></td>
              <td><?php echo $explainLine['ref']; ?></td>
              <td><?php echo number_format($explainLine['rows']);
?></td>
              <td><?php echo $explainLine['extra']; ?></td>
              </tr>
            <?php } ?>
            </tbody>
            </table>
```

```
          <?php } ?>
          </td>
          <td><?php echo $line['error']; ?></td>
          <td><?php echo number_format($line['affected']); ?></td>
          <td><?php echo number_format($line['numRows']); ?></td>
          <td><?php echo number_format($line['took']) . ' ms.';
?></td>
        </tr>
        <?php } ?>
      </tbody>
      </table>
    <?php } ?>
```

5. Finally, edit your `app/views/layouts/default.ctp` file and replace the line that reads `<?php echo $this->element('sql_dump'); ?>` with the following:

    `<?php echo $this->element('query_log'); ?>`

If we now browse to `http://localhost/profiles`, we should see the improved query log that includes the explanation of `SELECT` queries, as shown in the following screenshot:

How it works...

The SQL command EXPLAIN is used to obtain the execution plan for a SELECT query. When using EXPLAIN, MySQL includes information such as which tables are joined in the query, in which order they are joined, and what keys (if any) are used to optimize the query. This information can be used to optimize queries and considerably reduce their execution time.

The QueryLog component checks the debug setting to determine if it should process the query log, and uses the minimumTime setting to add more information about those queries that took a certain number of milliseconds, or more. In our example, we set this value to 0 when we added the component to AppController to make sure all SELECT queries are properly explained.

The component uses the beforeRender callback to perform its processing right before a view is to be rendered. It starts by using the ConnectionManager::sourceList() method to obtain a list of all available datasources (that is, the name of all connections defined in the app/config/database.php file). For each of those connection names, it gets the actual datasource object using the ConnectionManager::getDataSource() method. As we will see in other recipes in this chapter, a datasource may not implement all methods, so the component then uses the isInterfaceSupported() method, available in all datasources, to see if that particular source implements the getLog() method.

Using the getLog() method, the component obtains the list of queries issued on a particular source, and filters those to check for only SELECT queries that run for the minimum time specified in the minimumTime setting. Once it has the list of SELECT queries that need to be explained, it issues an EXPLAIN SQL statement, and processes the result into a more readable format, ensuring that all fields obtained are lower case.

Finally, and now that the query log is properly processed, it sets the appropriate view variable, which is utilized by the query_log.ctp element to show the log.

Parsing CSV files with a datasource

This recipe shows how to parse **comma-separated values** (**CSV**) files using a datasource, showing a clean approach to CSV processing.

Getting ready

We start by installing CakePHP's datasources plugin. Download the latest release from http://github.com/mariano/datasources/downloads and uncompress the downloaded file into your app/plugins folder. You should now have a directory named datasources inside app/plugins.

The datasources plugin, located at `http://github.com/cakephp/datasources`, is an official CakePHP plugin that offers several community-provided datasources, such as XML-RPC and SOAP. This and other recipes use a customized version of the plugin, modified for the purpose of this book.

We need some sample data to work with. Create a file named `contacts.csv` and place it in a folder of your choice (such as `/home/mariano`), with contents similar to the ones shown below. This example includes only two rows of data, but the file used in this recipe uses several more rows, and should include the starting header row:

```
name,email,country,gender,age
"John Doe","john.doe@email.com","United States of America","Male",34
"Jane Doe","jane.doe@email.com","United Kingdom","Female",25
```

How to do it...

1. We start by creating a connection to use the CSV datasource. Open your `app/config/database.php` file and add the following connection:

```php
public $csv = array(
    'datasource' => 'datasources.CsvSource',
    'path' => '/home/mariano/',
    'readonly' => true
);
```

2. Create a model named `Contact` in a file named `contact.php` and place it in your `app/models` folder with the following contents:

```php
<?php
class Contact extends AppModel
    {
        public $useDbConfig = 'csv';
    }
?>
```

3. Create its controller in a file named `contacts_controller.php` and place it in your `app/controllers` folder with the following contents:

```php
<?php
class ContactsController extends AppController
    {
        public function index()
            {
                $this->set('contacts', $this->paginate());
            }
    }
?>
```

4. Finally, we need to create the view. Create a folder named `contacts` in your `app/views` folder, and in that folder create a file named `index.ctp` with the following contents:

```
<p>
<?php echo $this->Paginator->prev(); ?> 
<?php echo $this->Paginator->numbers(); ?> 
<?php echo $this->Paginator->next(); ?>
</p>
<table>
<thead><tr>
    <th>ID</th>
    <th>Name</th>
    <th>Email</th>
    <th>Country</th>
    <th>Gender</th>
    <th>Age</th>
</tr></thead>
<tbody>
<?php foreach($contacts as $contact) { ?>
<tr>
    <td><?php echo $contact['id']; ?></td>
    <td><?php echo $contact['name']; ?></td>
    <td><?php echo $contact['email']; ?></td>
    <td><?php echo $contact['country']; ?></td>
    <td><?php echo $contact['gender']; ?></td>
    <td><?php echo $contact['age']; ?></td>
</tr>
<?php } ?>
</tbody>
</table>
```

If we now browse to `http://localhost/contacts`, we should see a paginated list, as shown in the following screenshot:

ID	Name	Email	Country	Gender	Age
1	John Doe	john.doe@email.com	United States of America	Male	34
2	Jane Doe	jane.doe@email.com	United Kingdom	Female	25
3	Jack Doe	jack.doe@email.com	United Kingdom	Male	22
4	Marie Doe	marie.doe@email.com	Ireland	Female	26
5	Linda Doe	linda.doe@email.com	Brazil	Female	19
6	Mark Doe	mark.doe@email.com	Mexico	Male	18
7	Peter Doe	peter.doe@email.com	India	Male	41
8	Jessica Doe	jessica.doe@email.com	Czech Republic	Female	35
9	Mathew Doe	mathew.doe@email.com	United States of America	Male	26
10	Chris Doe	chris.doe@email.com	United Kingdom	Male	26
11	Bettina Doe	bettina.doe@email.com	United States of America	Female	25
12	Dennis Doe	dennis.doe@email.com	United States of America	Male	27
13	Laura Doe	laura.doe@email.com	Portugal	Female	19
14	Claudia Doe	claudia.doe@email.com	Chile	Female	20
15	William Doe	william.doe@email.com	United States of America	Male	19
16	Valentina Doe	valentina.doe@email.com	Spain	Female	22

How it works...

We start by creating a new connection named `csv`, specifying `datasources.CsvSource` as its type, that is, a datasource named `CsvSource` that is a part of a plugin named `datasources`. We set the path to our CSV files to CakePHP's temporary directory using the `path` setting, and we specify that we don't want that path to be created if it doesn't exist, by setting `readonly` to true.

> The fork we are using in this recipe adds a feature to the original plugin: allowing one to change the CSV file used via the model property `table`

We then create the `Contact` model, specifying its underlying connection to be `csv` through the `useDbConfig` property. The CSV data source will then use the respective table name as the name of the file, attaching the `csv` extension to it. In this case, the CSV data source will use contacts for the `Contact` model, which can be changed through the model property `table`.

Using that file name, it will look for it in the path that was defined in the connection settings. If the file cannot be loaded, or if the path does not exist, it will throw a missing table error, just as any model with a missing table would.

> The default `csv` extension can be changed by specifying the `extension` setting in the connection.

Once the file is properly loaded, the datasource allows us to fetch records by issuing simple `find()` calls. It supports some of the most common find settings: `limit`, `page`, `fields`, and includes basic support for defining the setting `conditions` to limit the obtained records (see the *There's more* section below).

The rest of the recipe shows how we use our `Contact` model just as we would use any model, exemplifying this flexibility with a paginated list of parsed CSV records.

There's more...

Other than being able to define which page to obtain (through the `page` find setting) and how many records to obtain (using the `limit` find setting), the CSV datasource allows for some basic filtering, by means of the handy `Set::matches()` method. For example, we can modify our paginated list to obtain contacts whose ages are over 30, by adding the following `conditions` setting to our `index()` method:

```
public function index()
  {
    $this->paginate = array(
      'conditions' => array('age >' => 30)
   );
    $this->set('contacts', $this->paginate());
  }
```

Dynamic loading of CSV files

The example used in this recipe is bound to the file `contacts.csv` by means of the default table named for the `Contact` model, but what would be required if we needed to process several CSV files and we don't want to create a model for each of those files?

Using the `table` model property, we can dynamically change the underlying CSV file a model is importing from, and execute our `find` operations just as if we would've created a model specifically for this file. We start by creating a model that uses the `csv` connection, but that is not tied to any file:

```
<?php
class Csv extends AppModel
  {
    public $useDbConfig = 'csv';
    public $useTable = false;
  }
?>
```

Setting `useTable` to `false` allows us to avoid any file loading. We can then use the `listSources()` datasource method to obtain a list of all CSV files available for importing, and then dynamically change the `table` model property for each of those files, and fetch the actual records. We do this in the following `controller` method:

```
public function import()
  {
    $this->loadModel('Csv');
    $sources = array_flip($this->Csv->getDataSource()->listSources());
    foreach($sources as $source => $null)
      {
        $this->Csv->table = $source;
        $sources[$source] = $this->Csv->find('all');
      }
    debug($sources);
    exit;
  }
```

The list of files obtained through the `listSources()` method is fetched from the `path` setting specified in the datasource configuration, as defined in `app/config/database.php`. This path can be changed by first cleaning up the current connection, which releases the handle to the previously configured path, by using the datasource `setConfig()` method to change the `path` setting, and then calling it's `connect()` method to load the path:

```
$dataSource = $this->Csv->getDataSource();
$dataSource->close();
$dataSource->setConfig(array('path' => '/home/john/'));
$dataSource->connect();
```

Consuming RSS feeds with a datasource

This recipe shows how to get content from remote RSS feeds using a datasource.

Getting ready

We start by installing the fork of CakePHP's datasources plugin. Download the latest release from `http://github.com/mariano/datasources/downloads` and uncompress the downloaded file into your `app/plugins` folder. You should now have a directory named `datasources`. The fork used in this recipe uses a refactored version of the RSS datasource developed by Donatas Kairys, member of Loadsys Consulting. This modified version improves the datasource performance, and adds the possibility of changing the feed URL through a find setting. More information about the original datasource can be obtained at `http://blog.loadsys.com/2009/06/19/cakephp-rss-feed-datasource`.

How to do it...

1. We start by creating a connection to use the RSS datasource. Open your `app/config/database.php` file and add the following connection:

```php
public $feed = array(
    'datasource' => 'datasources.RssSource',
    'url' => 'http://marianoiglesias.com.ar/category/cakephp/feed/'
);
```

2. Create a model named `Post` in a file named `post.php` and place it in your `app/models` folder with the following contents:

```php
<?php
class Post extends AppModel {
    public $useDbConfig = 'feed';
}
?>
```

3. Create its controller in a file named `posts_controller.php` and place it in your `app/controllers` folder with the following contents:

```php
<?php
class PostsController extends AppController
    {
        public $helpers = array('Time');
        public function index()
            {
                $this->paginate = array(
                    'order' => array('pubDate' => 'desc'),
                    'limit' => 9
                );
                $this->set('posts', $this->paginate());
            }
    }
?>
```

4. Finally, we need to create the view. Create a folder named `posts` in your `app/views` folder, and in that folder create a file named `index.ctp` with the following contents:

```php
<p>
<?php echo $this->Paginator->prev(); ?> 
<?php echo $this->Paginator->numbers(); ?> 
<?php echo $this->Paginator->next(); ?>
</p>
<table>
<thead><tr><th>Title</th><th>Published</th></tr></thead>
<tbody>
```

```php
<?php foreach($posts as $post) { ?>
<tr>
   <td><?php echo $this->Html->link($post['Post']['title'],
$post['Post']['link']); ?></td>
   <td><?php echo $this->Time->nice($post['Post']['pubDate']);
?></td>
</tr>
<?php } ?>
</tbody>
</table>
```

If we now browse to `http://localhost/posts`, we should see a paginated list of posts, as shown in the following screenshot:

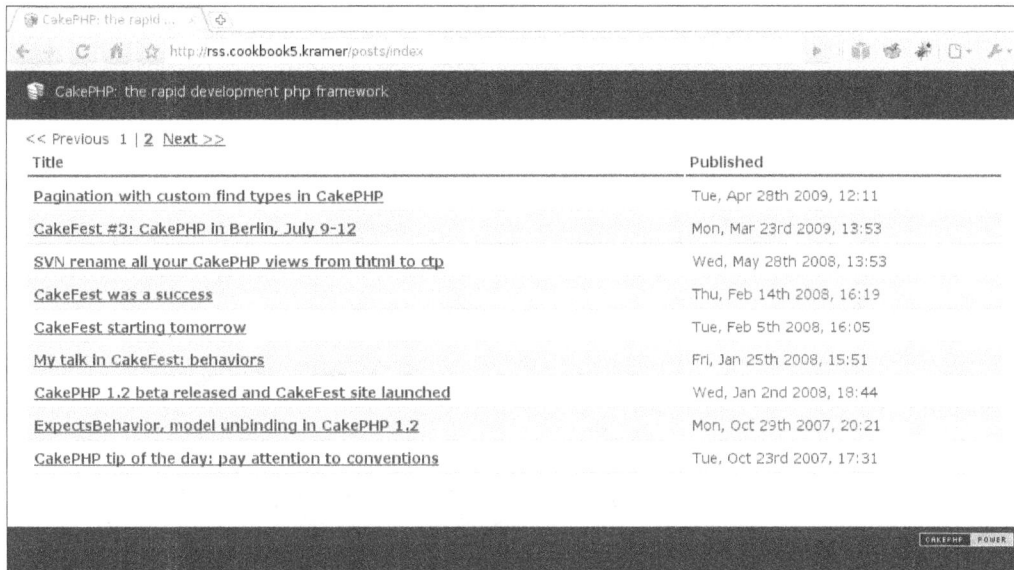

How it works...

We start by creating a new connection named `feed`, specifying `datasources.FeedSource` as its type. We use the setting `url` to specify the address of the feed source. Among other available connection settings we have:

- `encoding`: Sets the character encoding to use. Defaults to the CakePHP `App.encoding` configuration setting.
- `cache`: If set to `false`, no caching will be done. Otherwise this is the cache configuration name to use. Defaults to the configuration named `default`.

We then create the `Post` model, specifying its underlying connection to be `feed` through the `useDbConfig` property. We then proceed to setup a paginated list of posts sorting by publication date (`pubDate` field) in descending order, and limiting to nine posts per page.

Just as with the CSV datasource shown in the recipe, *Parsing CSV files with a datasource*, the RSS datasource allows some basic filtering. For example, to only show posts that were created in the year 2009 or later, we would add the following `conditions` setting to our `index()` method:

```
public function index()
  {
    $this->paginate = array(
      'conditions' => array('pubDate >=' => '2009-01-01'),
      'order' => array('pubDate' => 'desc'),
      'limit' => 9
    );
    $this->set('posts', $this->paginate());
  }
```

There's more...

There are cases where we might not be able to define the feed URL in a configuration file, for example, if the URL comes from a dynamic data source. Fortunately, for these cases we have the option to define the feed address through a custom find setting.

In the above example, we could remove the feed URL from the connection settings, and specify it as a find setting named `url`:

```
$this->paginate = array(
  'url' => 'http://marianoiglesias.com.ar/category/cakephp/feed/',
  'order' => array('pubDate' => 'desc'),
  'limit' => 9
);
$this->set('posts', $this->paginate());
```

Changing connection settings at runtime

We've seen how we can change the feed URL by using a custom find setting. However, we could also change this address by modifying the connection settings. Using the method `setConfig()`, available in all datasources, we can make changes to any connection setting. For example, instead of using the `url` custom find setting, we'll change the feed URL by changing the connection:

```
$this->Post->getDataSource()->setConfig(array(
  'url' => 'http://marianoiglesias.com.ar/category/cakephp/feed/'
));
```

```php
$this->paginate = array(
    'order' => array('pubDate' => 'desc'),
    'limit' => 9
);
$this->set('posts', $this->paginate());
```

Building a Twitter datasource

In this recipe we will learn how to implement our own datasource by providing a way to read from and post messages to a Twitter account.

Getting ready

We will integrate this datasource with OAuth, which is an authentication mechanism supported by Twitter. To do so, we will use a class named `HttpSocketOauth` developed by Neil Crookes, which is an extension to CakePHP's own `HttpSocket` class that adds OAuth support in a clean and elegant way. Download the file named `http_socket_oauth.php` from the URL `http://github.com/neilcrookes/http_socket_oauth/raw/master/ http_socket_oauth.php` and place it in your `app/vendors` folder.

There are other ways to communicate with an `OAuth` provider such as Twitter, most noticeably using the **PHP OAuth library** available at `http://code.google.com/p/oauth-php`. This recipe uses Neil's approach for its simplicity.

Let us continue by creating the `Tweet` model. Create a file named `tweet.php` and place it in your `app/models` folder with the following contents:

```php
<?php
class Tweet extends AppModel {
    public $useDbConfig = 'twitter';
}
?>
```

Create its controller in a file named `tweets_controller.php` and place it in your `app/controllers` with the following contents:

```php
<?php
class TweetsController extends AppController {
    public function index($twitter) {
        $tweets = $this->Tweet->find('all', array(
            'conditions' => array('username' => $twitter)
        ));
        $this->set(compact('tweets', 'twitter'));
    }
```

```
        public function add($twitter) {
            if (!empty($this->data)) {
                $this->Tweet->create();
                if ($this->Tweet->save($this->data)) {
                    $this->Session->setFlash('Succeeded');
                } else {
                    $this->Session->setFlash('Failed');
                }
            }
            $this->redirect(array('action'=>'index', $twitter));
        }
    }
    ?>
```

We now need the appropriate view. Create a folder named `tweets` in your `app/views` folder, and inside it, create a file named `index.ctp` with the following contents:

```
<?php
echo $this->Form->create(array('url' => array('action'=>'add',
$twitter)));
echo $this->Form->inputs(array(
    'status' => array('label'=>false)
));
echo $this->Form->end('Tweet this');
?>
<?php foreach($tweets as $tweet) { ?>
    <p><?php echo $tweet['Tweet']['text']; ?></p>
    <p><small>
    <?php echo $this->Html->link(
        date('F d, Y', strtotime($tweet['Tweet']['created_at'])),
        'http://www.twitter.com/' . $tweet['User']['screen_name'] . '/
status/' . $tweet['Tweet']['id']
    ); ?>
    with <?php echo $tweet['Tweet']['source']; ?>
    </small></p>
    <br />
<?php } ?>
```

Next, we will need to register our application on Twitter. Go to the URL `http://twitter.com/apps/new` and fill in the form (an example is shown in the following figure.) Make sure you specify a domain different than `localhost` when asked for your **Application Website**, and that you select **Read & Write** when asked for the **Default Access Type**. You will also need to specify **Browser** as the **Application Type**, and `http://localhost/tweets` as the **Callback URL**, replacing `localhost` with your own host. This callback won't actually be utilized, as we will define it at runtime, but it is mandatory, so we need to fill it in.

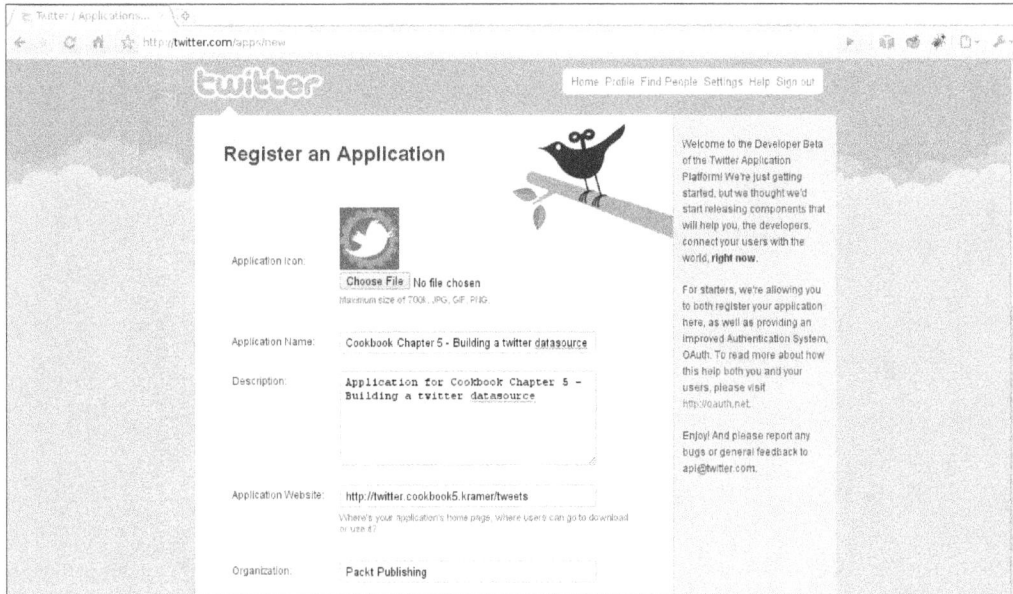

When you successfully submit this form, Twitter will give you some information regarding your newly registered application. In that screen, make sure to grab what is shown as **Consumer key** and **Consumer secret**, as we will need it when going through this recipe.

Add a new connection named `$twitter` to your `app/config/database.php`, by using the following contents and replacing KEY with your **Consumer key** and SECRET_KEY with the **Consumer secret** you obtained above:

```
public $twitter = array(
    'datasource' => 'twitter',
    'key' => 'KEY',
    'secret' => 'SECRET_KEY'
);
```

How to do it...

We start by fully implementing the datasource. Create a file named `twitter_source.php` and place it in your `app/models/datasources` folder with the following contents:

```php
<?php
App::import('Vendor', 'HttpSocketOauth');
class TwitterSource extends DataSource {
    public $_baseConfig = array(
        'key' => null,
        'secret' => null
```

```
        );
    protected $_schema = array(
        'tweets' => array(
            'id' => array(
                'type' => 'integer',
                'null' => true,
                'key' => 'primary',
                'length' => 11,
            ),
            'text' => array(
                'type' => 'string',
                'null' => true,
                'key' => 'primary',
                'length' => 140
            ),
            'status' => array(
                'type' => 'string',
                'null' => true,
                'key' => 'primary',
                'length' => 140
            ),
        )
    );
    public function __construct($config = null, $autoConnect = true) {
        parent::__construct($config, $autoConnect);
        if ($autoConnect) {
            $this->connect();
        }
    }
    public function listSources() {
        return array('tweets');
    }
    public function describe($model) {
        return $this->_schema['tweets'];
    }
    public function connect() {
        $this->connected = true;
        $this->connection = new HttpSocketOauth();
        return $this->connected;
    }
    public function close() {
        if ($this->connected) {
            unset($this->connection);
```

```
            $this->connected = false;
        }
    }
}
```

Now that we have the basic datasource skeleton, we need to add the ability for our datasorce to connect to Twitter, using OAuth. Add the following methods to the `TwitterSource`:

```
class created before:public function token($callback = null) {
    $response = $this->connection->request(array(
        'method' => 'GET',
        'uri' => array(
            'host' => 'api.twitter.com',
            'path' => '/oauth/request_token'
        ),
        'auth' => array(
            'method' => 'OAuth',
            'oauth_callback' => $callback,
            'oauth_consumer_key' => $this->config['key'],
            'oauth_consumer_secret' => $this->config['secret']
        )
    ));

    if (!empty($response)) {
        parse_str($response, $response);
        if (empty($response['oauth_token']) && count($response) == 1 &&
current($response) == '') {
            trigger_error(key($response), E_USER_WARNING);
        } elseif (!empty($response['oauth_token'])) {
            return $response['oauth_token'];
        }
    }
    return false;
}

public function authorize($token, $verifier) {
    $return = false;
    $response = $this->connection->request(array(
        'method' => 'GET',
        'uri' => array(
            'host' => 'api.twitter.com',
            'path' => '/oauth/access_token'
        ),
        'auth' => array(
            'method' => 'OAuth',
```

```
          'oauth_consumer_key' => $this->config['key'],
          'oauth_consumer_secret' => $this->config['secret'],
          'oauth_token' => $token,
          'oauth_verifier' => $verifier
      )
  ));

  if (!empty($response)) {
      parse_str($response, $response);
      if (count($response) == 1 && current($response) == '') {
          trigger_error(key($response), E_USER_WARNING);
      } else {
          $return = $response;
      }
  }
  return $return;
}
```

Our datasource is now able to connect by requesting the proper authorization from Twitter. The next step is adding support to fetch tweets by implementing the datasource `read()` method. Add the following method to the `TwitterSource`:

```
class:public function read($model, $queryData = array()) {
    if (
        empty($queryData['conditions']['username']) ||
        empty($this->config['authorize'])
    ) {
        return false;
    }
    $response = $this->connection->request(array(
        'method' => 'GET',
        'uri' => array(
            'host' => 'api.twitter.com',
            'path' => '1/statuses/user_timeline/' .
$queryData['conditions']['username'] . '.json'
        ),
        'auth' => array_merge(array(
            'method' => 'OAuth',
            'oauth_consumer_key' => $this->config['key'],
            'oauth_consumer_secret' => $this->config['secret']
        ), $this->config['authorize'])
    ));
    if (empty($response)) {
        return false;
```

```
    }
    $response = json_decode($response, true);
    if (!empty($response['error'])) {
        trigger_error($response['error'], E_USER_ERROR);
    }
    $results = array();
    foreach ($response as $record) {
        $record = array('Tweet' => $record);
        $record['User'] = $record['Tweet']['user'];
        unset($record['Tweet']['user']);
        $results[] = $record;
    }
    return $results;
}
```

The job would not be complete if we are unable to post new tweets with our datasource. To finish our implementation, add the following method to the `TwitterSource`:

```
class:public function create($model, $fields = array(), $values =
array()) {
    if (empty($this->config['authorize'])) {
        return false;
    }
    $response = $this->connection->request(array(
        'method' => 'POST',
        'uri' => array(
            'host' => 'api.twitter.com',
            'path' => '1/statuses/update.json'
        ),
        'auth' => array(
            'method' => 'OAuth',
            'oauth_token' => $this->config['authorize']['oauth_token'],
            'oauth_token_secret' => $this->config['authorize']['oauth_
token_secret'],
            'oauth_consumer_key' => $this->config['key'],
            'oauth_consumer_secret' => $this->config['secret']
        ),
        'body' => array_combine($fields, $values)
    ));
    if (empty($response)) {
        return false;
    }
    $response = json_decode($response, true);
    if (!empty($response['error'])) {
```

```
        trigger_error($response['error'], E_USER_ERROR);
    }
    if (!empty($response['id'])) {
        $model->setInsertId($response['id']);
        return true;
    }
    return false;
}
```

For the datasource to work, we will have to get OAuth authorization on all our requests to Twitter. To do so, we implement a method that will talk with the datasource to get the authorization keys, and handle the authorization callbacks Twitter will issue. Edit your app/controllers/tweets_controller.php and add the following contents at the beginning of the TweetsController class:

```
public function beforeFilter() {
    parent::beforeFilter();
    if (!$this->_authorize()) {
        $this->redirect(null, 403);
    }
}

protected function _authorize() {
    $authorize = $this->Session->read('authorize');
    if (empty($authorize)) {
        $source = $this->Tweet->getDataSource();
        $url = Router::url(null, true);
        if (
            !empty($this->params['url']['oauth_token']) &&
            !empty($this->params['url']['oauth_verifier'])
        ) {
            $authorize = $source->authorize(
                $this->params['url']['oauth_token'],
                $this->params['url']['oauth_verifier']
            );
            $this->Session->write('authorize', $authorize);
        } elseif (!empty($this->params['url']['denied'])) {
            return false;
        } else {
            $token = $source->token($url);
            $this->redirect('http://api.twitter.com/oauth/
authorize?oauth_token=' . $token);
        }
    }

    if (!empty($authorize)) {
```

```
        $this->Tweet->getDataSource()->setConfig(compact('authorize'));
    }
    return $authorize;
}
```

Assuming your twitter account name is **cookbook5**, we now browse to `http://localhost/tweets/index/cookbook5`, and should see a paginated list of our tweets as shown in the following figure:

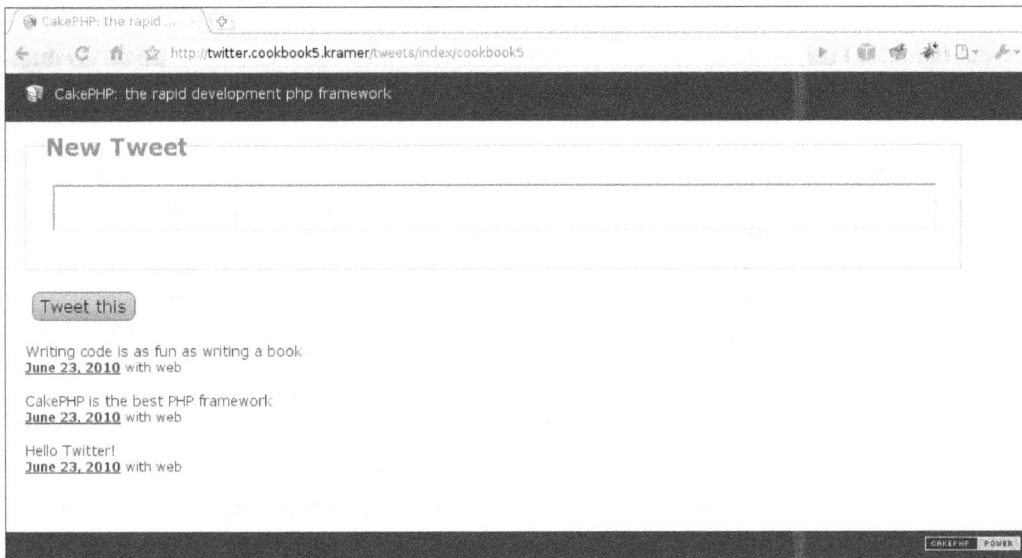

Using the form to post new tweets should submit our text to Twitter, and show us our new tweet in the listing.

How it works...

The Twitter datasource starts by specifying two new connection settings:

 ▸ `key`: A Twitter application consumer key
 ▸ `secret`: A Twitter application consumer secret key

It then defines a static schema, through the `_schema` property and the `listSources()` and `describe()` method implementations, to describe how a tweet post is built. This is done purely to add support for a Twitter based model to work with CakePHP's `FormHelper`. Doing so allows the `FormHelper` to determine what type of field to use when rendering a form for a Twitter-based model.

The `connect()` and `close()` methods simply instantiate and erase respectively an instance of the `HttpSocketOauth` class, which is our handler to communicate with the Twitter API.

OAuth is a complicated process, and understanding it may prove to be a challenge. If you wish to obtain more detailed information about this protocol, there is probably no better resource than the *Beginner's Guide to OAuth*, available at `http://hueniverse.com/oauth`.

The `token()` method uses the connection to request a token from Twitter, which is needed for our requests to be successful. When one is obtained, we take the user to a specific Twitter URL using this token (the redirection takes place in the controller's `_authorize()` method), which is then used by Twitter to request the user for authorization.

If the user allows the access to his/her Twitter account, the Twitter API will redirect the browser to the URL specified in the `callback` argument of the datasource `token()` method. This callback was set in `_authorize()` as the current URL.

After the user is brought back to our application, the `_authorize()` method will check for the existence of two parameters sent by Twitter: `oauth_token` and `oauth_verifier`. These parameters are passed as arguments to the datasource `authorize()` method, which talks back to the Twitter API for the final stage in the OAuth authorization procedure. This stage ends with Twitter giving back a valid token, and a token secret key. They are saved in the controller as a session variable, to avoid doing this on every request.

Once we have the authorization information, we set it as a connection setting by using the `setConfig()` method available in all datasources, and setting this information in a setting named `authorize`, because we won't be able to read from or post to our Twitter account without this authorization.

The datasource `read()` method is the implementation of all read procedures on our datasource. In our case, we only allow find operations that contain a condition on the field `username`. This condition tells us from which user account we want to obtain tweets. Using this account name and the authorization information, we make a request to the Twitter API to obtain the user timeline. Because the request was made using JSON, which can be identified from the request URL), we use PHP's `json_decode()` function to parse the response. We then browse through the resulting items (if no error was thrown) and change them into a more friendly format.

The datasource `write()` method is the implementation of save operations, that is, the creating of new tweets (modification of existing tweets is not supported in this implementation). Similarly to the `read()` method, we use the authorization information to make a POST request to the Twitter API, specifying as the tweet data whatever fields were sent to the method (combination of the `fields` and `values` arguments).

Adding transaction and locking support to the MySQL datasource

CakePHP's built-in MySQL datasource provides some basic transaction support by sending all unknown method calls directly to the datasource. However, this only enables us to use some basic transaction commands, and any locking would have to be performed through manual SQL queries.

> Table locking is a mechanism to effectively manage concurrent access to table contents by different client sessions. More information about locking in MySQL is available at `http://dev.mysql.com/doc/refman/5.5/en/internal-locking.html`.

This recipe shows how to modify an existing datasource by implementing better transaction support to the MySQL driver, adding locking operations, and finally allowing a recovery procedure for locked queries.

> More information about transaction support in MySQL databases is available at `http://dev.mysql.com/doc/refman/5.5/en/commit.html`.

Getting ready

To go through this recipe we need a sample table to work with. Create a table named `profiles` using the following SQL statement:

```
CREATE TABLE `profiles`(
    `id` INT UNSIGNED AUTO_INCREMENT NOT NULL,
    `name` VARCHAR(255) default NULL,
    PRIMARY KEY(`id`)
) ENGINE=InnoDb;
```

> The above query includes the specification of the MySQL database engine. Even when MyISAM (another available engine) can handle table level locking, row level locking is only possible on InnoDb tables. Furthermore, transactions are only supported on InnoDb. More information about the different engines and their supported features is available at `http://dev.mysql.com/doc/refman/5.5/en/storage-engines.html`.

Add some sample data using the following SQL statements:

```
INSERT INTO `profiles`(`id`, `name`) VALUES
    (1, 'John Doe'),
    (2, 'Jane Doe');
```

We proceed now to create the required model. Create the model `Profile` in a file named `profile.php` and place it in your `app/models` folder with the following contents:

```php
<?php
class Profile extends AppModel {
}
?>
```

Create its appropriate controller `ProfilesController` in a file named `profiles_controller.php` and place it in your `app/controllers` folder with the following contents:

```php
<?php
class ProfilesController extends AppController {
   public function index() {
   }
}
?>
```

How to do it...

1. We start by creating the skeleton of our datasource. Create a folder named `dbo` inside your `app/models/datasources` folder. In the `dbo` folder, create a file named `dbo_mysql_transaction.php` with the following contents:

```php
<?php
App::import('Core', 'DboMysql');
class DboMysqlTransaction extends DboMysql {
    protected $backAutoCommit;
    protected $lockTimeoutErrorCode = 1205;
    public function __construct($config = null, $autoConnect =
true) {
        $this->_baseConfig = Set::merge(array(
            'lock' => array(
                'log' => LOGS . 'locks.log',
                'recover' => true,
                'retries' => 1
            ),
            'autoCommit' => null
        ), $this->_baseConfig);

        $this->_commands = array_merge(array(
            'lock' => 'LOCK TABLES {$table} {$operation}',
            'unlock' => 'UNLOCK TABLES',
            'setAutoCommit' => 'SET @@autoCommit={$autoCommit}'
        ), $this->_commands);

        parent::__construct($config, $autoConnect);
```

```
    if (
        !is_null($this->config['autoCommit']) &&
        !$this->setAutoCommit($this->config['autoCommit'])
    ) {
        trigger_error('Could not set autoCommit', E_USER_
WARNING);
    }
  }
}
?>
```

2. We continue by adding methods to lock and unlock tables. Edit your app/models/
datasources/dbo/dbo_mysql_transaction.php file and add the following
methods to the DboMysqlTransaction class:

```
public function lock($model = null, $options = array()) {
    if (!is_object($model) && empty($options)) {
        $options = $model;
        $model = null;
    }
    if (empty($options) && !isset($model)) {
        trigger_error('Nothing to lock', E_USER_WARNING);
        return false;
    } elseif (!is_array($options)) {
        $options = array('table' => $options);
    } elseif (Set::numeric(array_keys($options))) {
        if (count($options) > 1) {
            $options = array('table' => $options[0], 'operation'
=> $options[1]);
        } else {
            if (!empty($options[0]) && is_array($options[0])) {
                $options = $options[0];
            } else {
                $options = array('table' => $options[0]);
            }
        }
    }
    if (empty($options['table']) && isset($model)) {
        $options = array_merge(array(
            'table' => $model->table,
            'alias' => $model->alias
        ), $options);
        if (!empty($options['operation']) &&
$options['operation'] == 'read') {
```

```
                    unset($options['alias']);
            }
        }

        $options = array_merge(array('alias'=>null,
'operation'=>'read', 'local'=>false, 'low'=>false), $options);
        if (!in_array(strtolower($options['operation']),
array('read', 'write'))) {
            trigger_error(sprintf('Invalid operation %s for locking',
$options['operation']), E_USER_WARNING);
            return false;
        }

        $table = $this->fullTableName($options['table']);
        if (!empty($options['alias'])) {
            $table .= ' AS ' . $this->name($options['alias']);
        }
        $operation = strtoupper($options['operation']);
        if ($options['operation'] == 'read' && $options['local']) {
            $operation .= ' LOCAL';
        } elseif ($options['operation'] == 'write' &&
$options['low']) {
            $operation = 'LOW_PRIORITY ' . $operation;
        }
        $sql = strtr($this->_commands['lock'], array(
            '{$table}' => $table,
            '{$operation}' => $operation
        ));
        return ($this->query($sql) !== false);
}
public function unlock($model = null, $options = array()) {
    return ($this->query($this->_commands['unlock']) !== false);
}
```

While still editing the DboMysqlTransaction class, add the
following methods to allow us to get and change the auto commit
status:

```
public function getAutoCommit($model = null) {
    if (is_null($this->config['autoCommit'])) {
        if (!$this->isConnected() && !$this->connect()) {
            trigger_error('Could not connect to database', E_USER_
WARNING);
            return false;
        }

        $result = $this->query('SELECT @@autocommit AS ' . $this-
>name('autocommit'));
        if (empty($result)) {
```

```
        trigger_error('Could not fetch autoCommit status from
database', E_USER_WARNING);
        return false;
    }
    $this->config['autoCommit'] = !empty($result[0][0]
['autocommit']);
  }
  return $this->config['autoCommit'];
}

public function setAutoCommit($model, $autoCommit = null) {
    if (!$this->isConnected() && !$this->connect()) {
        trigger_error('Could not connect to database', E_USER_
WARNING);
        return false;
    }

    if (is_bool($model)) {
        $autoCommit = $model;
        $model = null;
    } elseif (is_array($autoCommit)) {
        list($autoCommit) = $autoCommit;
    }

    $this->config['autoCommit'] = !empty($autoCommit);
    $sql = strtr($this->_commands['setAutoCommit'], array(
        '{$autoCommit}' => ($this->config['autoCommit'] ? '1' :
'0')
    ));
    return ($this->query($sql) !== false);
}
```

3. We will now add our basic transaction commands. Edit your app/models/
    datasources/dbo/dbo_mysql_transaction.php file and add the following
    methods to the DboMysqlTransaction class:

```
public function begin($model) {
    $this->_startTransaction();
    return parent::begin($model);
}
public function commit($model) {
    $result = parent::commit($model);
    $this->_endTransaction();
    return $result;
}
public function rollback($model) {
    $result = parent::rollback($model);
```

```
        $this->_endTransaction();
        return $result;
    }

    protected function _startTransaction() {
        if ($this->getAutoCommit()) {
            $this->backAutoCommit = $this->getAutoCommit();
            $this->setAutoCommit(false);
        }
    }

    protected function _endTransaction() {
        if (isset($this->backAutoCommit)) {
            $this->setAutoCommit($this->backAutoCommit);
            $this->backAutoCommit = null;
        }
    }

    public function query() {
        $args = func_get_args();
        if (!empty($args) && count($args) > 2 && in_array($args[0],
array_keys($this->_commands))) {
            list($command, $params, $model) = $args;
            if ($this->isInterfaceSupported($command)) {
                return $this->{$command}($model, $params);
            }
        }
        return call_user_func_array(array('parent', 'query'), $args);
    }
```

4. We end by adding methods to recover from a locked query, and to log those locks. Once again, edit your `app/models/datasources/dbo/dbo_mysql_transaction.php` file and add the following methods to the `DboMysqlTransaction` class:

```
public function _execute($sql, $retry = 0) {
    $result = parent::_execute($sql);
    $error = $this->lastError();
    if (
        !empty($error) &&
        $this->config['lock']['recover'] &&
        preg_match('/^\b' . preg_quote($this->lockTimeoutErrorCode)
. '\b/', $error)
    ) {
        if ($retry == 0) {
            $message = 'Got lock on query [' . $sql . ']';
            $queries = array_reverse(Set::extract($this->_queriesLog,
'/query'));
```

```
            if (!empty($queries)) {
                $message .= " Query trace (newest to oldest): \n\t";
                $message .= implode("\n\t", array_slice($queries, 0,
5));
            }
            $this->lockLog($message);
        }

        if ($retry < $this->config['lock']['retries']) {
            $result = $this->_execute($sql, $retry + 1);
        } elseif (!empty($this->config['lock']['log'])) {
            $this->lockLog('Failed after ' . number_format($retry) .
' retries');
        }
    } elseif (empty($error) && $retry > 0 && !empty($this-
>config['lock']['log'])) {
        $this->lockLog('Succeeded after ' . number_format($retry) .
' retries');
    }

    if (empty($error) && !$this->fullDebug && !empty($this-
>config['lock']['log'])) {
        $this->logQuery($sql);
    }
    return $result;
}

protected function lockLog($message) {
    $message = '['.date('d/m/Y H:i:s') . '] ' . $message . "\n";
    $handle = fopen($this->config['lock']['log'], 'a');
    if (!is_resource($handle)) {
        trigger_error(sprintf('Could not open log file %s', $this-
>config['lock']['log']), E_USER_WARNING);
        return false;
    }
    fwrite($handle, $message);
    fclose($handle);
    return true;
}
```

5. To test what happens when you reach a lock, edit your app/controllers/
profiles_controller.php file and add the following method to the
ProfilesController class:

```
public function index() {
    $this->Profile->setAutoCommit(false);
    if ($this->Profile->lock()) {
        $profile = $this->Profile->find('all');
```

```
          debug($profile);
          $this->Profile->unlock();
      }
      exit;
}
```

6. Open your MySQL client and issue the following SQL commands (don't close the client after you issue these commands as you may want to release the lock as shown later):

```
SET @@autocommit=0;
LOCK TABLE `profiles` WRITE;
```

7. If we now browse to `http://localhost/profiles` we should get an SQL error message that reads **SQL Error: 1205: Lock wait timeout exceeded; try restarting transaction**. A file named `locks.log` should have been created in your `app/tmp/logs` folder with the following contents (the database name `cookbook_chapter5_transaction` should change to the name of the database you are using):

```
[23/06/2010 09:14:11] Got lock on query [LOCK TABLES `profiles` AS
`Profile` READ] Query trace (newest to oldest):
        SET @@autocommit=0
        DESCRIBE `profiles`
        SHOW TABLES FROM `cookbook_chapter5_transaction`;
[23/06/2010 09:14:17] Failed after 1 retries
```

8. To test the recovery of locked queries, we could release the lock in our MySQL client by issuing the following command:

```
UNLOCK TABLES;
```

and do so somewhere between the first failed transaction and the next recovery attempt. To change how much time MySQL waits to see if a lock can be obtained, access MySQL documentation for the server setting `innodb_lock_wait_timeout`.

How it works...

As we are extending a DBO based datasource, we name our class using the `Dbo` prefix (`DboMysqlTransaction`), and place it in the `dbo` folder which is itself in our `app/models/datasources` folder.

The initial implementation includes two class properties:

► `backAutoCommit`:Utilized by the helper methods `_startTransaction()` and `_endTransaction()`, is used to temporarily change the auto commit setting.

► `lockTimeoutErrorCode`: Specifies MySQL's code number for identifying deadlock time expired errors.

Our first method is the class constructor, which is overridden to add our own connection settings, and the actual SQL commands to lock and unlock tables and to change the auto commit setting. The connection settings we added are:

- ▶ `lock`: It is a set of settings that specify what to do when dealing with locked queries. Its subset of settings are:
    - ❑ `log`: It is path to the file where to store logging information. If set to `false`, logging will be disabled. Defaults to a file named `locks.log` that is created in the `app/tmp/logs` directory.
    - ❑ `recover`: It decides whether to try to recover from locked queries. If set to `false`, no recovery will be attempted. Defaults to `true`.
    - ❑ `retries`: It decides if `recover` is set to `true`, how many attempts to rerun the failed (locked) query. Defaults to `1`.
- ▶ `autoCommit`: It gives the initial autocommit value (`true` for enabled, `false` for disabled). If set to `null`, it will get its value from the database server.

We then implement the `lock()` and `unlock()` methods. The `lock()` method allows us to lock a table for a certain operation. We can use it directly from a model to lock its underlying table for a `read` operation:

```
$this->Profile->lock();
```

We can change the locking operation to be `write`:

```
$this->Profile->lock(array('operation'=>'write'))
```

We can also use it to lock a specific table, using either the `lock()` method available on all models using this datasource, or directly invoking the method in the datasource:

```
$this->Profile->getDataSource()->lock(array(
    'table' => 'profiles',
    'operation'=>'write'
));
```

The `unlock()` method is used similarly, either through the model, or directly using the datasource) and unlocks all locked tables.

> When you do lock table, make sure you disable auto commit, by using the `setAutoCommit()` method, like so: `$this->Profile->setAutoCommit(false);`

In the next block of code, we add the implementation for starting, committing and rolling back transactions. There is not much detail needed for these methods except that they take care of disabling auto-commit upon starting a transaction, and reset its status after a transaction is finished.

The `query()` method is overridden to allow executing some of our datasource methods directly from our models. That is the case for the three methods we added: `lock()`, `unlock()`, and `setAutoCommit()`.

Finally, we override the `_execute()` method to detect when a lock wait timeout error is thrown. In these cases, we use the `lockLog()` method to LOG the situation, and we proceed to retry the query if we were told to do so.

6
Routing Magic

In this chapter, we will cover:

- ▸ Using `named` and `GET` parameters
- ▸ Using routes with prefixes
- ▸ Working with route elements
- ▸ Adding catch-all routes for profile pages
- ▸ Adding validation for catch-all routes
- ▸ Creating custom `Route` classes

Introduction

Almost every web-based application will eventually have to develop a successful strategy to obtain better search engine position through a technique known as **search engine optimization**.

This chapter starts by introducing some basic concepts of routing through the use of route parameters, and continues to build optimized routes to leverage our search engine placement.

The final section in this chapter shows us how to create highly optimized URLs for our user profiles, and how to build custom `Route` classes to obtain even more flexibility.

Using named and GET parameters

CakePHP already offers a very useful set of default routes that allow any set of URL elements to be sent to the controller action as arguments. For example, a URL such as `http://localhost/tags/view/cakephp` is interpreted as a call to the `TagsController::view()` method, sending `cakephp` as its first argument.

However, there are times when we need more flexibility when creating URLs with arguments, such as the ability to omit certain arguments or add others that may not have been specified in the method signature. `Named` and `GET` parameters allow us to have such flexibility, without losing the advantage of letting CakePHP deal with its automatic URL parsing.

Getting ready

To go through this recipe we need a sample table to work with. Create a table named `categories`, using the following SQL statement:

```sql
CREATE TABLE `categories`(
    `id` INT UNSIGNED AUTO_INCREMENT NOT NULL,
    `name` VARCHAR(255) NOT NULL,
    PRIMARY KEY(`id`)
);
```

Create a table named `articles`, using the following SQL statement:

```sql
CREATE TABLE `articles`(
    `id` INT UNSIGNED AUTO_INCREMENT NOT NULL,
    `category_id` INT UNSIGNED NOT NULL,
    `title` VARCHAR(255) NOT NULL,
    `body` TEXT NOT NULL,
    PRIMARY KEY(`id`),
    KEY `category_id`(`category_id`),
    FOREIGN KEY `articles__categories`(`category_id`) REFERENCES
`categories`(`id`)
);
```

Add some sample data, using the following SQL statements:

```sql
INSERT INTO `categories`(`id`, `name`) VALUES
    (1, 'Frameworks'),
    (2, 'Databases');

INSERT INTO `articles`(`id`, `category_id`, `title`, `body`) VALUES
    (1, 1, 'Understanding Containable', 'Body of article'),
    (2, 1, 'Creating your first test case', 'Body of article'),
```

```
(3, 1, 'Using bake to start an application', 'Body of article'),
(4, 1, 'Creating your first helper', 'Body of article'),
(5, 2, 'Adding indexes', 'Body of article');
```

We proceed now to create the required model. Create the model, `Article`, in a file named `article.php` and place it in your `app/models` folder, with the following contents:

```php
<?php
class Article extends AppModel {
    public $belongsTo = array(
        'Category'
    );
}
?>
```

Create its appropriate controller, `ArticlesController`, in a file named `articles_controller.php` and place it in your `app/controllers` folder, with the following contents:

```php
<?php
class ArticlesController extends AppController {
    public function view($id) {
        $article = $this->Article->find('first', array(
            'conditions' => array('Article.id' => $id)
        ));
        if (empty($article)) {
            $this->cakeError('error404');
        }
        $articles = $this->Article->find('all', array(
            'conditions' => array(
                'Category.id' => $article['Category']['id'],
                'Article.id !=' => $article['Article']['id']
            ),
            'order' => 'RAND()'
        ));
        $this->set(compact('article', 'articles'));
    }
}
?>
```

Create a folder named `articles` in your `app/views` folder, then create the view in a file named `view.ctp` and place it in your `app/views/articles` folder, with the following contents:

```php
<h1><?php echo $article['Article']['title']; ?></h1>
<p><?php echo $article['Article']['body']; ?></p>
<?php if (!empty($articles)) { ?>
```

```
      <br /><p>Related articles:</p>
      <ul>
      <?php foreach($articles as $related) { ?>
         <li><?php echo $this->Html->link(
            $related['Article']['title'],
            array(
               'action'=>'view',
               $related['Article']['id']
            )
         ); ?></li>
      <?php } ?>
      </ul>
   <?php } ?>
```

How to do it...

1. We start by adding the possibility to change the number of related articles through a GET parameter. Edit your app/controllers/articles_controller.php file and make the following changes to the view() method:

```
public function view($id) {
    $article = $this->Article->find('first', array(
        'conditions' => array('Article.id' => $id)
    ));
    if (empty($article)) {
        $this->cakeError('error404');
    }
    $limit = !empty($this->params['url']['related']) ?
        $this->params['url']['related'] :
        0;
    $articles = $this->Article->find('all', array(
        'conditions' => array(
            'Category.id' => $article['Category']['id'],
            'Article.id !=' => $article['Article']['id']
        ),
        'order' => 'RAND()',
        'limit' => $limit > 0 ? $limit : null
    ));
    $this->set(compact('article', 'articles', 'limit'));
}
```

2. If we now browse to `http://localhost/articles/view/1?related=2` we should see the article content, along with up to two related articles, as shown in the following screenshot:

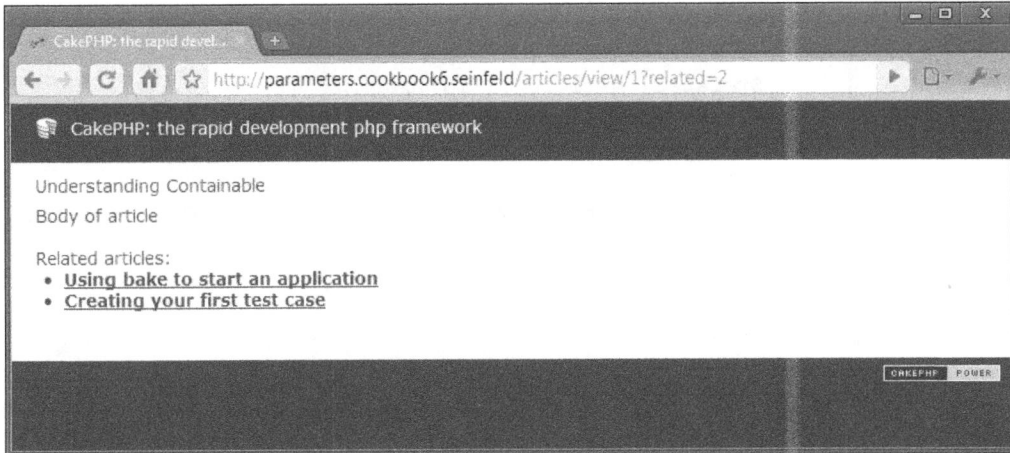

3. We will now use named parameters to pass a search engine-friendly version of the article title, even though it is not needed to show the article or its related content. Edit your `ArticlesController` class and add the following at the end of the `view()` method:

```php
$slug = !empty($this->params['named']['title']) ?
    $this->params['named']['title'] :
    null;
$categorySlug = !empty($this->params['named']['category']) ?
    $this->params['named']['category'] :
    null;
$this->set(compact('slug', 'categorySlug'));
```

4. Now edit the `app/views/articles/view.ctp` file and make the following changes:

```php
<?php if (!empty($slug)) { ?>
    Slug: <?php echo $this->Html->clean($slug); ?><br />
<?php } ?>
<?php if (!empty($categorySlug)) { ?>
    Category slug: <?php echo $this->Html->clean($categorySlug);
?><br />
<?php } ?>
<h1><?php echo $article['Article']['title']; ?></h1>
<p><?php echo $article['Article']['body']; ?></p>
<?php if (!empty($articles)) { ?>
    <br /><p>Related articles:</p>
```

```
<ul>
<?php foreach($articles as $related) { ?>
    <li><?php echo $this->Html->link(
        $related['Article']['title'],
        array(
            'action'=>'view',
            $related['Article']['id'],
            '?' => array('related' => $limit),
            'category' => strtolower(Inflector::slug($related['Cat
egory']['name'])),
            'title' => strtolower(Inflector::slug($related['Artic
le']['title']))
        )
    ); ?></li>
<?php } ?>
</ul>
<?php } ?>
```

5. If we hover over the links to the related articles, we will notice they include two new parameters: `category` and `title`. An example generated URL could be `http://localhost/articles/view/4/category:frameworks/title:creating_your_first_helper`. Clicking on this link would take us to the article page, which also shows the specified parameters.

How it works...

Both `GET` and `named` parameters work in a similar fashion, by being automatically available in our application code as an array. `GET` parameters are available in `$this->params['url']`, while named parameters are available in `$this->params['named']`. Checking the existence of a parameter is as simple as verifying that one of these given arrays contains a value whose key is the wanted parameter.

Creating links that specify either `named` or `GET` parameters (or both) is done by also specifying an indexed array of parameters (where the key is the parameter name, and the value its value.) For `GET` parameters, this array is set in the special `?` route index key, while for named parameters each parameter is specified as part of the actual array based URL.

There's more...

We learnt how to specify named parameters just by setting a `key => value` pair in the array-based URL. However, we may want to also specify which of the named parameters should actually be parsed, and to make sure they are only parsed when the value matches a certain regular expression.

As an example, we can define the `title` named parameter for all actions in the `articles` controller, so it is parsed only when it follows a certain regular expression, where title can only contain lower case letters, numbers, or the underscore sign. To do so, we add the following sentence to our `app/config/routes.php` file:

```
Router::connectNamed(
    array('title' => array('match' => '^[a-z0-9_]+$', 'controller' =>
'articles')),
    array('default' => true)
);
```

The first argument is an array, indexed by parameter name, and whose value contains another array that may include any of the following settings, all of which are optional:

Setting	Purpose
action	If specified, the named parameter will be parsed only for the given action.
controller	If specified, the named parameter will be parsed only for the given controller.
match	A regular expression that will be used to see if the provided value matches the named parameter. If specified, the named parameter will be parsed only when the value matches the expression.

The second argument to `Router::connectNamed()` is an optional array of settings, which may include any of the following:

Setting	Purpose
default	If set to `true`, it will also load the named parameters needed for pagination to work. If you call `Router::connectNamed()` several times, this is only needed once, unless you set the `reset` option to `true`. Defaults to `false`.
greedy	If set to `false`, it will only parse the named parameters that are explicitly defined through a `Router::connectNamed()` call. Defaults to `true`.
reset	If set to `true`, it will wipe out any named parameters defined prior to this call. Defaults to `false`.

To further understand the `greedy` option, we could still allow the URL to include the `category` and `title` parameters, but may want to only parse the `title` value. To do this, we would set `greedy` to `false` when defining the named parameter. That way, `$this->params['named']` would only contain the value for `title`, even when `category` is specified in the requested URL. We also want to do this only for the `view` action of the `articles` controller:

```
Router::connectNamed(
    array('title' => array('match' => '^[a-z0-9_]+$',
'controller'=>'articles', 'action'=>'view')),
```

```
    array('greedy' => false)
);
```

Notice how we had to specify the regular expression for the `title` named parameter again, even though we specified it before. This is because we are configuring a named parameter whose name already exists, so our definition would override the previous one.

See also

▸ *Working with route elements*

Using routes with prefixes

Often enough we find ourselves needing to separate different areas of our application, not only in terms of code and user interface, but also in terms of functionality. With CakePHP's flexible routing system, we can achieve this and more by using prefixes, which provide us with a way to reimplement certain controller actions in different ways, and reach a particular implementation depending on the prefix being used, if any.

Getting ready

To go through this recipe we need a sample table to work with. Create a table named `profiles`, using the following SQL statement:

```
CREATE TABLE `profiles`(
    `id` INT UNSIGNED AUTO_INCREMENT NOT NULL,
    `name` VARCHAR(255) NOT NULL,
    `email` VARCHAR(255) NOT NULL,
    `active` TINYINT(1) NOT NULL default 1,
    PRIMARY KEY(`id`)
);
```

Add some sample data, using the following SQL statements:

```
INSERT INTO `profiles`(`id`, `name`, `email`, `active`) VALUES
    (1, 'John Doe', 'john.doe@email.com', 1),
    (2, 'Jane Doe', 'jane.doe@email.com', 1),
    (3, 'Mark Doe', 'mark.doe@email.com', 0);
```

Next, create the required `ProfilesController` class in a file named `profiles_controller.php` and place it in your `app/controllers` folder, with the following contents:

```
<?php
class ProfilesController extends AppController {
    public function index() {
```

```
        $profiles = $this->paginate();
        $this->set(compact('profiles'));
    }

    public function edit($id) {
        if (!empty($this->data)) {
            if ($this->Profile->save($this->data)) {
                $this->Session->setFlash('Profile saved');
                $this->redirect(array('action'=>'index'));
            } else {
                $this->Session->setFlash('Please correct the errors');
            }
        } else {
            $this->data = $this->Profile->find('first', array(
                'conditions' => array('Profile.id' => $id),
                'recursive' => -1
            ));
        }
    }
}
?>
```

Create a folder named `profiles` in your `app/views` folder, then create the view in a file named `index.ctp` and place it in your `app/views/profiles` folder, with the following contents:

```
<p>
<?php echo $this->Paginator->prev(); ?> 
<?php echo $this->Paginator->numbers(); ?> 
<?php echo $this->Paginator->next(); ?>
</p>
<table>
<thead><tr><th>Name</th><th>Email</th><th>Actions</th></tr></thead>
<tbody>
<?php foreach($profiles as $profile) { ?>
    <tr>
        <td><?php echo $profile['Profile']['name']; ?></td>
        <td><?php echo $profile['Profile']['email']; ?></td>
        <td>
            <?php echo $this->Html->link('Edit', array('action'=>'edit',
$profile['Profile']['id'])); ?>
        </td>
    </tr>
<?php } ?>
</tbody></table>
```

Create the view for the `edit` action in a file named `edit.ctp` and place it in your `app/views/profiles` folder, with the following contents:

```php
<?php echo $this->Form->create('Profile'); ?>
    <?php echo $this->Form->input('name'); ?>
    <?php echo $this->Form->input('email'); ?>
<?php echo $this->Form->end('Save'); ?>
```

How to do it...

1. We start by adding two prefixes to CakePHP: `admin`, and `manager`. Edit your `app/config/core.php` file and look for the line that defines the `Routing.prefixes` setting. If it is commented out, uncomment it. Then change it to:

   ```php
   Configure::write('Routing.prefixes', array('admin', 'manager'));
   ```

2. Let us modify the `ProfilesController` class to add the overridden `index` and `edit` actions for both prefixes. We will also add a new action so that when accessed with the `admin` prefix, we can add new profile records. Edit your `app/controllers/profiles_controller.php` file and add the following methods at the beginning of the `ProfilesController` class:

```php
public function beforeFilter() {
    parent::beforeFilter();
    $prefixes = Configure::read('Routing.prefixes');
    if (!empty($prefixes)) {
        foreach($prefixes as $prefix) {
            $hasPrefix = false;
            if (!empty($this->params['prefix'])) {
                $hasPrefix = ($this->params['prefix'] == $prefix);
            }
            $prefixName = 'is' . Inflector::classify($prefix);
            $this->$prefixName = $hasPrefix;
            $this->set($prefixName, $hasPrefix);
        }
    }
}
public function manager_index() {
    $this->setAction('index');
}
public function manager_edit($id) {
    $this->setAction('edit', $id);
}
public function admin_index() {
```

```
        $this->setAction('index');
    }
    public function admin_edit($id) {
        $this->setAction('edit', $id);
    }
    public function admin_add() {
        $this->setAction('edit');
    }
    public function index() {
        $profiles = $this->paginate();
        $this->set(compact('profiles'));
    }
```

3. We now need to change the `edit` action so that it can handle the creation of new records. While still editing your app/controllers/profiles_controller.php file, make the following changes to the `edit()` method of the `ProfilesController` class:

```
public function edit($id = null) {
    if (!empty($id) && !$this->isAdmin && !$this->isManager) {
        $this->redirect(array('action' => 'index'));
    }
    if (!empty($this->data)) {
        if (empty($id)) {
            $this->Profile->create();
        }
        if ($this->Profile->save($this->data)) {
            $this->Session->setFlash('Profile saved');
            $this->redirect(array('action'=>'index'));
        } else {
            $this->Session->setFlash('Please correct the errors');
        }
    } elseif (!empty($id)) {
        $this->data = $this->Profile->find('first', array(
            'conditions' => array('Profile.id' => $id),
            'recursive' => -1
        ));
    }
}
```

4. The next step is changing the views. Edit your app/views/profiles/index.ctp view file and add the following at the end:

```
<?php
if ($isAdmin) {
```

```
    echo $this->Html->link('Create Profile', array('admin' => true,
'action'=>'add'));
}
?>
```

5. Finally, edit your `app/views/profiles/edit.ctp` view file and make the
   following changes:

```php
<?php echo $this->Form->create('Profile'); ?>
    <?php echo $this->Form->input('name'); ?>
    <?php echo $this->Form->input('email'); ?>
    <?php
    if ($isManager || $isAdmin) {
        echo $this->Form->input('active', array(
            'options' => array(1 => 'Yes', 0 => 'No')
        ));
    }
    ?>
<?php echo $this->Form->end('Save'); ?>
```

How it works...

Any set of values specified in the configuration setting, `Routing.prefixes`, act as routing
prefixes. In this example, we have added two prefixes: `admin` and `manager`. Whenever we
use a prefix in an URL (where the prefix precedes a normal CakePHP URL), CakePHP will set
the current prefix in `$this->params['prefix']` and execute an action whose name is the
same as if the prefix were not used, but preceded with the prefix and an underscore sign, in
the same controller as if the prefix were not used.

When we access `http://localhost/manager/profiles/index` in our example,
CakePHP will process this request by executing the action `manager_index` located in the
`ProfilesController`, and setting `$this->params['prefix']` to `manager`. Knowing
this, we can add controller and view variables to tell actions and views if we are accessing
the application as a manager (when the `manager` prefix is set) or as an administrator (when
the `admin` prefix is set.) We implement this through a more general approach by creating an
appropriate controller and view variable for each prefix (`isManager` for the `manager` prefix,
and `isAdmin` for the `admin` prefix) in the `beforeFilter` callback.

See also

▸ *Using prefixes for role based access controller* in Chapter 1, *Authentication*

Working with route elements

Even when GET and named parameters can be useful in most situations, we may need to further optimize our application URLs for better search engine rankings.

Fortunately, CakePHP provides us with route elements, a solution that maintains the flexibility of GET and named parameters, and improves the way intra-application URLs are built.

Getting ready

We need some sample data to work with. Follow the *Getting ready* section of the recipe *Using GET and named parameters*.

How to do it...

1. We want our article URLs to be further optimized for search engines, so we start by creating a new route. Edit your app/config/routes.php file and add the following route at the end of the file:

```php
Router::connect('/article/:category/:id-:title',
    array('controller' => 'articles', 'action' => 'view'),
    array(
        'pass' => array('id'),
        'id' => '\d+',
        'category' => '[^-]+',
        'title' => '[^-]+'
    )
);
```

2. As our route defines three elements (id, category, and title), we need to modify the view to specify the values for those elements. Edit your app/views/articles/index.ctp view file and make the following changes:

```php
<h1><?php echo $article['Article']['title']; ?></h1>
<p><?php echo $article['Article']['body']; ?></p>
<?php if (!empty($articles)) { ?>
    <br /><p>Related articles:</p>
    <ul>
    <?php foreach($articles as $related) { ?>
        <li><?php echo $this->Html->link(
            $related['Article']['title'],
            array(
                'action'=>'view',
                'id' => $related['Article']['id'],
```

```
                    'category' => strtolower(Inflector::slug($related['Cat
egory']['name'])),
                    'title' => strtolower(Inflector::slug($related['Artic
le']['title']))
            )
        ); ?></li>
    <?php } ?>
    </ul>
<?php } ?>
```

How it works...

CakePHP uses the routes defined in the `routes.php` configuration file to generate URLs, and parse requested URLs. When we want different URLs than those provided by the framework, we add new routes to this configuration file.

Routes are created by specifying up to three arguments when calling the `Router::connect()` method:

▶ The first argument is the route URL, a string representation of our route. It can include a wildcard and route elements.

▶ The second argument is utilized to specify the default route values, an array which may include `plugin`, `controller`, `action`, and action arguments. You may omit parts of these default values, for example, to define a route for all actions in a specific controller.

▶ The third argument defines the route elements, an optional array that defines the route elements a route utilizes. It may also include a list of those elements that are to be sent as arguments when calling the controller action

Using `Router::connect()`, we defined a route that includes all these arguments:

▶ We set `/article/:category/:id-:title` as our route URL. Notice how we are referring to route elements by prefixing their names with a colon.

▶ In the second argument, we specify that this route will match any link to the `view` action of the `articles` controller. Similarly, if a URL that matches the route URL specified in the first argument is requested, this is the action that will be executed.

▶ We specify three route elements in the third argument, with their respective regular expression matching expressions: `id` (a number), `category` (any string that does not include a dash), and `title` (also a string that does not include a dash.) We use the special `pass` option to specify which route elements are passed as regular action arguments.

When CakePHP finds a URL that includes the same default values as those specified in the first argument of our route, and also includes the route elements specified in its third argument, it will convert the route to our provided string representation. For example, if we create a link using the following statement:

```php
<?php echo $this->Html->link(
    'My article',
    array(
        'controller' => 'articles',
        'action' => 'view',
        'id' => 1,
        'category' => 'my_category',
        'title' => 'my_title'
    )
); ?>
```

We would be matching all our route requirements, and the resulting generated URL would look like `http://localhost/article/my_category/1-my_title`.

There's more...

When our controller action is executed as a result of a route that uses route elements, we can obtain the values for all the specified elements using the `$this->params` array available to every controller.

In our example, we set the `id` route element to be passed as a regular action argument, but we did not do so for the remaining elements (`category` and `title`.) To obtain the given value for `category`, we would do:

```php
$category = $this->params['category']
```

Using reverse routing

Even though CakePHP allows us to specify a string-based URL when creating links, it is recommended that we always use arrays to define link URLs unless the URL is an absolute reference to a foreign site.

URLs that are defined using an array allow for the reverse routing system to work, which is the part of the framework that allows us to use custom routes.

See also

- *Adding catch-all routes for profile pages*
- *Using GET and named parameters*

Adding catch-all routes for profile pages

Several websites include direct URLs to access user profiles, and those addresses live alongside a broad set of other URLs. For example, Twitter allows `http://twitter.com/ mgiglesias` to list tweets created by the user `mgiglesias`, while an address like `http://twitter.com/about` would take us to their service description.

This recipe shows us how to create direct URLs for our profile records, allowing the generated URLs to coexist with other application routes we may have.

Getting ready

To go through this recipe we need a sample table to work with. Create a table named `profiles`, using the following SQL statement:

```sql
CREATE TABLE `profiles`(
    `id` INT UNSIGNED AUTO_INCREMENT NOT NULL,
    `username` VARCHAR(255) NOT NULL,
    `name` VARCHAR(255) NOT NULL,
    PRIMARY KEY(`id`)
);
```

Add some sample data, using the following SQL statements:

```sql
INSERT INTO `profiles`(`id`, `username`, `name`) VALUES
    (1, 'john', 'John Doe'),
    (2, 'jane', 'Jane Doe');
```

Proceed now to create the required model. Create a file named `profile.php` and place it in your `app/models` folder, with the following contents:

```php
<?php
class Profile extends AppModel {
}
?>
```

Create the `ProfilesController` class in a file named `profiles_controller.php` and place it in your `app/controllers` folder, with the following contents:

```php
<?php
class ProfilesController extends AppController {
    public function index() {
        $profiles = $this->Profile->find('all');
        $this->set(compact('profiles'));
    }

    public function view($username) {
```

```
        $profile = $this->Profile->find('first', array(
            'conditions' => array('Profile.username' => $username)
        ));
        if (empty($profile)) {
            $this->cakeError('error404');
        }
        $this->set(compact('profile'));
    }
}
?>
```

Create a folder named `profiles` in your `app/views` folder. Create the view for the `index` action in a file named `index.ctp` and place it in your `app/views/profiles` folder, with the following contents:

```
<ul>
<?php foreach($profiles as $profile) { ?>
    <li><?php echo $this->Html->link($profile['Profile']['name'],
array(
        'action' => 'view',
        'userName' => $profile['Profile']['username']
    )); ?></li>
<?php } ?>
</ul>
```

Create the view for the `view` action in a file named `view.ctp` and place it in your `app/views/profiles` folder, with the following contents:

```
<h1><?php echo $profile['Profile']['name']; ?></h1>
Username: <?php echo $profile['Profile']['username']; ?>
<p><?php echo $this->Html->link('Profiles', array('action'=>'index'));
?></p>
```

How to do it...

Edit your `app/config/routes.php` file and add the following routes at the end of the file:

```
Router::connect('/:userName',
    array('controller' => 'profiles', 'action' => 'view'),
    array(
        'userName' => '[A-Za-z0-9\._-]+',
        'pass' => array('userName')
    )
);
```

```
Router::connect('/:controller/index/*', array('action' => 'index'));
```

If you now browse to `http://localhost/profiles/index`, you will see that the generated link for the `jane` user account is `http://localhost/jane`. Clicking on it should show us Jane's profile page, as shown in the following screenshot:

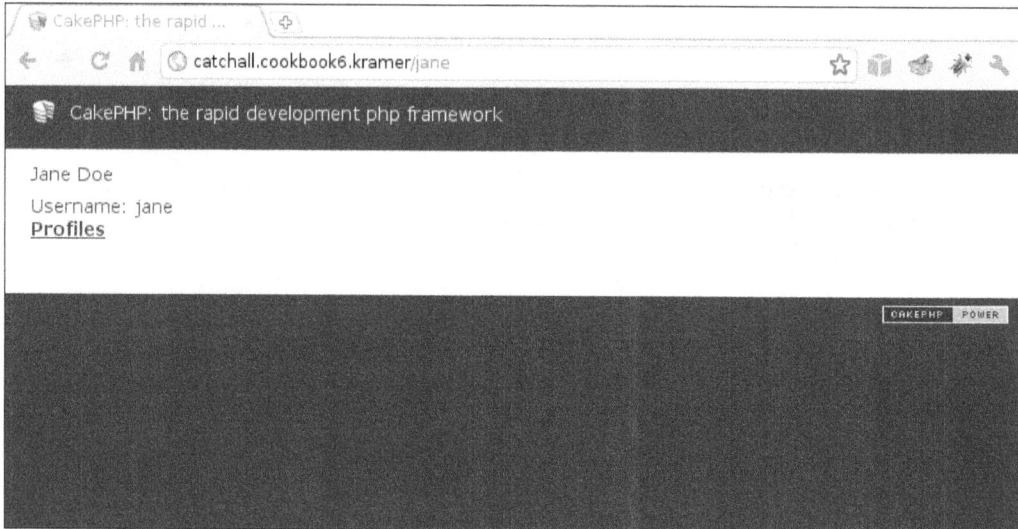

How it works...

We created two routes. The first one uses a route element called `userName` to set the URL as consisting solely on its value. Using a regular expression, our route guarantees that it is only used when the value for `userName` consists of letters, numbers, dots, dashes, or underscore signs. Using the `controller` and `action` settings, we link the route to the `view` action of the `profiles` controller. Finally, the `userName` element is set to be passed as a regular argument to the `ProfilesController::view()` method.

With this route defined, if we created a link with the following statement:

```php
<?php echo $this->Html->link('My Profile', array(
    'controller' => 'profiles',
    'action' => 'view',
    'userName' => 'john'
)); ?>
```

The generated URL would be `http://localhost/john`. Clicking on this link would execute the same action, using the same arguments, as if we used the URL `http://localhost/profiles/view/john`.

However, there is a noticeable problem. CakePHP provides a short URL for the index action for all our controllers. Because of it, we can access the `ProfilesController::index()` method using the URL `http://localhost/profiles`, the equivalent of the URL `http://localhost/profiles/index`. This default route would conflict with our custom route, as the word `profiles` matches our regular expression.

Fortunately, this functionality would not conflict with our route when generating a URL out of an array-based route. Because we linked our route to the `view` action of the `profiles` controller, CakePHP will only use our custom route when linking to this action and specifying the `userName` element.

We still need to fix the conflict that is produced when parsing a URL such as `http://localhost/profiles`. To do so, we create another route so CakePHP's built-in `index` routes are not utilized when producing a link. This route uses the special `:controller` route element (set to the controller the link points to), and forcing the `index` action as part of the URL. We link this route to all routes that use the `index` action, regardless of the controller.

> To learn about another, more effective approach to this problem, see Creating custom Route classes

After adding this route, if we created a link with:

```php
<?php echo $this->Html->link('Profiles', array(
    'controller' => 'profiles',
    'action' => 'index'
)); ?>
```

the generated URL would be `http://localhost/profiles/index`.

See also

- ▸ *Working with route elements*
- ▸ *Adding validation for catch-all routes*
- ▸ *Creating custom route classes*

Adding validation for catch-all routes

In the recipe *Adding catch-all routes for profile pages*, we created routes so that profile pages can be accessed, specifying only the username in the URL.

In this recipe, we will learn how to implement a custom validation method so that these usernames do not conflict with other custom routes.

Getting ready

We need some sample data to work with, and we need a catch-all route. Follow the entire recipe *Adding catch-all routes* for profile pages.

We also need the sign-up page, where new profile records are created. Edit your `app/controller/profiles_controller.php` file and place the following method inside the `ProfilesController` class definition:

```
public function add() {
    if (!empty($this->data)) {
        $this->Profile->create($this->data);
        if ($this->Profile->save()) {
            $this->Session->setFlash('Profile created');
            $this->redirect(array(
                'action'=>'view',
                'userName' => $this->data['Profile']['username']
            ));
        } else {
            $this->Session->setFlash('Please correct the errors below');
        }
    }
}
```

Create the appropriate view in a file named `add.ctp` and place it in your `app/views/profiles` folder, with the following contents:

```
<?php
echo $this->Form->create();
echo $this->Form->inputs(array(
    'username',
    'name'
));
echo $this->Form->end('Save');
?>
```

We also need a custom route to try out the validation. Edit your `app/config/routes.php` file and add the following route at the beginning:

```
Router::connect('/home', array(
    'controller' => 'pages', 'action' => 'display', 'home'
));
```

How to do it...

1. Edit your `app/models/profile.php` file and make the following changes:

```php
<?php
class Profile extends AppModel {
    public $validate = array(
        'username' => array(
            'notEmpty',
            'valid' => array(
                'rule' => 'validateUsername',
                'message' => 'This user name is reserved'
            )
        ),
        'name' => 'notEmpty'
    );
}
?>
```

2. While still editing your `app/models/profile.php` file, add the following method to the `Profile` class:

```php
public function validateUsername($value, $params) {
    $reserved = Router::prefixes();

    $controllers = array_diff(
        Configure::listObjects('controller'),
        (array) 'App'
    );
    if (!empty($controllers)) {
        $reserved = array_merge($reserved, array_
map(array('Inflector', 'underscore'), $controllers));
    }

    $routes = Router::getInstance()->routes;
    if (!empty($routes)) {
        foreach($routes as $route) {
            if (!empty($route->template) && preg_match('/^\/
([^\/:]+)/', $route->template, $matches)) {
                $reserved[] = strtolower($matches[1]);
            }
        }
    }

    return !in_array(strtolower(array_shift($value)), $reserved);
}
```

If you now browse to `http://localhost/profiles/add` and specify **home** as the user name and **Mark Doe** as the name, you will get a validation error message informing you that the username is reserved, as shown in the following screenshot:

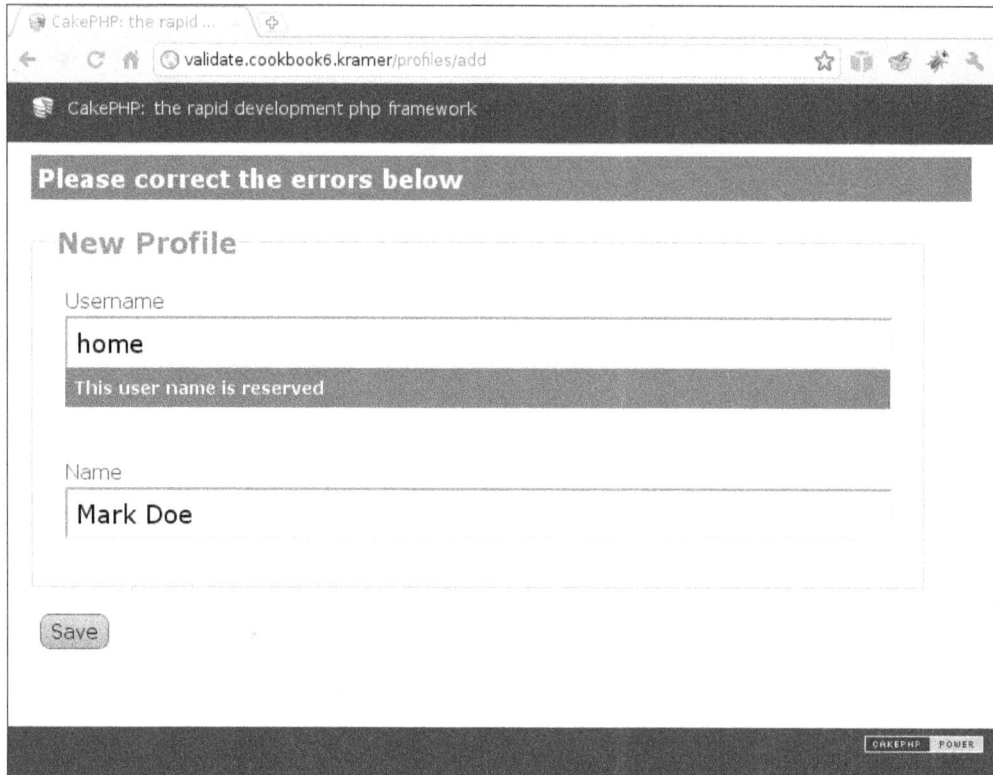

How it works...

First we add validation rules for two fields: `username`, and `name`. The validation for the `username` field consists of two rules: a built-in `notEmpty` rule, and a custom validation rule named `validateUsername`. The `name` field has only one rule: `notEmpty`.

In our `validateUsername` rule implementation, we start by storing all routing prefixes into a list of reserved words. We then get a list of all controllers, using the `Configure::listObjects()` method, and excluding the value `App`, which is the base of our controllers (and as such not directly accessible). Then we convert each name to its lower case, underscored form.

We then obtain the list of all defined routes by getting the instance of the `Router` class and accessing its `routes` public property, and for each of those routes we look for their `template` property.

This property stores the string representation of a route. For the route we defined during the *Getting ready* section, this would be /home. We are only interested in the starting portion of this value (that is, anything after the first slash, and before the second one), so we use a regular expression to match and extract that value, and then we add it to the list of reserved words.

In our example, the list of reserved words would be: pages, profiles, and home. The first two come from the list of our application controllers, and the last one comes from our custom route.

Once we have the list of reserved words, we set the field as valid only if the given value is not within this list.

See also

▸ *Adding catch-all routes for profile pages*

Creating custom Route classes

In the recipe *Adding catch-all routes for profile pages* we created routes so that profile pages can be accessed specifying only the user name in the URL. However, that implementation had a problem: we had to disallow the automatic access of the index action.

This recipe shows a different approach to our profile URL generation, by creating a custom route implementation that not only overcomes this problem, but makes sure the route is utilized only for existing profile records.

Getting ready

We need some sample data to work with. Follow the *Getting ready* section of the recipe *Adding catch-all routes for profile pages*.

How to do it...

1. Edit your app/config/routes.php file and add the following routes at the end of the file:

```
App::import('Lib', 'ProfileRoute');
Router::connect('/:userName',
    array('controller' => 'profiles', 'action' => 'view'),
    array(
        'routeClass' => 'ProfileRoute',
        'pass' => array('userName')
    )
);
```

2. Now create a file named `profile_route.php` and place it in your `app/libs` folder, with the following contents:

```php
<?php
App::import('Core', 'Router');
class ProfileRoute extends CakeRoute {
    public function match($url) {
        if (!empty($url['userName']) && $this->_
exists($url['userName'])) {
            return parent::match($url);
        }
        return false;
    }

    public function parse($url) {
        $params = parent::parse($url);
        if (!empty($params) && $this->_exists($params['userName']))
{
            return $params;
        }
        return false;
    }

    protected function _exists($userName) {
        $userNames = Cache::read('usernames');
        if (empty($userNames)) {
            $profiles = ClassRegistry::init('Profile')->find('all',
array(
                'fields' => array('username'),
                'recursive' => -1
            ));
            if (!empty($profiles)) {
                $userNames = array_map(
                    'strtolower',
                    Set::extract('/Profile/username', $profiles)
                );
                Cache::write('usernames', $userNames);
            }
        }
        return in_array($userName, (array) $userNames);
    }
}
?>
```

3. Next, edit your `app/models/profile.php` file and add the following methods to the `Profile` class:

```
public function afterSave($created) {
    parent::afterSave($created);
    Cache::delete('usernames');
}

public function afterDelete() {
    parent::afterDelete();
    Cache::delete('usernames');
}
```

You can now browse to `http://localhost/john` to see John's profile page. Specifying an invalid name in the URL (such as `http://localhost/kate`) would produce the regular CakePHP error page, while browsing to `http://localhost/profiles` will correctly take us to the profile index page.

How it works...

We start by first importing our custom route class file, and then defining a catch-all route for the `view` action of the `profiles` controller, using the custom `ProfileRoute` class, and setting the `userName` route element to be passed as a regular argument.

The `ProfileRoute` implementation implements two of the most typical route class methods:

1. `match()`: It is used during reverse routing to convert an array-based URL into its string representation. If the method returns `false`, then the provided URL does not fall into this route.

2. `parse()`: It is used when parsing a requested URL into an array-based URL, specifying `controller`, `action`, and other parameters. If the method returns `false`, then this tells CakePHP that the given URL is not handled by this route.

We created a helper method, called `_exists()`, to assist us, which looks for the given username amongst the registered records. We cache the list of usernames for obvious performance reasons, and we invalidate this cache whenever a record is created, modified, or deleted, by implementing the `afterSave` and `afterDelete` callbacks in the `Profile` model.

Our `match()` implementation first checks to make sure the `userName` route element is provided. If so, and if the given user exists, it will use the parent implementation to return the string representation. In any other case (no username provided, or nonexistent), it will not process the given URL.

The `parse()` implementation starts by calling its parent implementation to convert the string URL into an array based URL. If that call is successful (which means it contains the `userName` route element), and if the given user name exists, it returns the conversion. Otherwise it returns `false` to not process the given URL. Another route handler, or CakePHP's default route handler, will process it.

See also

▸ *Adding catch-all routes for profile pages*

▸ *Custom route classes*

7

Creating and
Consuming Web
Services

In this chapter, we will cover:

- ▶ Creating an RSS feed
- ▶ Consuming a JSON service
- ▶ Building REST services with JSON
- ▶ Adding authentication to REST services
- ▶ Implementing token-based authorization for API access

Introduction

Web services are essential when looking forward to expose application functionality to third-party applications, or when looking forward to integrate foreign services into our own applications. They offer a broad set of technologies and definitions so that systems written in different programming languages can communicate.

This chapter introduces a set of recipes to consume web services, and to expose parts of our application as web services.

Creating an RSS feed

RSS feeds are a form of web services, as they provide a service, over the web, using a known format to expose data. Due to their simplicity, they are a great way to introduce us to the world of web services, particularly as CakePHP offers a built in method to create them.

In the recipe *Consuming RSS feeds with a datasource* from *Chapter 5, Datasources*, we learned how to fetch content from a foreign RSS feed. In this recipe, will do exactly the opposite: produce a feed for our site that can be used by other applications.

Getting ready

To go through this recipe we need a sample table to work with. Create a table named `posts`, using the following SQL statement:

```sql
CREATE TABLE `posts`(posts
    `id` INT NOT NULL AUTO_INCREMENT,
    `title` VARCHAR(255) NOT NULL,
    `body` TEXT NOT NULL,
    `created` DATETIME NOT NULL,
    `modified` DATETIME NOT NULL,
    PRIMARY KEY(`id`)
);
```

Add some sample data, using the following SQL statements:

```sql
INSERT INTO `posts`(`title`,posts `body`, `created`, `modified`)
VALUES
    ('Understanding Containable', 'Post body', NOW(), NOW()),
    ('Creating your first test case', 'Post body', NOW(), NOW()),
    ('Using bake to start an application', 'Post body', NOW(), NOW()),
    ('Creating your first helper', 'Post body', NOW(), NOW()),
    ('Adding indexes', 'Post body', NOW(), NOW());
```

We proceed now to create the required controller. Create the class `PostsController` in a file named `posts_controller.php` and place it in your `app/controllers` folder, with the following contents:

```php
<?php
class PostsController extends AppController {
    public function index() {
        $posts = $this->Post->find('all');
        $this->set(compact('posts'));
    }
}
?>
```

Create a folder named `posts` in your `app/views` folder, and then create the `index` view in a file named `index.ctp` and place it in your `app/views/posts` folder, with the following contents:

```
<h1>Posts</h1>
<?php if (!empty($posts)) { ?>
    <ul>
    <?php foreach($posts as $post) { ?>
        <li><?php echo $this->Html->link(
            $post['Post']['title'],
            array(
                'action'=>'view',
                $post['Post']['id']
            )
        ); ?></li>
    <?php } ?>
    </ul>
<?php } ?>
```

How to do it...

1. Edit your `app/config/routes.php` file and add the following statement at the end:

    ```
    Router::parseExtensions('rss');
    ```

2. Edit your `app/controllers/posts_controller.php` file and add the following property to the `PostsController` class:

    ```
    public $components = array('RequestHandler');
    ```

3. While still editing `PostsController`, make the following changes to the `index()` method:

    ```
    public function index() {
        $options = array();
        if ($this->RequestHandler->isRss()) {
            $options = array_merge($options, array(
                'order' => array('Post.created' => 'desc'),
                'limit' => 5
            ));
        }
        $posts = $this->Post->find('all', $options);
        $this->set(compact('posts'));
    }
    ```

4. Create a folder named `rss` in your `app/views/posts` folder, and inside the `rss` folder create a file named `index.ctp`, with the following contents:

```php
<?php
$this->set('channel', array(
    'title' => 'Recent posts',
    'link' => $this->Rss->url('/', true),
    'description' => 'Latest posts in my site'
));

$items = array();
foreach($posts as $post) {
    $items[] = array(
        'title' => $post['Post']['title'],
        'link' => array('action'=>'view', $post['Post']['id']),
        'description' => array('cdata'=>true, 'value'=>$post['Post']
['body']),
        'pubDate' => $post['Post']['created']
    );
}

echo $this->Rss->items($items);
?>
```

5. Edit your `app/views/posts/index.ctp` file and add the following at the end of the view:

```php
<?php echo $this->Html->link('Feed', array('action'=>'index',
'ext'=>'rss')); ?>
```

If you now browse to `http://localhost/posts`, you should see a listing of posts with a link entitled **Feed**. Clicking on this link should produce a valid RSS feed, as shown in the following screenshot:

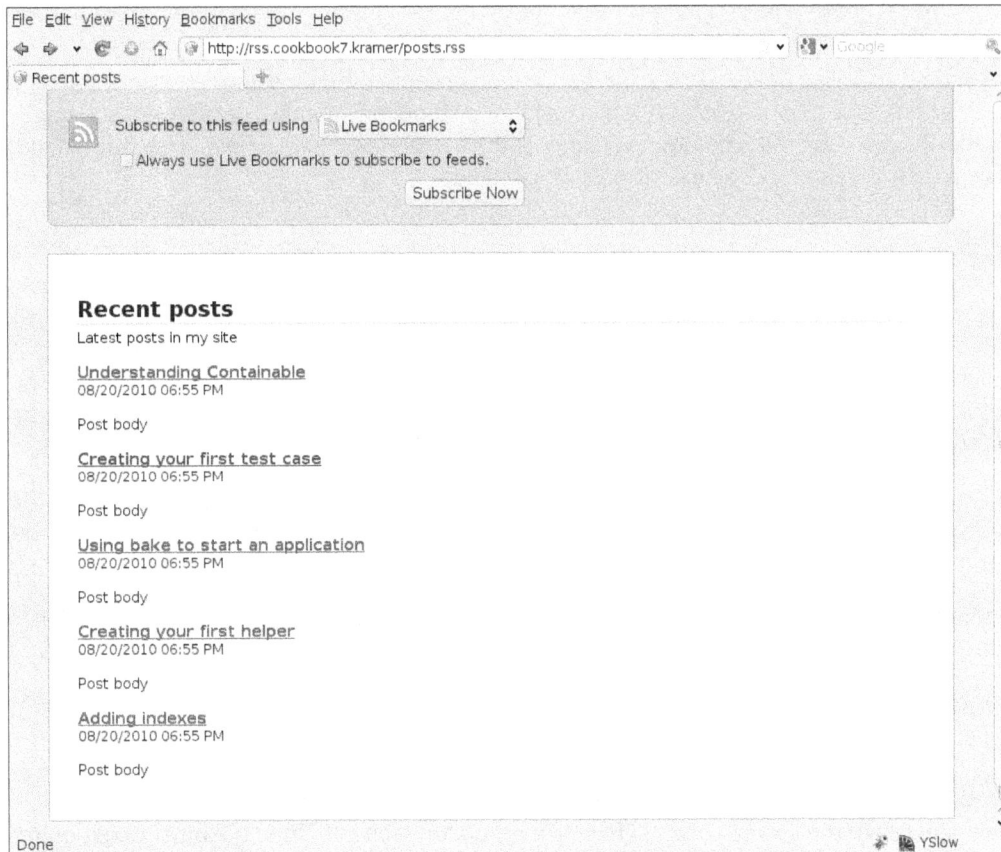

If you view the source of the generated response, you can see that the source for the first item within the RSS document is:

```
<item>
<title>Understanding Containable</title>
<link>http://rss.cookbook7.kramer/posts/view/1</link>
<description><![CDATA[Post body]]></description>
<pubDate>Fri, 20 Aug 2010 18:55:47 -0300</pubDate>
<guid>http://rss.cookbook7.kramer/posts/view/1</guid>
</item>
```

How it works...

We started by telling CakePHP that our application accepts the `rss` extension with a call to `Router::parseExtensions()`, a method that accepts any number of extensions. Using extensions, we can create different versions of the same view. For example, if we wanted to accept both `rss` and `xml` as extensions, we would do:

```
Router::parseExtensions('rss', 'xml');
```

In our recipe, we added `rss` to the list of valid extensions. That way, if an action is accessed using that extension, for example, by using the URL `http://localhost/posts.rss`, then CakePHP will identify `rss` as a valid extension, and will execute the `ArticlesController::index()` action as it normally would, but using the `app/views/posts/rss/index.ctp` file to render the view. The process also uses the file `app/views/layouts/rss/default.ctp` as its layout, or CakePHP's default RSS layout if that file is not present.

We then modify how `ArticlesController::index()` builds the list of posts, and use the `RequestHandler` component to see if the current request uses the `rss` extension. If so, we use that knowledge to change the number and order of posts.

In the `app/views/posts/rss/index.ctp` view, we start by setting some view variables. Because a controller view is always rendered before the layout, we can add or change view variables from the view file, and have them available in the layout. CakePHP's default RSS layout uses a `$channel` view variable to describe the RSS feed. Using that variable, we set our feed's `title`, `link`, and `description`.

We proceed to output the actual item files. There are different ways to do so, the first one is making a call to the `RssHelper::item()` method for each item, and the other one requires only a call to `RssHelper::items()`, passing it an array of items. We chose the latter method due to its simplicity.

While we build the array of items to be included in the feed, we only specify `title`, `link`, `description`, and `pubDate`. Looking at the generated XML source for the item, we can infer that the `RssHelper` used our value for the `link` element as the value for the `guid` (globally unique identifier) element.

Note that the `description` field is specified slightly differently than the values for the other fields in our item array. This is because our description may contain HTML code, so we want to make sure that the generated document is still a valid XML document.

By using the array notation for the `description` field, a notation that uses the `value` index to specify the actual value on the field, and by setting `cdata` to `true`, we are telling the `RssHelper` (actually the `XmlHelper` from which `RssHelper` descends) that the field should be wrapped in a section that should not be parsed as part of the XML document, denoted between a `<![CDATA[` prefix and a `]]>` postfix.

The final task in this recipe is adding a link to our feed that is shown in the index.ctp view file. While creating this link, we set the special ext URL setting to rss. This sets the extension for the generated link, which ends up being http://localhost/posts.rss.

Adding view caching to an RSS feed

Our feeds may be consumed by feed search crawlers. If we are lucky, we may get tons and tons of requests looking for updates to our blog. It is unlikely that we will update our blog so often that we would have new posts every second, so our server load may force us to add some caching.

When looking to improve performance, some developers are content to only cache their database queries. In our recipe, this would mean caching the results obtained from our $this->Post->find('all') call. Unless we have our database engine on a separate server that suffers from some considerable network latency, chances are this sort of caching will offer little or no benefit.

A much better solution is to use view caching. That is, caching the generated RSS feed, and using that cached document whenever a request is made to our feed, provided we are within the cache time. Fortunately, CakePHP offers us a view-caching implementation right from the dispatcher, speeding up the request considerably. If a cached view file is found, that file is rendered directly to the client, without any intervention by the controller, or the need to load models, components, or helpers.

We want to add caching only when our PostsController::index() action is accessed with the rss extension. That is, we don't want to cache the listing of posts, but its feed. So we will make sure to only specify caching information when a feed is requested. In fact, we are going to cache all actions in our PostsController whenever the rss extension is used.

The first thing we need to do is tell CakePHP to take view caching into account. Edit your app/config/core.php file and uncomment the following line:

```
Configure::write('Cache.check', true);
```

Next, edit your app/controllers/posts_controller.php file and add the Cache helper to the PostsController class. Without it, view caching will simply not work:

```
public $helpers = array('Cache');
```

While still editing the PostsController class, add the following method:

```
public function beforeFilter() {
    parent::beforeFilter();
    if ($this->RequestHandler->isRss()) {
        $this->cacheAction = array($this->action => '1 hour');
    }
}
```

In this `beforeFilter()` implementation, we are checking to see if the current request was made using the `rss` extension. If so, we add the current action (whatever that may be) to the list of cached actions, and set the cache time to be `1 hour`.

If we access the feed multiple times within the hour, we should see the same feed we have been getting so far, but coming from the cache instead of being built in real time.

See also

▸ *Consuming RSS feeds with a datasource* in *Chapter 5, Datasources*
▸ *Building REST services with JSON*

Consuming a JSON service

JSON (JavaScript Object Notation) is probably one of the best formats available for exposing data, due to its easy-to-read syntax, which greatly simplifies the parsing. In fact, PHP (as of its 5.2.0 release) provides built-in methods to convert data from a JSON-formatted string to a PHP native data type and from PHP types to JSON.

In this recipe, we will learn how to use the `HttpSocket` class to consume a JSON service from a foreign site. This time, we are going to use the YouTube JSON API to allow our users to search for YouTube videos that match a given search query.

The JSON service we will be consuming from YouTube uses a variant of JSON, called JSON-C. JSON-C is nothing more than JSON, but Google is making a distinction between what YouTube used to provide as JSON, and the new version it is now producing. YouTube's JSON-C-based responses are far simpler than their JSON service. Consequently, Google has decided to deprecate JSON in favor of JSON-C in the near future.

How to do it...

1. Start by creating the main controller in a file named `videos_controller.php` and place it in your `app/controllers` folder, with the following contents:

```php
<?php
class VideosController extends AppController {
    public function index() {
        if (!empty($this->data)) {
            $videos = $this->Video->search($this->data);
            $this->set(compact('videos'));
        }
    }
}
?>
```

2. Create the required model in a file named `video.php` and place it in your `app/models` folder, with the following contents:

```php
<?php
App::import('Core', 'HttpSocket');
class Video extends AppModel {
    public $useTable = false;
    protected $_httpSocket;

    public function __construct($id = false, $table = null, $ds =
null) {
        parent::__construct($id, $table, $ds);
        $this->_httpSocket = new HttpSocket();
    }
    public function search($data) {
        $query = !empty($data[$this->alias]['q']) ?
            $data[$this->alias]['q'] :
            '';

        $this->_httpSocket->reset();
        $response = $this->_httpSocket->get(
            'http://gdata.youtube.com/feeds/api/videos',
            array(
                'v' => '2',
                'alt' => 'jsonc',
                'q' => $query,
                'orderby' => 'updated'
            )
        );
        $videos = array();
        if (!empty($response)) {
            $response = json_decode($response);
            if (empty($response) || empty($response->data->items)) {
                return $videos;
            }
            foreach($response->data->items as $item) {
                $videos[] = array('Video' => array(
                    'url' => $item->player->default,
                    'title' => $item->title,
                    'uploaded' => strtotime($item->uploaded),
                    'category' => $item->category,
                    'description' => $item->description,
                    'thumbnail' => $item->thumbnail->sqDefault
                ));
```

```
            }
        }
        return $videos;
    }
}
?>
```

3. Create a view folder named videos in your `app/views` folder. Then, create a file named `index.ctp` and place it in your `app/views/videos` folder, with the following contents:

```php
<?php
echo $this->Form->create();
echo $this->Form->input('q', array('label'=>'Search terms:'));
echo $this->Form->end('Search');

if (!empty($videos)) {
    ?>
    <h1>Search results</h1>
    <?php foreach($videos as $video) { ?>
        <div style="float: left; clear: both; margin-bottom: 10px;">
        <h4><?php echo $this->Html->link($video['Video']['title'],
$video['Video']['url']); ?></h4>
        <?php echo $this->Html->image($video['Video']['thumbnail'],
array(
            'url' => $video['Video']['url'],
            'align' => 'left',
            'style' => 'margin-right: 10px;'
        )); ?>
        <p><?php echo $video['Video']['description']; ?></p>
        <br />
        <p><small>
        Uploaded on <?php echo date('F d, Y H:i', $video['Video']
['uploaded']); ?>
        in <?php echo $video['Video']['category']; ?>
        -
        <strong><?php echo $this->Html->link('PLAY', $video['Video']
['url']); ?></strong>
        </small></p>
        </div>
    <?php
    }
}
?>
```

If you now browse to `http://localhost/videos`, you will see a search form. Entering **CakePHP** and clicking the button **Search** should give you a set of results similar to those shown in the following screenshot:

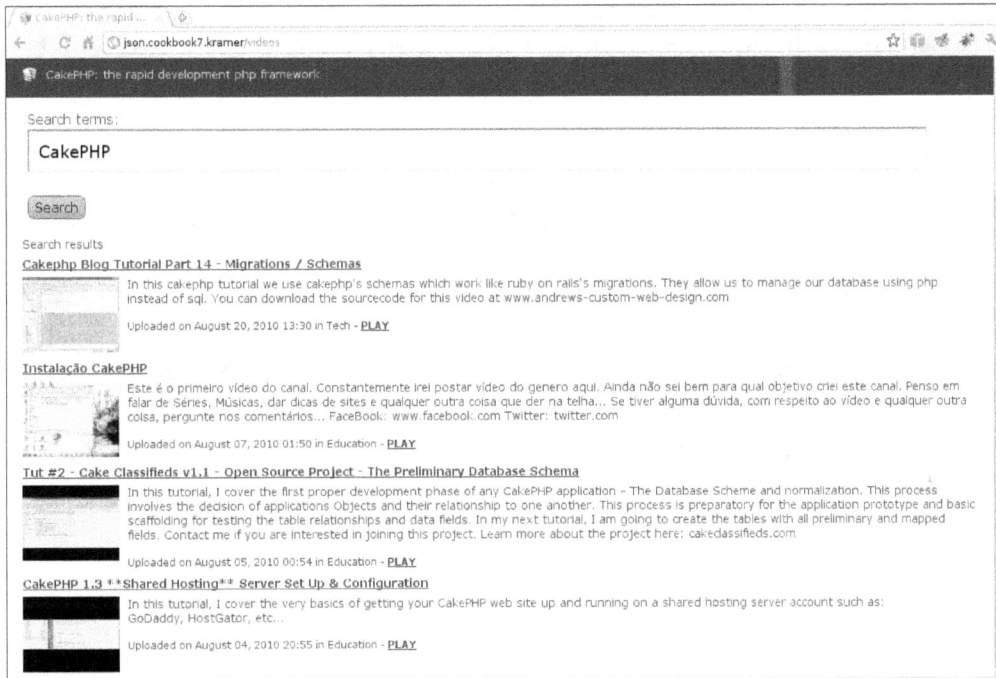

How it works...

The controller class (`ArticlesController`) and the view file (`index.ctp`) have no connection with the underlying web service we are consuming. In fact, if you look closely at their code, they look like a regular controller and a standard view file. This is because we decided to encapsulate the service logic in a model.

Doing so allows us to change how we communicate with the service provider without having to modify neither the controller nor the view. That is one of the many advantages of the MVC (Model View Controller) architecture that is the foundation of CakePHP.

We could have taken a more complex approach, and decided to build a datasource to interact with the server. Instead, we chose a simpler route, by creating a model method that would perform the actual search and return the results in a data format typical of any CakePHP application.

This is what the `Video` model is there for. As there's no underlying table for our videos, we set the model `$useTable` property to `false`. We also import the `HttpSocket` class, part of CakePHP's core, because it will be the mechanism we will use to communicate with the server.

The `search()` method is where the magic happens. The first thing we do is extract the search terms out of the submitted data. We then create an instance of `HttpSocket`, and use its get method to perform the request.

`HttpSocket::get()` takes three parameters:

 ▶ `$uri`: The URL to which we are making the request. This can be either a string, or an array that contains the different elements of the URL, such as `scheme`, `host`, `port`, and `path`.

 ▶ `$query`: An array of parameters to append to the URL. The indexes in this array are the parameter names and the values their respective values.

 ▶ `$request`: An array with any additional request information to send to the URL, such as `method`, `header`, and `body`.

In our case we specify the URL to the YouTube video API, and we set the following query parameters:

 ▶ `v`: The API version to use.

 ▶ `alt`: The format to get results in.

 ▶ `q`: The query to use for searching.

 ▶ `orderby`: The order in which to get the results.

Once we get the response, we decode it using PHP's `json_decode()` function, which converts a JSON string into a PHP object or to `null` if it is not a valid JSON string. For example, the following JSON:

```
{
    "name": "Mariano Iglesias",
    "profile": {
        "url": "http://marianoiglesias.com.ar"
    }
}
```

Would be evaluated to a PHP class with two public attributes: `name`, and `profile`. The `profile` attribute will itself be a class, with one public attribute: `url`. If we had the above JSON string in a variable called `$json`, the following code would output **Mariano Iglesias has a website in http://marianoiglesias.com.ar**:

```
$user = json_decode($json);
echo $user->name . ' has a website in ' . $user->profile->url;
```

Back to the `Video::search()` method. Once we have decoded the JSON response, we check to make sure there are resulting videos available in the `$response->data->items` property. If so, we iterate through them, and we add elements to our response array, specifying only a subset of the data we obtained.

Once we have the data prepared, we return it back to the controller, which sends it to the view to render the results.

See also

 ▶ *Chapter 5, Datasources*

 ▶ *Building REST services with JSON*

Building REST services with JSON

In the recipe *Consuming a JSON service*, we learnt how lightweight and convenient the JSON format can be for exchanging data. What happens if we not only want to expose data using JSON, but also allow the possibility to modify it? This is one of the reasons why the REST architecture exists. **REST** stands for **Representational State Transfer**, and is no more than a set of principles that guide the concepts that describe its proper implementation.

One of these main principles is that the client-server communication that is part of a REST request should be stateless. This means that no context exists in the server between requests from a specific client. All the information required to perform an operation is part of the request.

In this recipe, we will learn how to add REST services to an application, using JSON as their exchange format. These services will allow any foreign application to get data from a post, create new posts, or delete existing posts.

Getting ready

To go through this recipe we need sample data to work with. Follow the *Getting ready* section of the *Creating an RSS feed* recipe.

Create the `Post` model in a file named `post.php` and place it in your `app/models` folder, with the following contents. With the validation option, `required`, we are telling CakePHP that these fields should always be present when creating or modifying records:

```php
<?php
class Post extends AppModel {
    public $validate = array(
        'title' => array('required'=>true, 'rule'=>'notEmpty'),
        'body' => array('required'=>true, 'rule'=>'notEmpty')
```

```
        );
    }
    ?>
```

Let us add actions for creating, editing, and deleting posts. Edit your app/controllers/ posts_controller.php file and add the following methods to the PostsController class:

```php
public function add() {
    $this->setAction('edit');
}
public function edit($id=null) {
    if (!empty($this->data)) {
        if (!empty($id)) {
            $this->Post->id = $id;
        } else {
            $this->Post->create();
        }
        if ($this->Post->save($this->data)) {
            $this->Session->setFlash('Post created successfully');
            $this->redirect(array('action'=>'index'));
        } else {
            $this->Session->setFlash('Please correct the errors marked
below');
        }
    } elseif (!empty($id)) {
        $this->data = $this->Post->find('first', array(
            'conditions' => array('Post.id' => $id)
        ));
        if (empty($this->data)) {
            $this->cakeError('error404');
        }
    }
    $this->set(compact('id'));
}
public function delete($id) {
    $post = $this->Post->find('first', array(
        'conditions' => array('Post.id' => $id)
    ));
    if (empty($post)) {
        $this->cakeError('error404');
    }
    if (!empty($this->data)) {
        if ($this->Post->delete($id)) {
```

```
            $this->Session->setFlash('Post deleted successfully');
            $this->redirect(array('action'=>'index'));
        } else {
            $this->Session->setFlash('Could not delete post');
        }
    }
    $this->set(compact('post'));
}
```

We now need to add their respective views. Create a file named `edit.ctp` and place it in your `app/views/posts` folder, with the following contents:

```php
<?php
echo $this->Form->create();
echo $this->Form->inputs(array(
    'title',
    'body'
));
echo $this->Form->end('Save');
?>
```

Create a file named `delete.ctp` and place it in your `app/views/posts` folder, with the following contents:

```php
<p>Click the <strong>Delete</strong> button to delete
the post <?php echo $post['Post']['title']; ?></p>
<?php
echo $this->Form->create(array('url'=>array('action'=>'delete',
$post['Post']['id'])));
echo $this->Form->hidden('Post.id', array('value'=>$post['Post']
['id']));
echo $this->Form->end('Delete');
?>
```

Modify the `app/views/posts/index.ctp` to add links to these actions by changing the whole view to the following:

```php
<h1>Posts</h1>
<?php if (!empty($posts)) { ?>
    <ul>
    <?php foreach($posts as $post) { ?>
        <li>
            <?php echo $this->Html->link($post['Post']['title'], array(
                'action'=>'view',
                $post['Post']['id']
            )); ?>
            :
```

```php
<?php echo $this->Html->link('Edit', array(
    'action'=>'edit',
    $post['Post']['id']
)); ?>
-
<?php echo $this->Html->link('Delete', array(
    'action'=>'delete',
    $post['Post']['id']
)); ?>
</li>
<?php } ?>
</ul>
<?php } ?>
<?php echo $this->Html->link('Create new Post',
array('action'=>'add')); ?>
```

How to do it...

1. Edit your app/config/routes.php file and add the following statement at the end:

   ```php
   Router::parseExtensions('json');
   ```

2. Edit your app/controllers/posts_controller.php file and add the following property to the PostsController class:

   ```php
   public $components = array('RequestHandler');
   ```

3. Create a folder named json in your app/views/layouts folder, and inside the json folder, create a file named default.ctp, with the following contents:

   ```php
   <?php

   echo $content_for_layout;
   ?>
   ```

4. Create a folder named json in your app/views/posts folder, and inside the json folder, create a file named index.ctp, with the following contents:

   ```php
   <?php
   foreach($posts as $i => $post) {
       $post['Post']['url'] = $this->Html->url(array(
           'action'=>'view',
           $post['Post']['id']
       ), true);
       $posts[$i] = $post;
   }
   echo json_encode($posts);
   ?>
   ```

5. Edit your app/controllers/posts_controller.php file and add the following method to the end of the PostsController class:

```
protected function _isJSON() {
    return $this->RequestHandler->ext == 'json';
}
```

6. Edit the PostsController::index() method and make the following changes:

```
public function index() {
    if ($this->_isJSON() && !$this->RequestHandler->isGet()) {
        $this->redirect(null, 400);
    }

    $posts = $this->Post->find('all');
    $this->set(compact('posts'));
}
```

7. Add the following methods to the beginning of the PostsController class below the declaration of the components property:

```
public function beforeFilter() {
    parent::beforeFilter();
    if (
        $this->_isJSON() &&
        !$this->RequestHandler->isGet()
    ) {
        if (empty($this->data) && !empty($_POST)) {
            $this->data[$this->modelClass] = $_POST;
        }
    }
}

public function beforeRender() {
    parent::beforeRender();
    if ($this->_isJSON()) {
        Configure::write('debug', 0);
        $this->disableCache();
    }
}
```

8. Edit the PostsController::edit() method and make the following changes:

```
public function edit($id=null) {
    if ($this->_isJSON() && !$this->RequestHandler->isPost()) {
        $this->redirect(null, 400);
    }
```

```php
        if (!empty($this->data)) {
            if (!empty($id)) {
                $this->Post->id = $id;
            } else {
                $this->Post->create();
            }
            if ($this->Post->save($this->data)) {
                $this->Session->setFlash('Post created successfully');
                if ($this->_isJSON()) {
                    $this->redirect(null, 200);
                } else {
                    $this->redirect(array('action'=>'index'));
                }
            } else {
                if ($this->_isJSON()) {
                    $this->redirect(null, 403);
                } else {
                    $this->Session->setFlash('Please correct the errors
marked below');
                }
            }
        } elseif (!empty($id)) {
            $this->data = $this->Post->find('first', array(
                'conditions' => array('Post.id' => $id)
            ));
            if (empty($this->data)) {
                if ($this->_isJSON()) {
                    $this->redirect(null, 404);
                }
                $this->cakeError('error404');
            }
        }
        $this->set(compact('id'));
    }
```

9. Edit the `PostsController::delete()` method and make the following changes:

```php
public function delete($id) {
    if ($this->_isJSON() && !$this->RequestHandler->isDelete()) {
        $this->redirect(null, 400);
    }
    $post = $this->Post->find('first', array(
        'conditions' => array('Post.id' => $id)
```

```
    ));
    if (empty($post)) {
        if ($this->_isJSON()) {
            $this->redirect(null, 404);
        }
        $this->cakeError('error404');
    }

    if (!empty($this->data) || $this->RequestHandler->isDelete()) {
        if ($this->Post->delete($id)) {
            $this->Session->setFlash('Post deleted successfully');
            if ($this->_isJSON()) {
                $this->redirect(null, 200);
            } else {
                $this->redirect(array('action'=>'index'));
            }
        } else {
            if ($this->_isJSON()) {
                $this->redirect(null, 403);
            } else {
                $this->Session->setFlash('Could not delete post');
            }
        }
    }
    $this->set(compact('post'));
}
```

To test these services, we are going to create a small CakePHP shell that will create a new post, edit the created post, delete it, and show the list of posts throughout the process. Create a file named consume.php and place it in your app/vendors/shells folder, with the following contents:

```php
<?php
App::import('Core', 'HttpSocket');
class ConsumeShell extends Shell {
    protected static $baseUrl;
    protected static $httpSocket;

    public function main() {
        if (empty($this->args) || count($this->args) != 1) {
            $this->err('USAGE: cake consume <baseUrl>');
            $this->_stop();
        }

        self::$baseUrl = $this->args[0];
```

```php
        $this->test();
    }

    protected function test() {
        $this->request('/posts/add.json', 'POST', array(
            'title' => 'New Post',
            'body' => 'Body for my new post'
        ));

        $lastId = $this->listPosts();
        $this->hr();

        $this->request('/posts/edit/'.$lastId.'.json', 'POST', array(
            'title' => 'New Post Title',
            'body' => 'New body for my new post'
        ));

        $this->listPosts();
        $this->hr();

        $this->request('/posts/delete/'.$lastId.'.json', 'DELETE');

        $this->listPosts();
    }

    protected function request($url, $method='GET', $data=null) {
        if (!isset(self::$httpSocket)) {
            self::$httpSocket = new HttpSocket();
        } else {
            self::$httpSocket->reset();
        }

        $body = self::$httpSocket->request(array(
            'method' => $method,
            'uri' => self::$baseUrl . '/' . $url,
            'body' => $data
        ));

        if ($body === false || self::$httpSocket->response['status']
['code'] != 200) {
            $error = 'ERROR while performing '.$method.' to '.$url;
            if ($body !== false) {
                $error = '[' . self::$httpSocket->response['status']
['code'] . '] ' . $error;
            }
            $this->err($error);
            $this->_stop();
        }

        return $body;
    }
```

```php
    protected function listPosts() {
        $response = json_decode($this->request('/posts.json'));
        $lastId = null;
        foreach($response as $item) {
            $lastId = $item->Post->id;
            $this->out($item->Post->title . ': ' . $item->Post->url);
        }
        return $lastId;
    }
}
?>
```

To run this shell script, invoke it with one argument: the base URL of your application. So change `http://localhost` below to suit your application's URL:

▸ If you are on a GNU Linux / Mac / Unix system:

```
../cake/console/cake consume http://localhost
```

▸ If you are on Microsoft Windows:

```
..\cake\console\cake.bat consume http://localhost
```

The output should be similar to that shown in the following screenshot:

We can see that the first list of posts shows our newly created post entitled **New Post**. The second list shows how we successfully changed its title to **New Post Title**, and the third list shows how we deleted the post.

How it works...

Similarly to what was described in the *Creating an RSS feed* recipe, we started by specifying `json` as a valid extension and added the `RequestHandler` component to our list of components.

Unlike the `rss` and `xml` extensions, CakePHP does not provide a default layout for `json`, so we need to create one. Through the `beforeRender` callback, we turn debugging off, and we disable caching when a JSON request is made, to avoid any information that would break the JSON syntax and prevent client browsers from caching JSON requests.

> When a JSON request is made to a controller that uses the `RequestHandler` component, the component will automatically set the content type of the response to `application/json`.

Once we have our layout, we are ready to start implementing our JSON views. In this recipe, we only implement `index()` as a JSON action that returns JSON data through a view. All the other actions—`add()`, `edit()`, and `delete()`—will simply use HTTP status codes to communicate with the client. The JSON `index.ctp` view will simply add the full URL for each post, and echo the whole data structure as a JSON-formatted string using `json_encode()`.

As we will be changing some of the controller logic depending on the type of access (JSON versus normal access), we add a method named `_isJSON()` to our controller. This method uses the `ext` property of the `RequestHandler` component, which is set to the extension with which our action is requested. If no extension is used, and then it defaults to `html`. Using this property, we can check when a request is made using the `json` extension.

With `_isJSON()`, we can also add some extra checks to our methods, to make sure they are requested the proper way. For our `index` action, we make sure that if the request is made with JSON, we only allow GET requests to go through. If the request was made with any other method, for example, with POST, then we return an HTTP status of `400` (Bad Request), and we exit the application.

> When no data needs to be sent back to the client, HTTP status codes are a great way to inform if a REST request has succeeded or failed.

To help users of our REST requests, we should allow them to POST data without having to know how the data needs to be formatted for CakePHP to process it automatically. Therefore, we override the `beforeFilter` callback, so if a request is made with JSON that is not a GET request, and if CakePHP did not find any data properly formatted (when data was indeed posted), then we set what was posted as the controller data. This way, when creating or modifying posts, client code can simply use `title` to refer to the post `title` field, rather than having to use `data[Post][title]` as the name for the field.

We then proceed to make the necessary modifications to the `edit()` method. We start by making sure that we were accessing with the proper method (POST), and we change how we report success or failure: with an HTTP status of `200` (OK) when the post is saved, `403` (Forbidden) if the post cannot be saved, or `404` (Not Found) if trying to edit a post that does not exist.

The modifications to the `delete()` method are almost identical to the ones made to the `edit()` method. The two main differences are that the expected method is DELETED, and that we don't enforce data to be posted when being accessed through JSON.

To test the code in this recipe, we built a shell script to consume our REST services. This script uses the `HttpSocket` class to fetch the content. In this shell script, we built a generic `request()` function that takes a URL, a method (we use GET, POST, and DELETE), and an optional array of data to post.

We use the `request()` method to create a new post (notice how we specify the values for the `title` and `body` fields), get the list of posts that should include our newly created post, modify the created post, and finally delete it.

See also

▶ *Creating an RSS feed*

▶ *Adding authentication to REST services*

Adding authentication to REST services

In the previous recipe, *Building REST services with JSON,* we learnt how to enable JSON access to our actions, including the ability to create, modify, or delete posts with a simple JSON request.

Modification of data through REST requests can lead to sensitive data loss if we don't add some sort of authentication. This recipe shows us how to enforce that our data-changing REST services are only utilized by valid users using HTTP Basic Authentication.

Getting ready

To go through this recipe, we need some JSON-based REST services implemented. Follow the entire recipe *Building REST services with JSON*.

We also need a working authentication for our application. Follow the entire recipe *Setting up a basic authentication system* in the *Authentication* chapter.

How to do it...

Edit your app/controller/posts_controller.php file and make the following changes to the beforeFilter callback:

```php
public function beforeFilter() {
    parent::beforeFilter();

    if ($this->_isJSON()) {
        $this->Auth->allow($this->action);
        $this->Security->loginOptions = array(
            'type' => 'basic',
            'realm' => 'My REST services,services
            'login' => '_restLogin'
        );
        $this->Security->requireLogin($this->action);
        $this->Security->validatePost = false;
    }
    if (
        $this->_isJSON() &&
        !$this->RequestHandler->isGet()
    ) {
        if (empty($this->data) && !empty($_POST)) {
            $this->data[$this->modelClass] = $_POST;
        }
    }
}
```

While still editing the PostsController class, add the following method below the beforeFilter() method:

```php
public function _restLogin($credentials) {
    $login = array();
    foreach(array('username', 'password') as $field) {
        $value = $credentials[$field];
        if ($field == 'password' && !empty($value)) {
```

```
        $value = $this->Auth->password($value);
    }
    $login[$this->Auth->fields[$field]] = $value;
}
if (!$this->Auth->login($login)) {
    $this->Security->blackhole($this, 'login');
}
}
```

If we now browse to `http://localhost/posts`, we will be presented with a login screen. As there are no users in the system, we need to create one by browsing to `http://localhost/users/add`, and specifying the desired user name and password.

Let us run the test shell script (remember to change `http://localhost` to suit your application's base URL).

- If you are on a GNU Linux / Mac / Unix system:

    ```
    ../cake/console/cake consume http://localhost
    ```

- If you are on Microsoft Windows:

    ```
    ..\cake\console\cake.bat consume http://localhost
    ```

Its output would inform us that the creation of the post fails with a `401` (Unauthorized) status code, as shown in the following screenshot:

If you haven't done so already while following the recipe *Setting up a basic authentication system*, create a user account by browsing to `http://localhost/users/add` and specifying the desired username and password.

We need to modify the script to specify the user and password we created.

Edit your `app/vendors/shells/consume.php` shell script and add the following two properties to the `ConsumeShell` class:

```
protected static $user;
protected static $password;
```

While still editing the script, make the following changes to the main() method:

```
public function main() {
    if (empty($this->args) || count($this->args) != 3) {
        $this->err('USAGE: cake consume <baseUrl> <user> <password>');
        $this->_stop();
    }

    list(self::$baseUrl, self::$user, self::$password) = $this->args;

    $this->test();
}
```

Make the following changes to the request() method:

```
protected function request($url, $method='GET', $data=null) {
    if (!isset(self::$httpSocket)) {
        self::$httpSocket = new HttpSocket();
    } else {
        self::$httpSocket->reset();
    }

    $body = self::$httpSocket->request(array(
        'method' => $method,
        'uri' => self::$baseUrl . '/' . $url,
        'body' => $data,
        'auth' => array(
            'user' => self::$user,
            'pass' => self::$password
        )
    ));

    if ($body === false || self::$httpSocket->response['status']
['code'] != 200) {
        $error = 'ERROR while performing '.$method.' to '.$url;
        if ($body !== false) {
            $error = '[' . self::$httpSocket->response['status']
['code'] . '] ' . $error;
        }
        $this->err($error);
        $this->_stop();
    }

    return $body;
}
```

We can now run the script specifying the username and password we created. Change `http://localhost` to match your application's URL, `user` to match the username, and `password` to match the created password:

- If you are on a GNU Linux / Mac / Unix system:

    `../cake/console/cake consume http://localhost user password`

- If you are on Microsoft Windows:

    `..\cake\console\cake.bat consume http://localhost user password`

Running the script should give the same successful output as shown in the recipe *Building REST services with JSON*.

How it works...

We started by adding some special logic to the `beforeFilter` callback when being requested through JSON. In it, we start by telling the `Auth` component that the action being requested is public. If we didn't, the `Auth` component would render the login form to the client, which is obviously not a valid JSON response.

> This recipe uses a database-based authentication method. A simplier approach could have been taken by implementing basic HTTP authentication, a concept covered at `http://book.cakephp.org/view/1309/Basic-HTTP-Authentication`.

Once we have established that the `Auth` component will not handle authorization for any actions requested through JSON, we need to add support for HTTP Basic Authentication. We do so by first configuring the `loginOptions` property of the `Security` component with the following settings:

- `type`: Type of HTTP Authentication to use, which can be either `basic` or `digest`. We chose `basic`.

- `realm`: A descriptive name of the system being accessed.

- `login`: An optional function that is called when a client is trying to login through HTTP authentication. As we will use the `Auth` component to validate a login, we specify our own custom function, named `_restLogin`, to validate a user.

Once we configured `Security`, we use its `requireLogin()` method to mark the current action as one that requires HTTP authentication.

We also need to take into account a special check the `Security` component performs on certain requests. When data is posted, the component will look for a special token that should be saved in the session, and also posted as part of the request. This is a great feature that prevents the manipulation of hidden fields, because the token contains a hash of all known form values.

Naturally, this is something that should not be applicable for REST requests because as we learnt while describing the REST architecture in the introduction to the recipe *Building REST services with JSON*, REST requests are stateless. Therefore, we disable this feature by setting the `validatePost` property of the `Security` component to `false`.

The final step is implementing the method that is called by the `Security` component whenever an HTTP authentication login is attempted. We named this method `_restLogin()`, prefixing it with an underscore to prevent direct access to it. This method takes only one parameter, an indexed array with two mandatory keys: `username`, and `password`.

As the `Auth` component can be configured to use any field names for the `username` and `password` fields, we need to make sure we use the configured field names prior to attempting the login. The `fields` property of the `Auth` component contains this configuration in an array, indexed by `username`, and `password`.

When we receive a call to `_restLogin()`, the value for the `password` field is plain text, as this is the standard way HTTP Basic Authentication works. However, the `Auth` component only takes hashes as passwords, so we need to hash the given password by utilizing the `password()` method of the `Auth` component.

Once the correct field names are utilized, and the password is hashed, we are ready to attempt the login. We call the `login()` method of the `Auth` component, which returns `true` if the login is successful, or `false` otherwise. If the login fails, we use the `blackHole()` method of the `Security` component, specifying the reason for failure (`login`, which translates to a 401 HTTP status code), which stops the client request.

Implementing token-based authorization for API access

In the previous recipe, *Adding authentication to REST services*, we built a REST API using JSON for our `PostsController` actions. With it, clients that utilize our REST services use a user account to validate their requests.

Without neglecting the need to authorize all requests, several companies take a different approach when publishing their APIs: the use of API tokens. The advantage of using API tokens is that our user accounts are not exposed in client scripts, so the authorization information can't be used to log in to the site.

In this recipe we will take our authenticated REST service system and enable the use of tokens to use the exposed API. We will also add a usage limit, so client API usage is only allowed within a certain time and number of uses threshold.

Getting ready

To go through this recipe, we need some JSON-based REST services implemented with authentication in place, so follow the previous recipe.

How to do it...

1. We start by adding some fields to our `users` table. Issue the following SQL statements:

```
ALTER TABLE `users`users
    ADD COLUMN `token` CHAR(40) default NULL,
    ADD COLUMN `token_used` DATETIME default NULL,
    ADD COLUMN `token_uses` INT NOT NULL default 0,
    ADD UNIQUE KEY `token`(`token`);
```

2. Edit your `app/controllers/users_controller.php` file and add the following method to the `UsersController` class:

```php
public function token() {
    $token = sha1(String::uuid());
    $this->User->id = $this->Auth->user('id');
    if (!$this->User->saveField('token', $token)) {
        $token = null;
        $this->Session->setFlash('There was an error generating this token');
    }
    $this->set(compact('token'));
}
```

3. Create its view in a file named `token.ctp` and place it in your `app/views/users` folder, with the following contents:

```php
<h1>API access token</h1>
<?php if (!empty($token)) { ?>
    <p>Your new API access token is: <strong><?php echo $token; ?></strong></p>
<?php } ?>
```

4. Let us add the parameters that will define the API access limits. Edit your `app/config/bootstrap.php` file and add the following at the end:

```
Configure::write('API', array(
    'maximum' => 6,
    'time' => '2 minutes'
));
```

5. Edit your `app/controllers/posts_controller.php` file and change the `_restLogin()` method, replacing it with the following contents:

```
public function _restLogin($credentials) {
    $model = $this->Auth->getModel();
    try {
        $id = $model->useToken($credentials['username']);
        if (empty($id)) {
            $this->redirect(null, 503);
        }
    } catch(Exception $e) {
        $id = null;
    }
    if (empty($id) || !$this->Auth->login(strval($id)))  {
        $this->Security->blackhole($this, 'login');
    }
}
```

6. Create the `User` model in a file named `user.php` and place it in your `app/models` folder, with the following contents:

```
<?php
class User extends AppModel {
    public function useToken($token) {
        $user = $this->find('first', array(
            'conditions' => array($this->alias.'.token' => $token),
            'recursive' => -1
        ));
        if (empty($user)) {
            throw new Exception('Token is not valid');
        }

        $apiSettings = Configure::read('API');
        $tokenUsed = !empty($user[$this->alias]['token_used']) ?
$user[$this->alias]['token_used'] : null;
        $tokenUses = $user[$this->alias]['token_uses'];
        if (!empty($tokenUsed)) {
            $tokenTimeThreshold = strtotime('+' .
$apiSettings['time'], strtotime($tokenUsed));
```

```
        }
        $now = time();
        if (!empty($tokenUsed) && $now <= $tokenTimeThreshold &&
$tokenUses >= $apiSettings['maximum']) {
            return false;
        }
        $id = $user[$this->alias][$this->primaryKey];
        if (!empty($tokenUsed) && $now <= $tokenTimeThreshold) {
            $this->id = $id;
            $this->saveField('token_uses', $tokenUses + 1);
        } else {
            $this->id = $id;
            $this->save(
                array('token_used'=>date('Y-m-d H:i:s'), 'token_
uses'=>1),
                false,
                array('token_used', 'token_uses')
            );
        }
        return $id;
    }
}
?>
```

7. Edit your app/vendors/shells/consume.php test script, remove the $user and $password properties, and then add the following property:

    ```
    protected $token;
    ```

8. While still editing the shell script, make the following changes to its main() method:

    ```
    public function main() {
        if (empty($this->args) || count($this->args) != 2) {
            $this->err('USAGE: cake consume <baseUrl> <token>');
            $this->_stop();
        }
        list(self::$baseUrl, self::$token) = $this->args;
        $this->test();
    }
    ```

9. Finally, make the following changes to the request() method:

    ```
    protected function request($url, $method='GET', $data=null) {
        if (!isset(self::$httpSocket)) {
            self::$httpSocket = new HttpSocket();
        } else {
    ```

```
            self::$httpSocket->reset();
        }
        $body = self::$httpSocket->request(array(
            'method' => $method,
            'uri' => self::$baseUrl . '/' . $url,
            'body' => $data,
            'auth' => array(
                'user' => self::$token,
                'pass' => ''
            )
        ));

        if ($body === false || self::$httpSocket->response['status']
['code'] != 200) {
            $error = 'ERROR while performing '.$method.' to '.$url;
            if ($body !== false) {
                $error = '[' . self::$httpSocket->response['status']
['code'] . '] ' . $error;
            }
            $this->err($error);
            $this->_stop();
        }
        return $body;
    }
```

If you now browse to `http://localhost/users/token`, you will be asked to Log in. Log in with the user account you created during the *Getting Started* section and you will then obtain an API token.

Let us now run the testing script with the following command. Change `http://localhost` to match your application's URL, and token to match the API token you just generated:

- ▸ If you are on a GNU Linux / Mac / Unix system:

    `../cake/console/cake consume http://localhost token`

- ▸ If you are on Microsoft Windows:

    `..\cake\console\cake.bat consume http://localhost token`

If we specified the right token, we will get the same successful output as shown in the recipe *Building REST services with JSON*.

If you run the script again within 2 minutes since the last run, you will get a `503` (Service Unavailable) HTTP status error, indicating that we are overusing our API token. We will have to wait two minutes to be able to successfully run the script again, because each run makes six requests to the API, and six is the maximum allowed requests within two minutes, as configured in `app/config/bootstrap.php`.

How it works...

We start by adding three fields to the `users` table:

- ▶ `token`: The API access token, unique to each user. This is what a user will use to use our API services.
- ▶ `token_used`: The last time the API usage counter (`token_uses`) was reset.
- ▶ `token_uses`: The number of API uses since the date and time specified in `token_used`.

We then create an action called `token` in the `UsersController` class to allow users to get new API access tokens. This action will simply create a new token by hashing a **UUID** (**Universally Unique Identifier**), and saving it to the `users` table record.

We proceed to set our application configuration in `bootstrap.php` by defining the API access limits with two settings:

- ▶ `maximum`: The maximum number of API requests allowed within a given time frame.
- ▶ `time`: The time frame that is used to check for API overuse. Any string that can be used by the PHP function `strtotime()` is allowed.

We set `time` to 2 minutes, and `maximum` to 6 requests, which means that we will allow up to six API requests per user, every two minutes.

As we are no longer using real accounts to authenticate our API users, we changed the `_restLogin()` method in `ProfilesController` to only use the given `username` field value. This value is in fact a user's API token. The `password` field is therefore ignored, which allows our test client script to simply pass an empty value as the password.

We use the method `useToken()` of the `User` model to check the validity of the token. If the method throws an `Exception`, then the given token does not exist, so we end the request with a `401` status (Unauthorized) by calling the `blackhole()` method of the `Security` component. If the `useToken()` method returns `false`, then the token is being overused, so we send back a `503` (Service Unavailable) status. If we are given back a valid user ID, we convert this value to a string, and pass it to the `login()` method of the `Auth` component, which will log in a user with a given ID if the specified parameter is a string.

As we can see, the whole token usage logic relies on the `User::useToken()`. This method starts by looking for a user record with the given token. If none is found, it throws an `Exception`. If a valid token is being used, it checks to see if the token has been used. If so, we set the time limit since the first update of the token usage in the `$tokenTimeThreshold` local variable. If we are within this time frame, and if the number of token uses exceeds the configured setting, we return `false`.

If none of the above conditions are met, then the token use is valid, so we either increment the number of uses if `$tokenTimeThreshold` is within the current time frame, or reset it.

8

Working with Shells

In this chapter, we will cover:

- ▶ Building and running a shell
- ▶ Parsing command line parameters
- ▶ Creating reusable shell tasks
- ▶ Sending e-mails from shells
- ▶ Creating Non-interactive tasks with the robot plugin

Introduction

One of the most powerful, yet unknown, features of CakePHP is its shell framework. It provides applications with all that is required for building command-line tools, which can be used to perform intensive tasks and any other type of non-interactive processing.

This chapter introduces the reader to CakePHP shells by starting with the process of building basic shells, and then moving on to more advanced features, such as sending e-mails and running controller actions from shells. It finishes by presenting the robot plugin, which offers a fully featured solution for scheduling and running tasks.

Building and running a shell

In this recipe, we will learn how to build and run a custom shell, which will ask for a username and a password, and add the given account to a list of user accounts. Based on the system created in the recipe *Setting up a basic authentication system* from *Chapter, Authentication*, this shell is a great help when looking to create test accounts.

Getting ready

To go through this recipe we need an authentication system. Follow the entire recipe *Setting up a basic authentication system* from *Authentication* chapter.

How to do it...

Create a file named `user.php` and place it in your `app/vendors/shells` folder, with the following contents:

```php
<?php
App::import('Core', 'Security');

class UserShell extends Shell {
    public $uses = array('User');
    public function main() {
        $user = $this->in('Enter the username (ENTER to abort):');
        if (empty($user)) {
            $this->_stop();
        }

        $defaultPassword = $this->_randomPassword();;
        $password = $this->in('Enter the password (ENTER to use
generated):', null, $defaultPassword);

        $this->out();
        $this->out('USER: '.$user);
        $this->out('PASSWORD: '.$password);
        $this->out();

        if (strtoupper($this->in('Proceed?', array('Y', 'N'), 'N')) !=
'Y') {
            $this->_stop();
        }

        $user = array('User' => array(
            'username' => $user,
            'password' => Security::hash($password, null, true)
        ));

        $this->User->create();
        if ($this->User->save($user)) {
            $this->out('User created.');
        } else {
            $this->error('Error while creating user.');
        }
    }

    protected function _randomPassword($size=10) {
```

```
$chars = '@!#$_';
foreach(array('A'=>'Z', 'a'=>'z', '0'=>'9') as $start => $end) {
    for ($i=ord($start), $limiti=ord($end); $i <= $limiti; $i++)
{

        $chars .= chr($i);
      }
  }
$totalChars = strlen($chars);
$password = '';
for($i=0; $i < $size; $i++) {
    $password .= $chars[rand(0, $totalChars-1)];
}
return $password;
    }
  }
?>
```

We are now ready to run our shell. Open a terminal window, and access the directory where your application resides. Inside this directory you should have your `app/` and `cake/` folders. For example, if your application is installed in `/var/www/myapp`, then `/var/www/myapp/app` should be your `app/` folder, and `/var/www/myapp/cake` your `cake/` folder. While standing in your application's main directory (`/var/www/myapp` in this example), run:

> To learn more about setting the right path when running shells, or how to add the cake shell script to your PATH environment variable see `http://book.cakephp.org/view/1106/The-CakePHP-Console`

If you are on a GNU Linux / Mac / Unix system:

    ../cake/console/cake user

If you are on Microsoft Windows:

    ..\cake\console\cake.bat user

> If you receive an error message such as **Error: Class UserShell could not be loaded**, this means that CakePHP is unable to find your `app/` folder, which is probably because you have a different name for the `app/` folder. In this case, you can specify the folder with the app argument, like so: $ `cake/console/cake -app /var/www/myapp/app user`.

Once the shell is run, it will ask us for the desired username and password, and will wait for a final confirmation before creating the account, as shown in the following screenshot:

```
Welcome to CakePHP v1.3.3 Console
-----------------------------------------------------------
------
App : basic
Path: /var/www/cookbook/chapter8/./basic
-----------------------------------------------------------
------
Enter the username (ENTER to abort):
> mariano
Enter the password (ENTER to use generated):
[VR4krScvcs] > secret

USER: mariano
PASSWORD: secret

Proceed? (Y/N)
> Y
User created.
[17:06] mariano@kramer:/var/www/cookbook/chapter8$
```
chapter8 : bash

We are now able to use this account when logging in through our application's login page.

How it works...

We started by importing the Security class, which is used for hashing the password prior to saving the user record. We then created a class named UserShell, extending it from CakePHP's Shell class, which offers us a set of methods and properties that are helpful when building shells. One of such properties is uses, which works the same way as a controller's uses property—by defining a list of application models that should be instantiated and ready to use from any method in the shell.

Our shell's entry point is the main() method. This comes as no surprise if you have any experience developing C, C++, or Java applications, as main() is also their entry function. If you have no such experience, then all there is to know is that main() will be automatically executed by CakePHP when our shell is invoked through the command line.

Our main() method starts by asking the user for their desired username. To ask for user input, we use the in() method (available through the Shell parent class), which takes up to three arguments:

- prompt: The message that is shown to the user before asking for their input.
- options: An optional set of values that the user should be restricted to when entering their input.

- ▶ `default`: An optional default value that is to be used if the user enters no input by clicking *Enter* at the prompt.

If the user does not specify a user name, we exit the application by calling the `_stop()` method, available to all CakePHP classes that descend from `Object`, `Shell` being one of them.

Once we have our username, we need to ask for a password. As a useful alternative, we want to offer the user an automatically generated password. To generate this password, we implement a method called, not surprisingly, `_randomPassword()`.

This method takes one argument, the size of the generated password, and builds it by randomly selecting an element from a defined set of characters. This set is constructed by including all characters between the letters A and Z, a and z, and 0 and 9. For more secure passwords, we also included the symbols @ ! # $ and _ as valid characters.

When we use the `in()` method to ask the user for a password, we use this default generated password as its third argument (`default`.) After asking for the password, we show the user the choice for username and password, and ask for confirmation, utilizing the `options` argument in our call to `in()`.

If the user confirms the operation, we proceed to create the user record, hashing the entered password with the `Security::hash()` method, which takes up to three arguments:

- ▶ `string`: The string to be hashed.
- ▶ `method`: The method to use for hashing, which can be any of: `sha1`, `sha256`, `md5`, or any other method supported by the `hash()` PHP function. Defaults to the following PHP functions, depending on their availability: `sha1()` (also used if `sha1` is the chosen method), `mhash()` (also used if `sha256` is the chosen method), `hash()`, and finally `md5()`.
- ▶ `salt`: If `true`, prefixes the string with the application's salt (available in the `Configure` setting `Security.salt`). If a string is specified, it is prefixed to the password being hashed in place of the application's `Security.salt` setting. If `false`, hashes the given string without a prefix.

If a record is created, we inform the user that the operation succeeded. Otherwise we use the `error()` method (available through the `Shell` parent class) which sends an error message through the standard error stream and exits the application.

Using the Auth component for hashing passwords

In this recipe, we called the `Security::hash()` method to hash passwords, by specifying the same exact arguments that are utilized in the `Auth` component. If we did not do so, we would have different hash values for the same passwords, which would render our shell useless, as any user account created with it wouldn't be able to log in.

The problem with this approach is that if the method that is used by the `Auth` component to hash passwords is changed, we would need to reflect such changes in our shell. Therefore, we may want to use the `Auth` component to do the hashing instead. This solution requires a bit of extra effort, as components are not natively available in a shell. Edit your `app/vendors/shells/user.php` file and remove the import of the `Security` class, and then add the following import statement at the beginning of the file:

```
App::import('Component', 'Auth');
```

We now need to instantiate the `AuthComponent` class. Add the following code to the beginning of the `main()` method:

```
$this->Auth = new AuthComponent();
```

Finally change the definition of the data that is used for creating the `User` record, so its `password` field is hashed using the `Auth` component:

```
$user = array('User' => array(
    'username' => $user,
    'password' => $this->Auth->password($password)
));
```

See also

▶ *Parsing command line parameters*

Parsing command line parameters

The recipe *Building and running a shell* showed us how to create a shell that adds records based on user-provided information. This recipe adds support to import accounts from a CSV file, while allowing the user to configure different settings through the use of command-line parameters.

Getting ready

To go through this recipe we need the user shell implemented. Follow the entire recipe *Building and running a shell*.

We will also need a sample CSV file from which to import records. Create a file named `users.csv` and place it in a directory of your choice (for example, in the application's `app/tmp` directory) with the following contents:

```
"john","John","Doe"
"jane","Jane","Doe"
"mark","Mark","Doe"
```

```
"mathew","Mathew","Doe"
"peter","Peter","Doe"
"roland","Roland","Doe"
```

How to do it...

1. Edit your `app/vendors/shells/user.php` file, and change the name of the method `main()` to `add()`.

2. Add the following method right below the `add()` method:

```php
public function help() {
    $this->out('USAGE: $ cake '.$this->shell.' <import <path/to/
file> [-limit N | -size N | -verbose] | add>');
    $this->out('where:');
    $this->out();
    $this->out('-limit N: import up to N records');
    $this->out('-size N: size of generated password');
    $this->out('-verbose: Verbose output');
}
```

3. Now add the following method above the `_randomPassword()` method:

```php
protected function _parseCSV($path) {
    $file = fopen($path, 'r');
    if (!is_resource($file)) {
        $this->error('Can\'t open '.$file);
    }
    $rows = array();
    while($row = fgetcsv($file)) {
        $rows[] = $row;
    }
    fclose($file);
    return $rows;
}
```

4. Finally, add the following below the `help()` method:

```php
public function import() {
    $this->_checkArgs(1);
    $defaults = array(
        'limit' => null,
        'size' => 10,
        'verbose' => false
    );
```

```php
    $options = array_merge(
        $defaults,
        array_intersect_key($this->params, $defaults)
    );

    $path = $this->args[0];
    if (!is_file($path) || !is_readable($path)) {
        $this->error('File '.$path.' cannot be read');
    }

    $users = array();
    foreach($this->_parseCSV($path) as $i => $row) {
        $users[$row[0]] = $this->_randomPassword($options['size']);
        if (!empty($options['limit']) && $i + 1 == $options['limit']) {
            break;
        }
    }

    if ($options['verbose']) {
        $this->out('Will create '.number_format(count($users)).'
accounts');
    }

    foreach($users as $userName => $password) {
        if ($options['verbose']) {
            $this->out('Creating user '.$userName.'... ', false);
        }

        $user = array('User' => array(
            'username' => $userName,
            'password' => Security::hash($password, null, true)
        ));

        $this->User->create();
        $saved = ($this->User->save($user) !== false);
        if (!$saved) {
            unset($users[$userName]);
        }

        if ($options['verbose']) {
            $this->out($saved ? 'SUCCESS' : 'FAIL');
        }
    }

    $this->out('Created accounts:');
    foreach($users as $userName => $password) {
        $this->out($userName.' : '.$password);
    }
}
```

If we run the shell without arguments, CakePHP will say that there is no known command, and suggest that we get help by specifying `help` as an argument to our shell. Doing so will display our help message, as shown in the following screenshot:

If we run our shell with the `add` argument, we will see exactly the same functionality implemented in the recipe *Building and running a shell*.

Executing the shell with the `import` argument and the `verbose` parameter, and specifying the path to our CSV file with a command such as the following:

```
$ cake/console/cake user import app/tmp/users.csv -verbose
```

would import the users listed in the CSV file, generating an output similar to what is shown in the following screenshot:

How it works...

We started by changing the name of the entry method to `add()`. Doing so means we no longer have an entry method, so how does CakePHP find what to run when our shell is invoked? Through the use of commands.

If there is no entry method defined in a shell, CakePHP will assume that the first argument used when executing a shell is a command. A command is nothing more than a public method that does not start with an underscore sign. As such, a method named `add()` is executed when the shell is invoked with the `add` argument. If no argument is specified, CakePHP complains, as there is no command to run, and suggests the user use the `help` argument, which is nothing more than a way to call the `help()` method in our shell (as `help` is a regular command).

We use the `help()` method to show usage instructions for our shell, listing the available commands (`add`, and `import`), and the parameters for each of those commands. While the `add` command has no available parameters, we support the following parameters for our `import` command:

Setting	Purpose
`limit`	A maximum number of records to process from the CSV file. If omitted, all records will be processed.
`size`	The maximum length for the generated passwords. Defaults to `10`.
`verbose`	If specified, the shell will output information as its creating the user records.

The `_parseCSV()` method is our helper method to parse a CSV file, returning an array of rows found in a file, where each row is itself an array of values. This method uses PHP's `fgetcsv()` function to parse a record from a file handle, obtained with the use of PHP's `fopen()` function, and closed with `fclose()` once the parsing is finished.

We continue by implementing the `import()` method, the body of our `import` command. This method uses the `_checkArgs()` method (available through the `Shell` class) to make sure that the command receives at least the specified number of arguments, in our case 1. If the method finds that the user did not specify the minimum number of arguments, it will throw an error message and abort the execution. This is a way for us to make sure that at least the path to the CSV file is provided.

If the number of arguments is correct we proceed to process the optional parameters. To do so, we use the `params` property. This property is available to all shells, and includes the following values even when no parameters are provided:

Setting	Purpose
app	The name of the app/ directory.
root	The full path to our application's root directory, which would contain the app/ and cake/ directories.
webroot	The name of the webroot/ directory, which is inside the app/ directory.
working	The full path to the app/ directory.

However, we are only interested in the parameters given by the user through the command line. Therefore, we define the set of valid parameters with their default values, and we merge the values for those parameters that are available in the params property. We store this merged values in an array named options.

Using the is_file() and is_readable() PHP functions, we make sure we were given a valid file. If not, we use the error() method to print out an error message and abort the application.

We then proceed to use _importCSV() to get a list of parsed rows, and for each of those rows we assign a random password, using the size option. We stop generating passwords once we reach the value of the limit option, if one is provided. By the end of this loop, we will have an array named users where its index is a username, and its value is the password for the given user.

For each of the values in the users array, we create the account record similar to the way we do it in the add command, while outputting the status of each creation if the verbose option is set. If we get an error while creating a specific record, we remove the problematic user from the users array.

Once the creation process is finalized, we output the list of successfully created usernames, together with their generated passwords.

See also

▸ *Parsing CSV files with a datasource* in *Chapter 5, Datasources*
▸ *Creating reusable shell tasks*

Creating reusable shell tasks

Just as we have components to share functionality amongst controllers, we also have behaviors for models, and helpers for views. What about shells? CakePHP offers the concept of tasks, which are classes that also extend from the Shell class, but can be reused from other shells.

In this recipe, we will learn how to build a task that handles argument and parameter processing for our shell, can auto-generate help messages, and check the definition of mandatory arguments and optional parameters. We will implement this task in the most generic fashion, so we can use it for any future shells we may decide to build.

Getting ready

To go through this recipe we need a shell that accepts parameters and has different commands available. Follow the entire recipe *Parsing command line parameters*.

How to do it...

1. Edit your `app/vendors/shells/user.php` file and add the following right below the declaration of the `uses` property:

```php
public $tasks = array('Help');
public static $commands = array(
    'add',
    'import' => array(
        'help' => 'Import user records from a CSV file',
        'args' => array(
            'path' => array(
                'help' => 'Path to CSV file',
                'mandatory' => true
            )
        ),
        'params' => array(
            'limit' => array(
                'type' => 'int',
                'help' => 'import up to N records'
            ),
            'size' => array(
                'value' => 10,
                'type' => 'int',
                'help' => 'size of generated password'
            ),
            'verbose' => array(
                'value' => false,
                'type' => 'bool',
                'help' => 'Verbose output'
            )
        )
    )
);
```

2. While still editing the shell, remove the `help()` method, and remove the following lines from the beginning of the `import()` method:

```php
$this->_checkArgs(1);

$defaults = array(
    'limit' => null,
    'size' => 10,
    'verbose' => false
);
$options = array_merge(
    $defaults,
    array_intersect_key($this->params, $defaults)
);

$path = $this->args[0];
```

3. Add the following lines at the beginning of the `import()` method:

```php
$options = $this->Help->parameters;
extract($this->Help->arguments);
```

4. Create a file named `help.php` and place it in your `app/vendors/shells/tasks`, with the following contents:

```php
<?php
class HelpTask extends Shell {
    public $parameters = array();
    public $arguments = array();
    protected $commands = array();

    public function initialize() {
        $shellClass = Inflector::camelize($this->shell).'Shell';
        $vars = get_class_vars($shellClass);

        if (!empty($vars['commands'])) {
            foreach($vars['commands'] as $command => $settings) {
                if (is_numeric($command)) {
                    $command = $settings;
                    $settings = array();
                }
                if (!empty($settings['args'])) {
                    $args = array();
                    foreach($settings['args'] as $argName => $arg) {
                        if (is_numeric($argName)) {
                            $argName = $arg;
                            $arg = array();
                        }
                        $args[$argName] = array_merge(array(
```

```
                                'help' => null,
                                'mandatory' => false
                            ), $arg);
                        }
                        $settings['args'] = $args;
                    }
                    if (!empty($settings['params'])) {
                        $params = array();
                        foreach($settings['params'] as $paramName =>
$param) {
                            if (is_numeric($paramName)) {
                                $paramName = $param;
                                $param = array();
                            }
                            $params[$paramName] = array_merge(array(
                                'help' => null,
                                'type' => 'string'
                            ), $param);
                        }
                    }
                    $this->commands[$command] = array_merge(array(
                        'help' => null,
                        'args' => array(),
                        'params' => array()
                    ), $settings);
                }
            }

        if (empty($this->command) && !in_array('main', get_class_
methods($shellClass))) {
                $this->_welcome();
                $this->_help();
        } elseif (!empty($this->command) && array_key_exists($this-
>command, $this->commands)) {
                $command = $this->commands[$this->command];

                $number = count(array_filter(Set::extract(array_
values($command['args']), '/mandatory')));
                if ($number > 0 && (count($this->args) - 1) < $number) {
                    $this->err('WRONG number of parameters');
                    $this->out();
                    $this->_help($this->command);
                } elseif ($number > 0) {
                    $i = 0;
                    foreach($command['args'] as $argName => $arg) {
```

```
                    if ($number >= $i && isset($this->args[$i+1])) {
                        $this->arguments[$argName] = $this->args[$i+1];
                    }
                    $i++;
                }
            }

            $values = array_intersect_key($this->params,
    $command['params']);
            foreach($command['params'] as $settingName => $setting) {
                if (!array_key_exists($settingName, $values)) {
                    $this->parameters[$settingName] = array_key_
    exists('value', $setting) ?
                        $setting['value'] :
                        null;
                } elseif ($setting['type'] == 'int' && !is_
    numeric($values[$settingName])) {
                    $this->err('ERROR: wrong value for '.$settingName);
                    $this->out();
                    $this->_help($this->command);
                } else {
                    if ($setting['type'] == 'bool') {
                        $values[$settingName] =
    !empty($values[$settingName]);
                    }
                    $this->parameters[$settingName] =
    $values[$settingName];
                }
            }
        }
    }
```

5. Add the following methods to the created `HelpTask` class:

```
 public function execute() {
    $this->_help(!empty($this->args) ? $this->args[0] : null);
}

protected function _help($command = null) {
    $usage = 'cake '.$this->shell;
    if (empty($this->commands)) {
        $this->out($usage);
        return;
    }
    $lines = array();
    $usages = array();
```

```
      if (empty($command) || !array_key_exists($command, $this-
>commands)) {
          foreach(array_keys($this->commands) as $currentCommand) {
              $usages[] = $this->_usageCommand($currentCommand);
              if (!empty($lines)) {
                  $lines[] = null;
              }
              $lines = array_merge($lines, $this->_
helpCommand($currentCommand));
          }
      } else {
          $usages = (array) $this->_usageCommand($command);
          $lines = $this->_helpCommand($command);
      }

          if (!empty($usages)) {
          $usage .= ' ';

          if (empty($command)) {
              $usage .= '<';
          }

          $usage .= implode(' | ', $usages);

          if (empty($command)) {
              $usage .= '>';
          }
      }

      $this->out($usage);
      if (!empty($lines)) {
          $this->out();
          foreach($lines as $line) {
              $this->out($line);
          }
      }
      $this->_stop();
  }
```

6. While still editing the `HelpTask` class, add the following helper methods to the class:

```
protected function _usageCommand($command) {
    $usage = $command;
    if (!empty($this->commands[$command]['args'])) {
        foreach($this->commands[$command]['args'] as $argName =>
$arg) {
            $usage .= ' ' . ($arg['mandatory'] ? '<' : '[');
            $usage .= $argName;
            $usage .= ($arg['mandatory'] ? '>' : ']');
```

```php
        }
    }
    if (!empty($this->commands[$command]['params'])) {
        $usages = array();
        foreach(array_keys($this->commands[$command]['params']) as
$setting) {
            $usages[] = $this->_helpSetting($command, $setting);
        }
        $usage .= ' ['.implode(' | ', $usages).']';
    }
    return $usage;
}
protected function _helpCommand($command) {
    if (
        empty($this->commands[$command]['args']) &&
        empty($this->commands[$command]['params'])
    ) {
        return array();
    }
    $lines = array('Options for '.$command.':');
    foreach($this->commands[$command]['args'] as $argName => $arg)
{
        $lines[] = "\t".$argName . (!empty($arg['help'])) ?
"\t\t".$arg['help'] : '');
    }
    foreach(array_keys($this->commands[$command]['params']) as
$setting) {
        $lines[] = "\t".$this->_helpSetting($command, $setting,
true);
    }
    return $lines;
}
protected function _helpSetting($command, $settingName, $useHelp =
false) {
    $types = array('int' => 'N', 'string' => 'S', 'bool' => null);
    $setting = $this->commands[$command]['params'][$settingName];
    $type = array_key_exists($setting['type'], $types) ?
$types[$setting['type']] : null;
    $help = '-'.$settingName . (!empty($type) ? ' '.$type : '');
    if ($useHelp && !empty($setting['help'])) {
        $help .= "\t\t".$setting['help'];
        if (array_key_exists('value', $setting) && !is_
null($setting['value'])) {
```

```
                    $help .= '. DEFAULTS TO: ';
                    if (empty($type)) {
                        $help .= $setting['value'] ? 'Enabled' : 'Disabled';
                    } else {
                        $help .= $setting['value'];
                    }
                }
            }
        return $help;
    }
```

If you now run the shell without any parameters, with a command such as the following:

```
$ cake/console/cake user
```

we would get the thorough help message shown in the following screenshot:

```
Welcome to CakePHP v1.3.3 Console
-----------------------------------------------------------------
App : tasks
Path: /var/www/cookbook/chapter8/./tasks
-----------------------------------------------------------------
cake user <add | import <path> [-limit N | -size N | -verbose]>

Options for import:
        path            Path to CSV file
        -limit N                import up to N records
        -size N         size of generated password. DEFAULTS TO: 10
        -verbose                Verbose output. DEFAULTS TO: Disabled
[11:36] mariano@kramer:/var/www/cookbook/chapter8$ 
```

We can also obtain detailed help for a specific command. Running the shell with a command such as the following:

```
$ cake/console/cake user help import
```

would show us the help message for the `import` command, as shown in the following screenshot:

```
Welcome to CakePHP v1.3.3 Console
-----------------------------------------------------------------
App : tasks
Path: /var/www/cookbook/chapter8/./tasks
-----------------------------------------------------------------
cake user import <path> [-limit N | -size N | -verbose]

Options for import:
        path             Path to CSV file
        -limit N              import up to N records
        -size N          size of generated password. DEFAULTS TO: 10
        -verbose              Verbose output. DEFAULTS TO: Disabled
[13:54] mariano@kramer:/var/www/cookbook/chapter8$ █
```

chapter8 : bash

Running the shell with the same parameters as the ones used in the recipe *Parsing command line parameters* to import CSV files should work as expected.

How it works...

When a shell includes the property `tasks` in its declaration, it is said to use the specified tasks. Tasks are stored in the `app/vendors/shells/tasks` folder, and are accessible in the shell as instances. In our case, we add a task named `Help`, which should be implemented in a class named `HelpTask` and placed in a file named `help.php` in the `tasks` folder, and we refer to it as `$this->Help` from within the shell.

Before proceeding, a point has to be made regarding the naming of this particular task. As we want our task to automatically generate help messages for our shell, we somehow need to catch the call to the `help()` command. This is only achievable if we first understand how the shell dispatching process works. Let us assume the following invocation:

```
$ cake/console/cake user import
```

The shell dispatcher, implemented in the file `cake/console/cake.php`, would go through the following steps:

1. Instantiate the shell class `UserShell`.

2. Call its `initialize()` method.

3. Load all tasks defined in the `tasks` property of the shell.

4. For each of those tasks, call their `initialize()` method, and load any tasks that they themselves may be using.

If the given command (`import` in this case) is the name of one of the included tasks, call the task's `startup()` method, and then its `execute()` method.

If the given command is not a task name, then call the shell's `startup()` method, and execute the command's method, if it exists, or the entry method `main()` if the command is not implemented.

This means that if we have a task named `Help` included in our shell, and the user launches the shell with the following command:

```
$ cake/console/cake user help
```

Then the shell dispatcher would call the `execute()` method of the `HelpTask` class, because the command, `help`, is actually the name of one of the shell's tasks. Knowing this, we can remove the `help()` implementation of our `User` shell, and have the `Help` task handle the display of help messages.

Furthermore, our `Help` task needs to be generic enough to not be tied to a specific shell. Therefore, we need a way to tell it about our available commands, expected arguments, and optional parameters. This is what the `commands` property is there for: an array of commands, where the key is the command name and the value any of the following settings:

Setting	Purpose
help	The help message describing the purpose of the command. Defaults to no message.
args	The list of mandatory and optional arguments the command takes. Defaults to no arguments.
params	The list of optional parameters the command accepts. Defaults to no parameters.

Notice, however, that the `add` command is defined in a different fashion: instead of being defined in the key, it is simply the name of the command added to the `commands` array. This means that the command has no help message, no arguments, and no parameters.

The `args` command setting is an array of arguments, indexed by argument name. Each argument may define any of the following settings:

Setting	Purpose
help	The help message that describes the argument. Defaults to no message.
mandatory	If `true`, this argument must be present. If `false`, the argument may be omitted. Defaults to `false`.

Similarly, the `params` command setting is also an array, indexed by parameter name, where each parameter may define any of the following settings:

Setting	Purpose
`help`	The help message that describes the parameter. Defaults to no message.
`type`	The type of data this parameter holds. May be `int`, `bool`, or `string`. Any other type is interpreted as `string`. Defaults to `string`.
`value`	A default value to use if the parameter is not specified. Defaults to no default value.

Using the `commands` property in the `UserShell` class, we define the set of available arguments and parameters for our `import` command, and we then modify the `import()` method so that the options are obtained from the `parameters` property of the `Help` task. We also use the `extract()` PHP function to convert any arguments that are defined in the `arguments` property of the `Help` task to local variables. This way, the `path` argument will be available to the method as the variable `$path`.

These were all the modifications required in the `UserShell` class. Notice how we not only removed the `help()` method implementation, but also the processing of parameters, and the check for the right number of arguments from the `import()` method. This is all done automatically by the `Help` task now, based on what we define in our `commands` property.

This means that our `Help` task is indeed the Swiss Army knife of our shells, with most of its work being done in its `initialize()` method. This method starts by utilizing the PHP method, `get_class_vars()`, to obtain the `commands` property defined in the shell, because our task has no way of getting a hold of the instance of the `UserShell` class. It then proceeds to go through the list of commands, and normalizes all arguments and parameters thereby defined, assigning the resulting array to the `commands` property of the `HelpTask` class.

Once we have all our commands ready to be checked, we establish if the user has indeed selected a command to be executed through the `command` property, available to all classes that extend from `Shell`, and set to the current command. If the user has not, and if there is no `main()` method implemented in the shell, we use the `_help()` method to display the help.

If users have indeed specified a command that is within the list of available commands, we make sure that the specified arguments match the minimum number of mandatory arguments, if any, aborting the execution with a proper error message if the check fails. If the number of arguments is correct, we store the value of each given argument in the `arguments` property of the task.

Once the arguments are processed, we proceed to deal with the parameters. Going through the specified parameters, we check their provided value against the data type, if any, aborting the shell with a proper error message if the value given is of an incorrect type. If no value is given, the default value is used, if any. The resulting array of parameters and values is stored in the `parameters` property of the task.

The `execute()` method is the one called whenever the `Help` task is invoked, which is whenever the `help` command is used when calling the shell. Therefore, this method will simply display the help message by calling the `_help()` method, optionally passing to it the first argument, which would provide the user with the help message for the given command.

The `_help()` method builds the help message, for the entire shell or a specific command. It uses the command information stored in the `commands` property, and calls the `_usageCommand()` helper method to get the usage message for a given command, and the `_helpCommand()` method to get the help message for all available parameters and arguments in the command.

Sending e-mails from shells

E-mail sending is not a task that requires any interaction by visitors to our web applications, so it is pointless to make them wait for their delivery, which is exactly what we would do if we were to send an e-mail from a controller's action.

Deferring e-mail sending to a shell makes real sense both from a performance perspective and from the administrator point of view, as we may also add the ability to re-send failed e-mails.

This recipe uses the `Email` component provided by CakePHP to send a fictitious newsletter, adding the ability to test the sending process through a shell parameter.

Getting ready

To go through this recipe we need some data to work with. Create a `subscribers` table with the following SQL statement:

```
CREATE TABLE `subscribers`(
    `id` INT UNSIGNED AUTO_INCREMENT NOT NULL,
    `name` VARCHAR(255) NOT NULL,
    `email` VARCHAR(255) NOT NULL,
    PRIMARY KEY(`id`)
);
```

Create a `newsletters` table with the following statement:

```
CREATE TABLE `newsletters`(
    `id` INT UNSIGNED AUTO_INCREMENT NOT NULL,
    `title` VARCHAR(255) NOT NULL,
    `body` TEXT NOT NULL,
    `sent` TINYINT(1) UNSIGNED NOT NULL default 0,
    PRIMARY KEY(`id`)
);
```

Create a `newsletters_subscribers` table with the following statement:

```
CREATE TABLE `newsletters_subscribers`(
    `id` INT UNSIGNED AUTO_INCREMENT NOT NULL,
    `newsletter_id` INT UNSIGNED NOT NULL,
    `subscriber_id` INT UNSIGNED NOT NULL,
    `sent` TINYINT(1) UNSIGNED NOT NULL default 0,
    PRIMARY KEY(`id`)
);
```

Now add some sample data to these tables with the following statements:

```
INSERT INTO `subscribers`(`name`, `email`) VALUES
    ('John Doe', 'john.doe@email.com'),
    ('Jane Doe', 'jane.doe@email.com');

INSERT INTO `newsletters`(`title`, `body`) VALUES
    ('My first newsletter', 'This is the body for <strong>my first
newsletter</strong>');
```

Create a file named `newsletter.php` and place it in your `app/models` folder, with the following contents:

```php
<?php
class Newsletter extends AppModel {
    public $hasMany = array('NewslettersSubscriber');
}
?>
```

How to do it...

Create a file named `email.php` and place it in your `app/vendors/shells`, with the following contents:

```php
<?php
App::import('Component', 'Email');
class EmailShell extends Shell {
    public $uses = array('Newsletter', 'Subscriber');

    public function startup() {
        $this->Email = new EmailComponent();
        $this->Email->delivery = 'smtp';
        $this->Email->smtpOptions = array(
            'host' => 'smtp.email.com',
            'username' => 'smtpUser',
            'password' => 'smtpPassword'
        );
```

```
    }

    public function main() {
        $email = !empty($this->params['to']) ? $this->params['to'] :
array();

        $newsletter = $this->Newsletter->find('first', array(
            'conditions' => array('sent' => false),
            'recursive' => -1
        ));
        if (empty($newsletter)) {
            $this->out('All newsletters have been sent');
            $this->_stop();
        }

        $this->out('Sending newsletter "'.$newsletter['Newsletter']
['title'].'"');

        $subscribers = $this->Subscriber->find('all');
        foreach($subscribers as $subscriber) {
            $this->out('Sending to '.$subscriber['Subscriber']
['email'].'... ', false);

            $currentEmail = !empty($email) ? $email :
$subscriber['Subscriber']['email'];

            if (!empty($email)) {
                $this->Email->headers['Destination'] =
$subscriber['Subscriber']['email'];
            }

            $this->Email->sendAs = 'html';
            $this->Email->subject = $newsletter['Newsletter']['title'];
            $this->Email->from = 'My Application <info@email.com>';
            $this->Email->to = $subscriber['Subscriber']['name'] . '
<'.$currentEmail.'>';

            $sent = $this->Email->send($newsletter['Newsletter']
['body']));
            if ($sent) {
                $this->out('DONE');
            } else {
                $error = !empty($this->Email->smtpError) ? $this->Email-
>smtpError : '';
                $this->out('ERROR' . (!empty($error) ? ': '.$error : ''));
            }

            $this->Newsletter->NewslettersSubscriber->create(array(
                'newsletter_id' => $newsletter['Newsletter']['id'],
                'subscriber_id' => $subscriber['Subscriber']['id'],
                'sent' => $sent
```

```
        ));
        $this->Newsletter->NewslettersSubscriber->save();

        $this->Email->reset();
    }

    $this->Newsletter->id = $newsletter['Newsletter']['id'];
    $this->Newsletter->saveField('sent', true);
    }
}
?>
```

Make sure to change the following lines in the `startup()` function to match your settings:

```
$this->Email->delivery = 'smtp';
$this->Email->smtpOptions = array(
    'host' => 'smtp.email.com',
    'username' => 'smtpUser',
    'password' => 'smtpPassword'
);
```

If you wish to use PHP's `mail()` function instead of SMTP, change the `delivery` property of the `Email` component to `mail`. Once configured, you can run the shell with the following command to force all e-mails to go to your specific address (in this case, `my@email.com`):

```
$ cake/console/cake email -to my@email.com
```

As all e-mails are forced to be sent to `my@email.com` through the use of the shell parameter, we need a way to tell if each e-mail will be going to the real e-mail address. Use your e-mail program to view the headers of the e-mail, and you will notice the following header lines:

```
To: John Doe <my@email.com>
From: My Application <info@email.com>
Subject: My first newsletter
X-Mailer: CakePHP Email Component
X-Destination: john.doe@email.com
```

From these headers we can tell that the **X-Destination** header is set to the address to which the e-mail was originally intended for.

How it works...

The `EmailShell` starts by implementing the `startup()` method, which is called before any shell command or its entry method is executed. In this method, we create an instance of the `Email` component. Once we have the instance, we configure its delivery settings through the properties `delivery` and `smtpOptions`.

The entry method `main()` checks to see if the `to` parameter is given. If so, this will be the e-mail to which all e-mails will be sent to, a basic way to test the sending process. It continues to fetch the first newsletter that has not yet been sent, and the list of subscribers that should receive the newsletter.

For each of those subscribers, we set the appropriate properties of the `Email` component:

Property	Purpose
sendAs	Type of e-mail to send. Can be text, `html`, or `both`. We set it to `html` to specify that we are sending an HTML-only e-mail.
subject	The subject of the e-mail.
from	The address sending the e-mail.
to	The destination address. If the parameter is provided, this is the e-mail to send `to`, otherwise we use the e-mail of the subscriber.

Finally, we proceed to send the actual e-mail through the component's `send()` method, informing the user of the result of the operation, and resetting the e-mail contents with the component's `reset()` method prior to the next loop in the `for` operation. We end the shell by marking that the newsletter is sent.

See also

▶ *Sending an e-mail* in *Chapter 11, Utility Classes and Tools*

Non-interactive tasks with the robot plugin

As our application grows in size and complexity, we will find ourselves in the need to create and automate certain tasks, deferring the processing of non-interactive tasks for later execution. While we can create shells to perform these operations, some of our needs may be met by the Robot plugin.

> While this recipe shows a pure CakePHP approach, there are more involved and scalable alternatives. One of the most used tools is **Gearman**, available at `http://gearman.org/`.

The Robot plugin allows us to schedule tasks for later execution, and have those tasks run by a shell. The tasks themselves are actually CakePHP controller actions, which are run by the shell at the specified time.

This recipe shows us how to use the Robot plugin to send an e-mail after a user has signed up for our newsletters, and how to have the shell in the Robot plugin periodically check for pending tasks and run them as they become available.

Getting ready

To go through this recipe we need some data to work with. Follow the *Getting ready* section of the previous recipe.

We need to download the Robot plugin. Go to `http://github.com/mariano/robot/downloads` and download the latest release. Uncompress the downloaded file into your `app/plugins` folder. You should now have a directory named `robot` inside `app/plugins`.

Run the SQL statements found in the `app/plugins/robot/config/sql/robot.sql` file to create the tables required by the Robot plugin.

How to do it...

1. Create a file named `subscribers_controller.php` and place it in your `app/controllers` folder, with the following contents:

```php
<?php
class SubscribersController extends AppController {
    public function add() {
        if (!empty($this->data)) {
            $this->Subscriber->create();
            if ($this->Subscriber->save($this->data)) {
                $this->Session->setFlash('You have been subscribed!');
                $this->redirect('/');
            } else {
                $this->Session->setFlash('Please correct the errors');
            }
        }
    }
    public function welcome() {
    }
}
?>
```

2. Create a folder named `subscribers` in your `app/views` folder. Create a file named `add.ctp` and place it in the folder `app/views/subscribers`, with the following contents:

```php
<?php
echo $this->Form->create();
echo $this->Form->inputs(array(
    'legend' => 'Subscribe',
    'name',
    'email'
));
```

```
    echo $this->Form->end('Submit');
    ?>
```

3. Create a file named `welcome.ctp` and place it in the `app/views/subscribers` folder, with the following contents:

```
<h1>Welcome to my site!</h1>
```

4. Add the following property to the beginning of the `SubscribersController` class (change the delivery settings of the `Email` component to match your needs):

```
public $components = array(
    'Email' => array(
        'delivery' => 'smtp',
        'smtpOptions' => array(
            'host' => 'smtp.email.com',
            'username' => 'smtpUser',
            'password' => 'smtpPassword'
        )
    )
);
```

5. Edit the `add()` method of the `SubscribersController` class and make the following changes:

```
public function add() {
    if (!empty($this->data)) {
        $this->Subscriber->create();
        if ($this->Subscriber->save($this->data)) {
            ClassRegistry::init('Robot.RobotTask')->schedule(
                array('action'=>'welcome'),
                array(
                    'name' => $this->data['Subscriber']['email'],
                    'email' => $this->data['Subscriber']['email']
                )
            );
            $this->Session->setFlash('You have been subscribed!');
            $this->redirect('/');
        } else {
            $this->Session->setFlash('Please correct the errors');
        }
    }
}
```

6. While still editing the `SubscribersController` class, replace the `welcome()` method with the following contents:

```
public function welcome() {
    if (isset($this->params['robot'])) {
        $subscriber = $this->params['robot'];

        $this->Email->sendAs = 'html';
        $this->Email->subject = 'Welcome to my site!';
        $this->Email->from = 'My Application <info@email.com>';
        $this->Email->to = $subscriber['name'] . '
<'.$subscriber['email'].'>';

        return ($this->Email->send('Hi, and <strong>welcome</strong>
to my site!') !== false);
    }
}
```

You can now browse to `http://localhost/subscribers/add` and enter your name and e-mail address. Now run the robot shell with the following command:

If you are on a GNU Linux / Mac / Unix system:

```
../cake/console/cake robot.robot run
```

If you are on Microsoft Windows:

```
..\cake\console\cake.bat robot.robot run
```

You should get an output similar to what is shown in the following screenshot:

```
[17:29] mariano@kramer:/var/www/cookbook/chapter8/robot$ ../cake/console/cake -app `pw
d` robot.robot run
[09/02/2010 17:30:01] --------------------------------------------------------
[09/02/2010 17:30:01] Robot Runner v1.3 - A CakePHP shell based task runner
[09/02/2010 17:30:01] --------------------------------------------------------
[09/02/2010 17:30:01] Action: run
[09/02/2010 17:30:01]
[09/02/2010 17:30:01] Fetching next pending task... DONE
[09/02/2010 17:30:01] Processing task 4c80093f-36f4-4553-9f8e-637994a56bba
[09/02/2010 17:30:01] Running /subscribers/welcome... DONE (5,484.94 ms.)
[09/02/2010 17:30:06] Setting task 4c80093f-36f4-4553-9f8e-637994a56bba as completed
[09/02/2010 17:30:07] Fetching next pending task... DONE
[09/02/2010 17:30:07]
[09/02/2010 17:30:07] TOTAL TIME: 5,963.41 ms.
[17:30] mariano@kramer:/var/www/cookbook/chapter8/robot$
```

robot ; php

The robot is informing us that a task executed the CakePHP URL `/subscribers/welcome` successfully, after which we should receive a welcome e-mail.

How it works...

We started with a basic controller that takes new subscriptions and saves them, redirecting to a welcome screen after the record is created. Then we added the `Email` component to our controller, as it will be used for sending e-mails.

We continued by modifying the `add()` method to create the scheduled task. We scheduled a task using the `schedule()` method of the `RobotTask` model located in the Robot plugin. This method takes up to three arguments:

Argument	Purpose
`action`	The URL to a CakePHP action, which can be given as a string or as an array.
`parameters`	Optional parameters to send to the controller action specified in `action`. Defaults to no parameters.
`scheduled`	The time at which the action should be executed. This can be either a specific time stamp (in seconds since the Unix Epoch, which is January 1, 1970 00:00:00 GMT), or any string that can be used by the PHP function `strtotime()`. Defaults to `null`, which means the task should be executed as soon as possible.

In our `add()` method, we set the `action` argument to the `welcome` action of the current controller, and send two parameters: `name`, and `email`. These parameters are available to the called action through the `$this->params['robot']` array.

In fact, whenever a controller action is called through the robot shell, `$this->params['robot']` will be available. If no parameters were specified when scheduling the task, this array will be empty, hence the check with `isset()` instead of `!empty()` in the `welcome()` method.

When called through the robot shell, the `welcome()` method uses the given parameters to build and send the e-mail. It returns a Boolean value to indicate the success of the executed task. If no value is returned, the task is assumed to have succeeded.

To test the Robot plugin, we ended the recipe by signing up as a subscriber, and then running the robot. Naturally, the application should not have to wait for us to manually run the robot shell in order for e-mails to go out. We need to add the shell to our list of automated tasks, commonly known as CRON tasks on most operative systems.

Assuming your application lives at `/var/www/myapp`, and that the path to your PHP binary is `/usr/bin/php`, the following would be the command that should be included as an automated task in your operative system:

```
/usr/bin/php -q /var/www/myapp/cake/console/cake.php -app /var/www/
myapp/app robot.robot run -silent
```

Notice the `silent` option. This tells the robot plugin to output no messages unless an error is found. This is particularly important when adding this command to our list of automated tasks, as it may be configured to e-mail the output of any executed command.

When adding this command to our list of automated tasks, we have to decide how often we want the robot to check for tasks. If we are interested in immediate results, we should set the robot to run every minute. However, what happens if at second 0 of a given minute the robot finds no tasks? We will have 59 seconds of idle time.

Fortunately, the plugin offers an interesting solution to this problem. Using the parameter `daemon`, we tell the Robot plugin to wait for tasks even if there are none available. If we try to manually run it with this option using the following command:

```
$ cake/console/cake robot.robot run -daemon
```

we will notice the shell complains, saying that there is no limit specified. This is because the robot should not be set to wait for tasks indefinitely, as any PHP fatal error that may be provoked by a called action could render the robot useless.

Instead, we can use the `time` parameter to limit the number of seconds to which the robot should wait for tasks. If we wanted to run the robot every minute, this limit should be set to 59 seconds:

```
$ cake/console/cake robot.robot run -daemon -time 59
```

This means that we would have a robot waiting up to 59 seconds for tasks, after which the next robot run will be triggered.

9
Internationalizing Applications

In this chapter, we will cover:

- ▶ Internationalizing controller and view texts
- ▶ Internationalizing model validation messages
- ▶ Translating strings with dynamic content
- ▶ Extracting and translating text
- ▶ Translating database records with the Translate behavior
- ▶ Setting and remembering the language

Introduction

This chapter includes a set of recipes that allow the reader to internationalize all aspects of their CakePHP applications, including static content, such as those available in views, and dynamic content, such as database records.

The first two recipes show how to allow text that is part of any CakePHP view or model validation messages to be ready for translation. The third recipe shows how to translate more complex expressions. The fourth recipe shows how to run CakePHP's built-in tools to extract all static content that needs translation, and then translate that content to different languages. The fifth recipe shows how to translate database records. Finally, the last recipe shows how to allow users to change the current application language.

Internationalizing controller and view texts

In this recipe, we will learn how to internationalize text that is located in our application views, and have that content ready for translation.

Getting ready

To go through this recipe, we need some data to work with. Create a table named `articles` with the following SQL statement:

```
CREATE TABLE `articles`(
    `id` INT UNSIGNED AUTO_INCREMENT NOT NULL,
    `title` VARCHAR(255) NOT NULL,
    `body` TEXT NOT NULL,
    `created` DATETIME NOT NULL,
    `modified` DATETIME NOT NULL,
    PRIMARY KEY(`id`)
);
```

Now add some sample data to this table with the following statement:

```
INSERT INTO `articles`(`title`, `body`, `created`, `modified`) VALUES
    ('First Article', 'Body for first article', NOW(), NOW()),
    ('Second Article', 'Body for second article', NOW(), NOW()),
    ('Third Article', 'Body for third article', NOW(), NOW());
```

Create the controller for this table in a file named `articles_controller.php` and place it in your `app/controllers` folder, with the following contents:

```php
<?php
class ArticlesController extends AppController {
    public function index() {
        $this->paginate['limit'] = 2;
        $articles = $this->paginate();
        $this->set(compact('articles'));
    }
    public function add() {
        if (!empty($this->data)) {
            $this->Article->create();
            if ($this->Article->save($this->data)) {
                $this->Session->setFlash('Article saved');
                $this->redirect(array('action'=>'index'));
            } else {
                $this->Session->setFlash('Please correct the errors');
            }
```

```
        }
    }
    public function view($id) {
        $article = $this->Article->find('first', array(
            'conditions' => array('Article.id' => $id)
        ));
        if (empty($article)) {
            $this->cakeError('error404');
        }
        $this->set(compact('article'));
    }
}
?>
```

Create a file named `article.php` and place it in your `app/models` folder, with the following contents:

```
<?php
class Article extends AppModel {
    public $validate = array(
        'title' => 'notEmpty',
        'body' => 'notEmpty'
    );
}
?>
```

Create a folder named `articles` in your `app/views` folder, and inside that folder create a file named `index.ctp` with the following contents:

```
<h1>Articles</h1>
<p>
<?php echo $this->Paginator->counter(); ?>
 - 
<?php echo $this->Paginator->prev(); ?>
 
<?php echo $this->Paginator->numbers(); ?>
 
<?php echo $this->Paginator->next(); ?>
</p>
<p>
<?php echo count($articles) . ' articles: '; ?>
</p>
<ul>
<?php foreach($articles as $article) { ?>
    <li><?php echo $this->Html->link(
        $article['Article']['title'],
```

```
        array('action'=>'view', $article['Article']['id'])
    ); ?></li>
<?php } ?>
</ul>
<p><?php echo $this->Html->link('Create article',
array('action'=>'add')); ?></p>
```

Create a file named `add.ctp` and place it in your `app/views/articles` folder, with the following contents:

```
<?php
echo $this->Form->create();
echo $this->Form->inputs(array(
    'title',
    'body'
));
echo $this->Form->end('Save');
?>
```

Create a file named `view.ctp` and place it in your `app/views/articles` folder, with the following contents:

```
<h1><?php echo $article['Article']['title']; ?></h1>
<?php echo $article['Article']['body']; ?>
```

How to do it...

1. Edit the `articles_controller.php` file located in your `app/controllers` folder and make the following changes to the `add()` method:

```
public function add() {
    if (!empty($this->data)) {
        $this->Article->create();
        if ($this->Article->save($this->data)) {
            $this->Session->setFlash(__('Article saved', true));
            $this->redirect(array('action'=>'index'));
        } else {
            $this->Session->setFlash(__('Please correct the errors',
true));
        }
    }
}
```

2. Edit the file `add.ctp` located in your `app/views/articles` folder and make the following changes:

```php
<?php
echo $this->Form->create();
echo $this->Form->inputs(array(
    'legend' => __('New Article', true),
    'title' => array('label' => __('Title:', true)),
    'body' => array('label' => __('Body:', true))
));
echo $this->Form->end(__('Save', true));
?>
```

3. Finally, edit the file `index.ctp` located in your `app/views/articles` folder and make the following changes:

```php
<h1><?php __('Articles'); ?></h1>
<p>
<?php echo $this->Paginator->counter(__('Showing records %start%-
%end% in page %page% out of %pages%', true)); ?>
 - 
<?php echo $this->Paginator->prev(__('<< Previous', true)); ?>
 
<?php echo $this->Paginator->numbers(); ?>
 
<?php echo $this->Paginator->next(__('Next >>', true)); ?>
</p>
<p>
<?php
$count = count($articles);
echo $count . ' ' . __n('article', 'articles', $count, true) . ':
';
?>
</p>
<ul>
<?php foreach($articles as $article) { ?>
    <li><?php echo $this->Html->link(
        $article['Article']['title'],
        array('action'=>'view', $article['Article']['id'])
    ); ?></li>
<?php } ?>
</ul>
<p><?php echo $this->Html->link(__('Create article', true),
array('action'=>'add')); ?></p>
```

If you now browse to `http://localhost/articles`, you should see a paginated list of articles, as shown in the following screenshot:

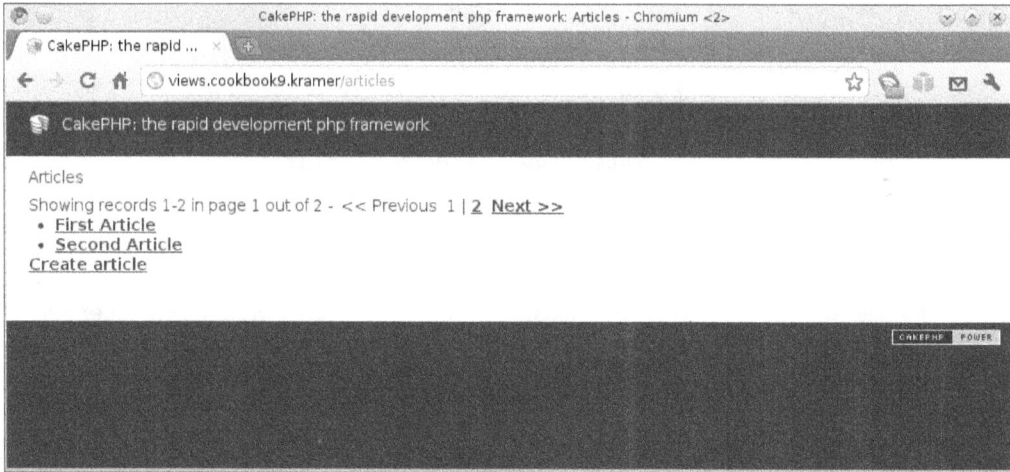

How it works...

CakePHP offers two main methods (amongst others) to allow developers to specify content that can be translated: `__()` and `__n()`. The naming of these methods may seem a bit odd, but they are largely influenced by Perl's implementation of `gettext`, a tool that is part of the GNU Translation Project.

The `__()` method is used to translate static text, and takes up to two arguments:

Argument	Purpose
singular	Text that should be translated to the current language.
return	If set to `true`, the translated text will be returned instead of echoed to the client. Defaults to `false`.

The `__n()` method is used to translate static text that could change if a certain value is either singular or plural, and takes up to four arguments:

Argument	Purpose
singular	Text that should be used if the given value in `count` is `singular`, and that will be translated to the current language when used.
plural	Text that should be used if the given value in `count` is `plural`, and that will be translated to the current language when used.

Argument	Purpose
count	A variable or numeric value that holds the value that should be used to determine if either the singular or plural text is to be used.
return	If set to true, the translated text will be returned instead of echoed to the client. Defaults to false.

We start by changing the flash messages in the ArticlesController class to use the __() method, specifying that the translated string should be returned rather than echoed to the client. We continue by modifying the add.ctp view so that all labels and the form legend can be translated.

Similarly, we wrap the title in the index.ctp view with the translator function. We then use the first parameter of the counter(), next(), and prev() methods that are part of the PaginatorHelper class to pass the translated version of the appropriate pagination text. Finally, we use the __n() function to choose the correct translated text depending on the value of the count variable.

> When using the __n() function you should only use a variable as its third parameter. Using expressions (including array indexes) may produce unexpected results when running CakePHP's extractor shell, which is covered in the recipe *Extracting and translating text*.

Domains and categories

The translation functions used in this recipe are actually wrappers around the translate() method of CakePHP's built-in I18n class. This method not only allows simple translations, but also allows the developer to specify the domain from which translated texts are obtained, and the category to which the text to be translated belongs to.

Domains allow you to separate groups of translation text into separate files. By default, when no domain is specified, CakePHP assumes a domain named default. If you want to specify the domain in which a translated text should be looked for, use the __d() and __dn() translation functions. For example, to look for a translated text in the my_plugin domain, you would do:

```
$translated = __d('my_plugin', 'Hello World', true);
```

Categories allow for a further grouping of translated texts by grouping the translation files into separate directories, and provide further meaning to the translated text. By default, CakePHP will assume that translated texts belong to the `LC_MESSAGES` category. If you wish to change the category, use the `__dc()` and `__dcn()` translator functions, by setting its next-to-last argument, `return`, to the desired category, which can be any of the following defined constants with the respective fixed value:

- `LC_ALL: 0`
- `LC_COLLATE: 1`
- `LC_CTYPE: 2`
- `LC_MONETARY: 3`
- `LC_NUMERIC: 4`
- `LC_TIME: 5`
- `LC_MESSAGES: 6`

For example, to look for a translated text in the `default` domain and the `LC_MESSAGES` category you would do:

```
$translated = __dc('default', 'Hello World', 6, true);
```

> When looking forward to using categories, always use the category value previously given in the list rather than the constant name, as this constant is platform-dependent.

See also

- *Internationalizing model validation messages*
- *Extracting and translating text*

Internationalizing model validation messages

In this recipe, we will learn different approaches for the same need: translating model validation messages.

Getting ready

To go through this recipe, we need a basic application skeleton to work with. Go through the previous recipe.

How to do it...

Edit the file `article.php` located in your `app/models` folder and make the following changes to the `validate` property:

```
public $validate = array(
    'title' => array(
        'required' => 'notEmpty'
    ),
    'body' => array(
        'required' => 'notEmpty'
    )
);
```

There are two ways to have validation messages translated. The first one requires you to override the model constructor by adding the following implementation to the `Article` class defined in your `app/models/article.php` file:

```
public function __construct($id = false, $table = null, $ds = null) {
    foreach($this->validate as $field => $rules) {
        if (!is_array($rules)) {
            $rules = (array) $rules;
        }
        foreach($rules as $key => $rule) {
            if (!is_array($rule)) {
                $rules[$key] = compact('rule');
            }
        }
        $this->validate[$field] = $rules;
    }

    $this->validate = Set::merge($this->validate, array(
        'title' => array(
            'required' => array('message' => __('A title must be specified', true))
        ),
        'body' => array(
            'required' => array('message' => __('You must define the body', true))
        )
    ));

    parent::__construct($id, $table, $ds);
}
```

The alternative way to translate validation messages is to move these messages to the view. Instead of overriding and defining the messages in the model constructor, edit your app/views/articles/add.ctp view file and make the following changes to it:

```php
<?php
echo $this->Form->create();
echo $this->Form->inputs(array(
    'title' => array(
        'label' => __('Title:', true),
        'error' => array(
            'required' => __('A title must be specified', true)
        )
    ),
    'body' => array(
        'label' => __('Body:', true),
        'error' => array(
            'required' => __('You must define the body', true)
        )
    )
));
echo $this->Form->end(__('Save', true));
?>
```

Both ways should produce the same result. If you now browse to http://localhost/articles/add and submit the form without entering any values, you should see the validation messages shown in the following screenshot:

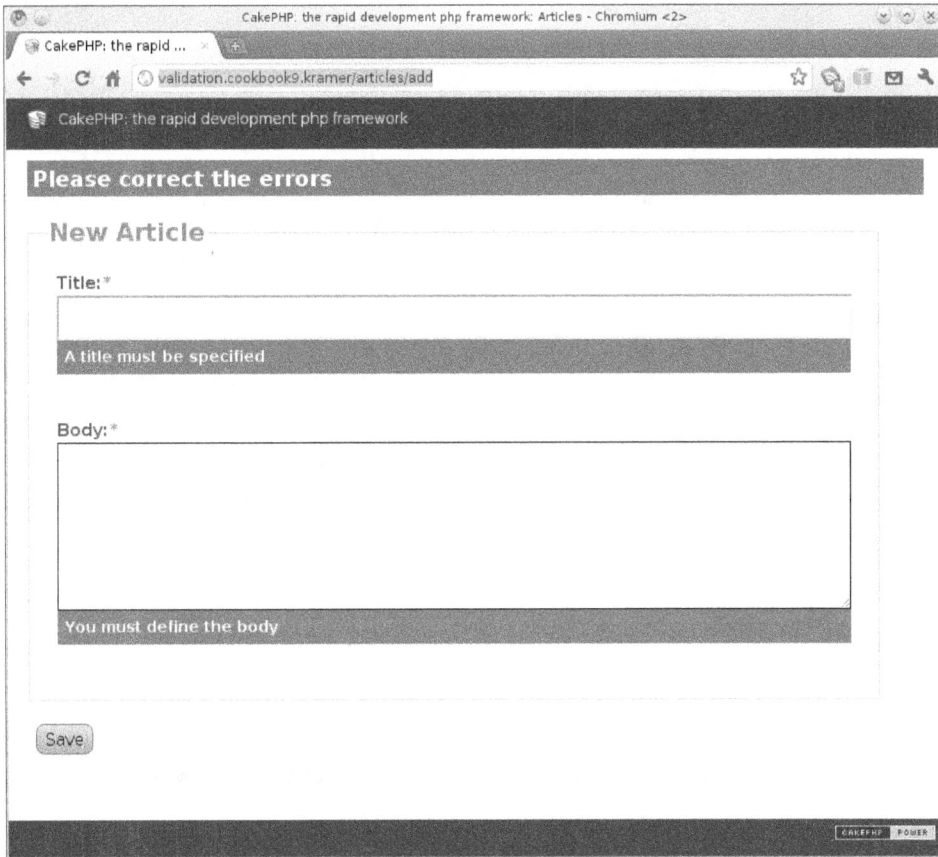

How it works...

Before attempting to provide the error messages for each validation rule, we need to name each of our rules. We do so by modifying the `Article` model so that each rule defined is indexed by a name. In our case we choose `required` as the name for the validation based on CakePHP's built-in `notEmpty` rule.

The first method we used to specify the validation messages shows a practical approach when we want to centralize all validation messages in the model. We override the model constructor so that from within this constructor we specify the error messages that should be translated. We needed to implement the constructor because class property values cannot use an expression other than a static assignment, so the following block of code would produce a PHP syntax error:

```php
public $validate = array(
    'title' => array(
        'required' => array(
```

```
                'rule' => 'notEmpty',
                'message' => __('Nothing defined!', true) // SYNTAX ERROR
            )
        )
    );
```

In this constructor implementation, we start by making sure that the `validate` property is an array of rules, indexed by field name, and that each set of rules is itself an array indexed by name, having as its value another array where at the very least the `rule` setting is defined.

Once we are sure that the `validate` property has the right format, we merge the validation messages for each rule using the `__()` translator function to translate the messages. Finally, we call the parent constructor to ensure that the model is built properly.

The second method described in this recipe moves the responsibility of declaring each validation error message to the view, by means of the `error` setting available in the `input()` method of the `FormHelper` class. This setting is set to an array, indexed by validation name, and the value is set to the error message shown when the respective validation fails.

See also

▶   *Extracting and translating text*

Translating strings with dynamic content

In this recipe, we will learn how to allow strings consisting of parts that are not static, such as variable values, to be translatable.

Getting ready

To go through this recipe, we need a basic application skeleton to work with. Go through the entire recipe *Internationalizing controller and view texts*.

How to do it...

1. Edit the file `articles_controller.php` located in your `app/controllers` folder and make the following changes to the `add()` method:

```
public function add() {
    if (!empty($this->data)) {
        $this->Article->create();
        if ($this->Article->save($this->data)) {
```

```
                    $this->Session->setFlash(
                        sprintf(__('Article "%s" saved', true), $this-
    >Article->field('title'))
                    );
                    $this->redirect(array('action'=>'index'));
                } else {
                    $this->Session->setFlash('Please correct the errors');
                }
            }
        }
```

2. Edit the view file `index.ctp` located in your `app/views/articles` folder and
    make the following changes:

```
<h1><?php __('Articles'); ?></h1>
<p>
<?php echo $this->Paginator->counter(__('Showing records %start%-
%end% in page %page% out of %pages%', true)); ?>
 - 
<?php echo $this->Paginator->prev(__('<< Previous', true)); ?>
 
<?php echo $this->Paginator->numbers(); ?>
 
<?php echo $this->Paginator->next(__('Next >>', true)); ?>
</p>
<p>
<?php
$count = count($articles);
printf(__n('%d article', '%d articles', $count, true), $count);
?>
</p>
<ul>
<?php foreach($articles as $article) { ?>
    <li><?php echo $this->Html->link(
        $article['Article']['title'],
        array('action'=>'view', $article['Article']['id'])
    ); ?></li>
<?php } ?>
</ul>
<p><?php echo $this->Html->link(__('Create article', true),
array('action'=>'add')); ?></p>
```

When looking forward to including dynamic information, such as the value of a variable, or in this case, the value of a table field in the database, one can be tempted to simply append the variable to the string that is sent to the translator function:

```
$translated = __('Hello ' . $name, true); // This is wrong
```

This is not a valid expression, as CakePHP's extractor, shown in the recipe *Extracting and translating text*, expects only static strings as arguments to the translator functions, and other languages may need to re-order the sentence. Therefore, we need to use some way of string interpolation, so we chose to use the most common ones offered by PHP: the `printf()` and `sprintf()` functions.

Both functions take the same number and type of arguments. The first argument is mandatory and specifies the string to use for interpolation, while any subsequent argument is used to produce the final string. The only difference between `printf()` and `sprintf()` is that the former will output the resulting string, while the later simply returns it.

We start by changing the success message given by the `ArticlesController` class whenever an article is created. We use `sprintf()` as we need to send it through to the `setFlash()` method of the `Session` component. In this case, we use the expression `%s` to interpolate the value of the `title` field for the newly created article.

Similarly, our latest change uses `%d` to interpolate the decimal value of the variable `count`, and uses `printf()` to output the result string.

Reordering and reusing interpolation arguments

When using expressions such as `%s` or `%d` to tell `printf()` and `sprintf()` where to place the value of an argument, we have no flexibility in terms of value positioning, and no practical way to reuse a value, as each of those expressions needs to match a specific argument. Let us assume the following expression:

```
printf('Your name is %s and your country is %s', $name, $country);
```

The first `%s` expression gets replaced with the value of the `name` variable, while the last `%s` expression is replaced with the value of the `country` variable. What if we wanted to change the order of these values in the string without altering the order of the arguments that are sent to `printf()`?

We can instead specify which argument is used by an interpolation expression by referring to an argument number (`name` being the argument number 1, and `country` argument number 2):

```
printf('You are from %2$s and your name is %1$s', $name, $country);
```

This also allows us to reuse an argument without having to add it as an extra argument to `printf()`:

```
printf('You are from %2$s and your name is %1$s . Welcome %1$s!',
$name, $country);
```

See also

▶ *Extracting and translating text*

Extracting and translating text

In this recipe, we will learn how to extract all strings that need translation from our CakePHP applications and then perform the actual translations using free software.

Getting ready

To go through this recipe, we need a basic application skeleton to work with. Go through the entire recipe *Internationalizing controller and view texts*.

We also need to have **Poedit** installed in our system. Go to `http://www.poedit.net/download.php` and download the appropriate file for your operative system.

How to do it...

From the command line, and while in your `app/` directory, issue the following command:

If you are on a GNU Linux / Mac / Unix system:

```
../cake/console/cake i18n extract
```

If you are on Microsoft Windows:

```
..\cake\console\cake.bat i18n extract
```

You should accept the default options, as shown in the following screenshot:

After answering the final question, the shell should go through your application files and generate a translation template in a file named `default.pot`, placing it in your `app/locale` folder.

Open Poedit, and then click on the menu **File**, and option **New catalog from POT file**. You should now see an open file dialog box. Browse to your `app/locale` folder, select the `default.pot` file, and click the **Open** button. A setting window should appear, as shown in the following screenshot:

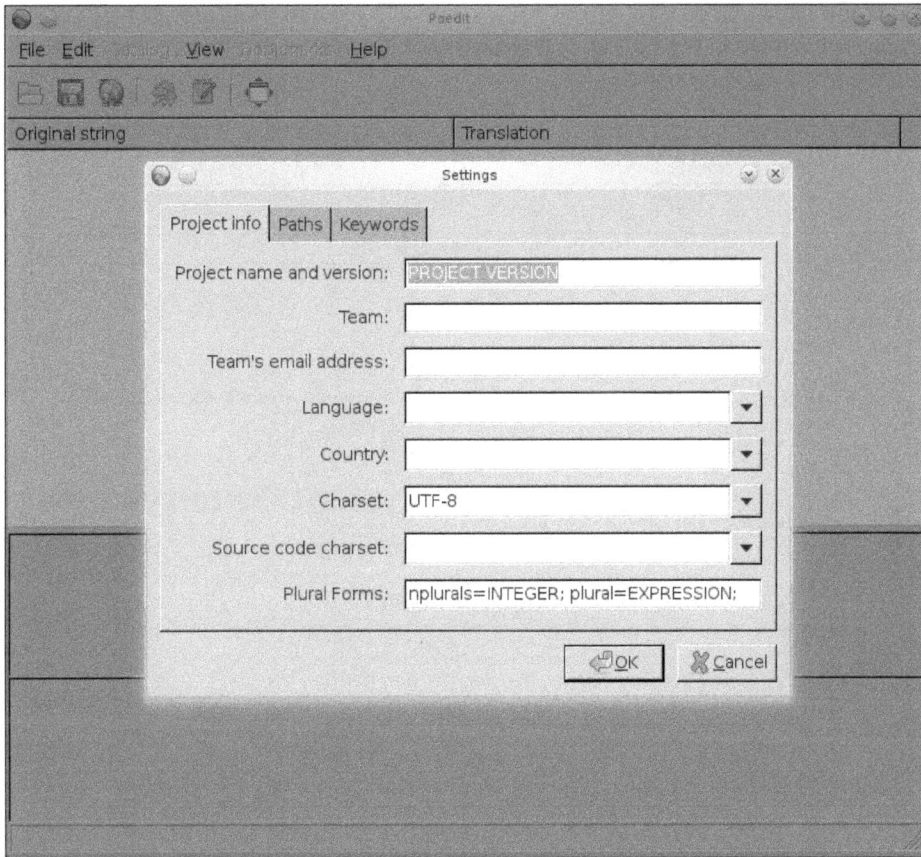

In the **Settings** window, enter the desired project name and project information. In the **Plural Forms** field you should enter an expression that tells Poedit how to recognize plural translations. For most languages, such as English, Spanish, German and Portuguese, you should enter the following expression:

```
nplurals=2; plural=(n != 1);
```

> More information about plural forms and which value should be given, depending on the language you are translating to, is available at http://drupal.org/node/17564.

Once you have entered all the desired details, click on the **OK** button. You will now be asked where to store the translated file. Create a folder named spa and place it in your app/locale folder. Inside the spa folder, create a folder named LC_MESSAGES. Then, while in Poedit's dialog box, select the folder app/locale/spa/LC_MESSAGES and click the button **Save** without changing the file name, which should be default.po.

Poedit will now show you all the original strings, and allow you to translate each by entering the desired translation in the bottom text area. After you enter your translations, Poedit may look like the following screenshot:

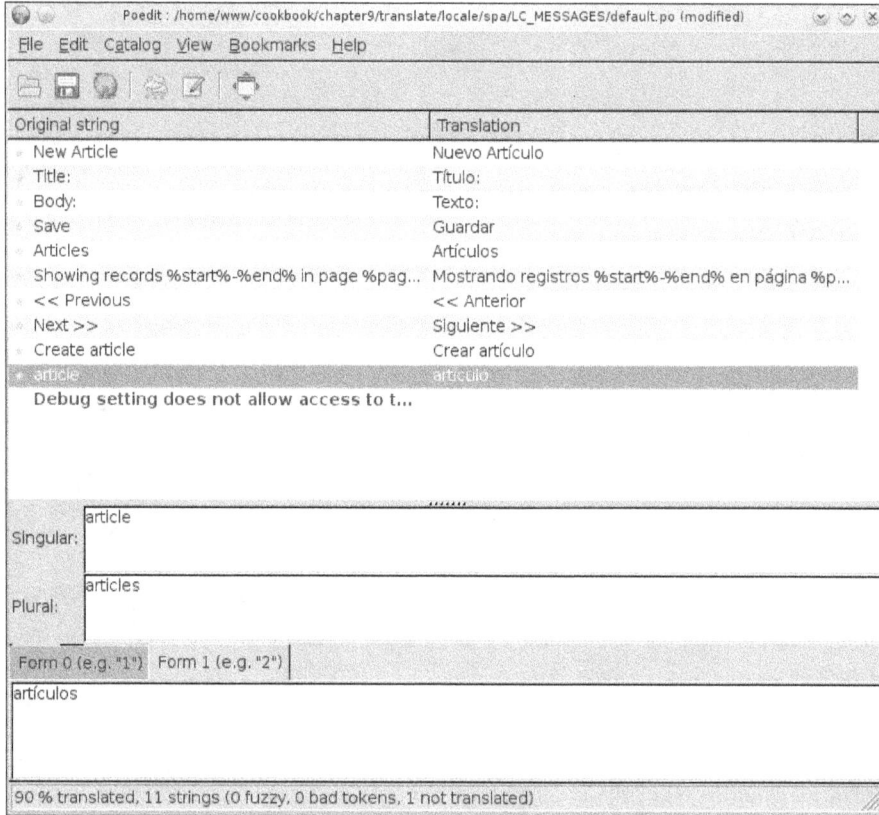

Click on the menu **File**, and then option **Save** to save the translated file. There should now be two files in your `app/locale/spa/LC_MESSAGES` folder: `default.po` and `default.mo`.

How it works...

CakePHP's extractor will first ask which paths to process. When all paths have been specified, it will browse recursively through its directories and look for any use of a translator function (any of `__()`, `__n()`, `__d()`, `__dn()`, `__dc()`, `__dcn()`, and `__c()`) in PHP and view files. For each found usage, it will extract the strings that need translation (first argument on calls to `__()` and `__c()`; the second argument on calls to `__d()` and `__dc()`; the first and second arguments on calls to `__n()`; and the second and third arguments on calls to `__dn()` and `__dcn()`.

> It is important to only use static strings, avoiding any PHP expressions, on the arguments the extractor looks for. If you want to learn how to interpolate variable values in the strings that need translation, see the recipe *Translating strings with dynamic content*.

Once CakePHP's extractor has obtained all strings that need translation, it will create the appropriate translation template files. If you used any translator function that specifies a domain (`__d()`, `__dn()`, `__dc()`, and `__dcn()`), you can optionally merge all strings into one template file, or have each domain create a separate template file. Template files have the `pot` extension, and use the domain name as its filename (`default.pot` being the default template file).

If you open `default.pot` with a text editor, you will notice that it starts with a header that includes several settings, and then includes two lines for each string that needs translation: a line that defines a `msgid` (the string to be translated), and a line that has an empty string for `msgstr` (the translated string).

We then use Poedit to open this template file, translate the strings, and save it in the appropriate directory (`app/locale/spa/LC_MESSAGES`), where Poedit will create two files: `default.po` and `default.pot`. If you open `default.po` with a text editor, you will notice it almost looks exactly as the template file does, except that the header settings have changed to what we defined, and the `msgid` lines are filled with our translations. The `default.mo` file is a binary version of the `default.po` file, also generated by Poedit, and is used by CakePHP to speed processing of the translation file.

Translating database records with the Translate behavior

In this recipe, we will learn how to allow translation of database records by means of CakePHP's `Translate` behavior.

Getting ready

To go through this recipe, we need a basic application skeleton to work with. Go through the entire recipe *Internationalizing controller and view texts*.

How to do it...

From the command line, and while in your `app/` directory, issue the following command:

If you are on a GNU Linux / Mac / Unix system:

```
../cake/console/cake i18n initdb
```

If you are on Microsoft Windows:

```
..\cake\console\cake.bat i18n initdb
```

Accept all the default answers. The shell should finish by creating a table named i18n, as shown in the following screenshot:

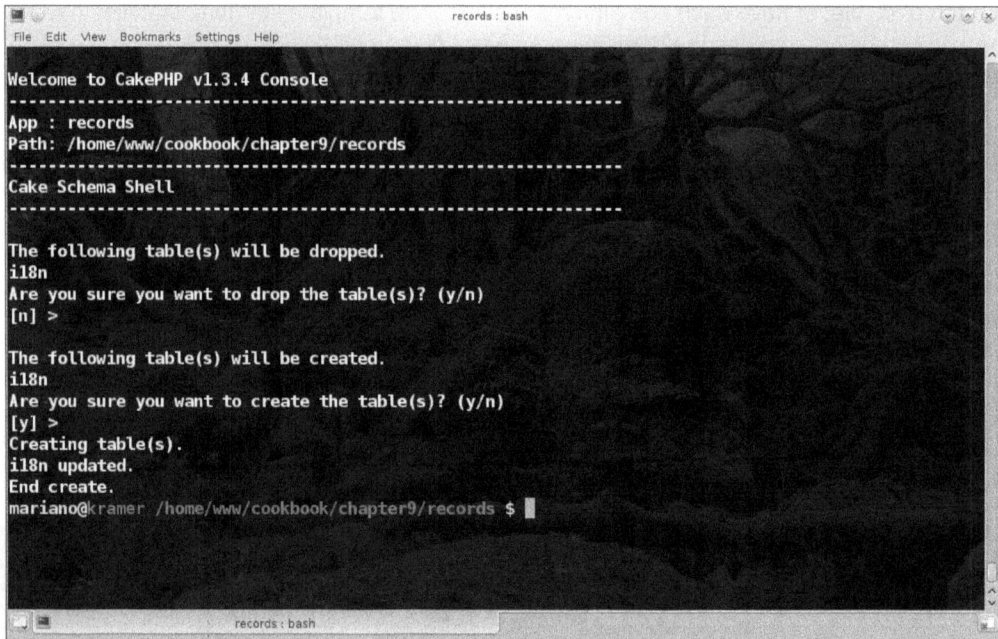

Edit your app/models/article.php file and add the following property:

```php
<?php
class Article extends AppModel {
    public $validate = array(
        'title' => 'notEmpty',
        'body' => 'notEmpty'
    );
    public $actsAs = array(
        'Translate' => array('title', 'body')
    );

}
?>
```

We now need to move the values for the `title` and `body` fields from the `articles` table to the `i18n` table, and then drop those fields from the `articles` table. Issue the following SQL statements:

```
INSERT INTO `i18n`(`locale`, `model`, `foreign_key`, `field`,
`content`)
SELECT 'eng', 'Article', `articles`.`id`, 'title', `articles`.`title`
FROM `articles`;

INSERT INTO `i18n`(`locale`, `model`, `foreign_key`, `field`,
`content`)
SELECT 'eng', 'Article', `articles`.`id`, 'body', `articles`.`body`
FROM `articles`;

ALTER TABLE `articles`
    DROP COLUMN `title`,
    DROP COLUMN `body`;
```

Add the Spanish translations for our articles by Issuing the following SQL statements:

```
INSERT INTO `i18n`(`locale`, `model`, `foreign_key`, `field`,
`content`) VALUES
    ('spa', 'Article', 1, 'title', 'Primer Artículo'),
    ('spa', 'Article', 1, 'body', 'Cuerpo para el primer Artículo'),
    ('spa', 'Article', 2, 'title', 'Segundo Artículo'),
    ('spa', 'Article', 2, 'body', 'Cuerpo para el segundo Artículo'),
    ('spa', 'Article', 3, 'title', 'Tercer Artículo'),
    ('spa', 'Article', 3, 'body', 'Cuerpo para el tercer Artículo');
```

Finally, edit your `app/config/bootstrap.php` file and add the following above the PHP closing tag:

```
Configure::write('Config.language', 'eng');
```

If you now browse to `http://localhost/articles`, you should see the same listing of articles, as shown in the first screenshot (recipe *Internationalizing controller and view texts*).

How it works...

We start by using the shell to create the table required by the `Translate` behavior. This table is by default named `i18n`, and contains (besides its primary key) the following fields:

Field	Purpose
locale	The locale (language) this particular record field is being translated to.
model	The model where the record being translated belongs.
foreign_key	The ID (primary key) in `model` that identifies the record being translated.
field	The field being translated.
content	The translated value for the record field.

We then add the `Translate` behavior to our `Article` model, and set it to translate the `title` and `body` fields. This means that these fields will no longer be a part of the `articles` table, but instead be stored in the `i18n` table. Using the `model` and `foreign_key` values in the `i18n` table, the `Translate` behavior will fetch the appropriate values for these fields whenever an `Article` record is obtained matching the application language.

We copy the values of the `title` and `body` fields into the `i18n` table, and we then remove these fields from the `articles` table. No change is needed in the `find()` call that is used in our `ArticlesController` class. Furthermore, the creation of articles will continue to work transparently, as the `Translate` behavior will use the current language when saving records through the `Article` model.

The final step is telling CakePHP which is the default application language, by setting the `Config.language` configuration setting. If this step is omitted, CakePHP will obtain the current language by looking into the `HTTP_ACCEPT_LANGUAGE` header sent by the client browser.

Using separate translation tables

Any model that uses the `Translate` behavior will by default use this `i18n` table to store the different translations for each of its translated fields. This could be troublesome if we have a large number of records, or a large number of translated models. Fortunately, the `Translate` behavior allows us to configure a different translation model.

As an example, let us assume that we want to store all article translations in a table called `article_translations`. Create the table and then copy the translated records from the `i18n` table by issuing the following SQL statements:

```
CREATE TABLE `article_translations`(
    `id` INT UNSIGNED AUTO_INCREMENT NOT NULL,
    `model` VARCHAR(255) NOT NULL,
    `foreign_key` INT UNSIGNED NOT NULL,
    `locale` VARCHAR(6) NOT NULL,
    `field` VARCHAR(255) NOT NULL,
```

```
    `content` TEXT default NULL,
    KEY `model__foreign_key`(`model`, `foreign_key`),
    KEY `model__foreign_key__locale`(`model`, `foreign_key`, `locale`),
    PRIMARY KEY(`id`)
);

INSERT INTO `article_translations`
SELECT `id`, `model`, `foreign_key`, `locale`, `field`, `content`
FROM `i18n`;
```

Create a file named `article_translation.php` and place it in your `app/models` folder, with the following contents:

```php
<?php
class ArticleTranslation extends AppModel {
    public $displayField = 'field';
}
?>
```

The `displayField` property in the translation model tells the `Translate` behavior which field in the table holds the name of the field being translated.

Finally, edit your `app/models/article.php` file and make the following changes:

```php
<?php
class Article extends AppModel {
    public $validate = array(
        'title' => 'notEmpty',
        'body' => 'notEmpty'
    );
    public $actsAs = array(
        'Translate' => array('title', 'body')
    );
    public $translateModel = 'ArticleTranslation';

}
?>
```

See also

► *Setting and remembering the language*

Setting and remembering the language

In this recipe, we will learn how to allow users to change the current language and have their language selection be remembered through the use of cookies.

Getting ready

To go through this recipe we need a fully internationalized application to work with.
Go through the entire recipe *Translating database records with the Translate behavior*.

We also need an application layout that we can modify. Copy the file `default.ctp` from `cake/libs/view/layouts` to your `app/views/layouts` directory.

How to do it...

1. Edit your `app/config/bootstrap.php` file and add the following right above the PHP closing tag:

```
Configure::write('Config.languages', array(
    'eng' => __('English', true),
    'spa' => __('Spanish', true)
));
```

2. Edit the `default.ctp` layout file located in your `app/views/layouts` folder and add the following where you want the list of languages to be included (such as right above the call to the `flash()` method of the `Session` component):

```
<div style="float: right">
<?php
$links = array();
$currentLanguage = Configure::read('Config.language');
foreach(Configure::read('Config.languages') as $code => $language)
{
    if ($code == $currentLanguage) {
        $links[] = $language;
    } else {
        $links[] = $this->Html->link($language, array('lang' =>
$code));
    }
}
echo implode(' - ', $links);
?>
</div>
```

[✎ The Config.language setting used earlier was specified in the `app/config/`
`bootstrap.php` file while going through the *Translating database records*
with the Translate behavior.]

3. Create a file named `app_controller.php` and place it in your `app/` folder, with the
   following contents:

```php
<?php
class AppController extends Controller {
    public $components = array('Language', 'Session');
}
?>
```

4. Finally, create a file named `language.php` and place it in your `app/controller/`
   `components` folder, with the following contents:

```php
<?php
class LanguageComponent extends Object {
    public $controller = null;
    public $components = array('Cookie');
    public $languages = array();
    public function initialize($controller) {
        $this->controller = $controller;
        if (empty($languages)) {
            $this->languages = Configure::read('Config.languages');
        }
        $this->set();
    }
    public function set($language = null) {
        $saveCookie = false;
        if (empty($language) && isset($this->controller)) {
            if (!empty($this->controller->params['named']['lang'])) {
                $language = $this->controller->params['named']
['lang'];
            } elseif (!empty($this->controller->params['url']
['lang'])) {
                $language = $this->controller->params['url']['lang'];
            }
            if (!empty($language)) {
                $saveCookie = true;
            }
        }
        if (empty($language)) {
            $language = $this->Cookie->read('language');
            if (empty($language)) {
                $saveCookie = true;
            }
        }
```

```
            if (empty($language) && !array_key_exists($language, $this-
    >languages)) {
                $language = Configure::read('Config.language');
            }
            Configure::write('Config.language', $language);
            if ($saveCookie) {
                $this->Cookie->write('language', $language, false, '1
    year');
            }
        }
    }
?>
```

If you now browse to `http://localhost/articles` you should see the list of articles, and in the top-right area, a link to switch the current language to **Spanish**. Clicking on it should display the Spanish version of the articles, and change all available texts to the selected language, as shown in the following screenshot:

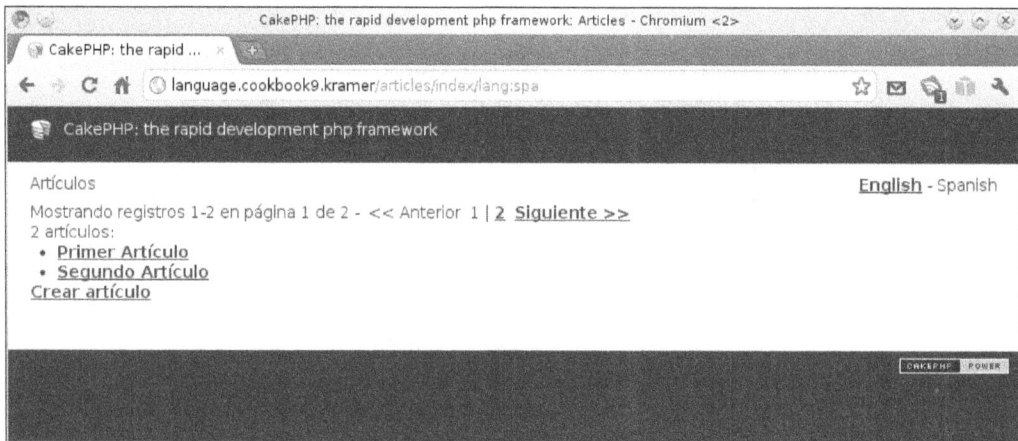

How it works...

We start by defining all available languages so that we can easily include a link to switch the current language. We use this list to construct the list of links and place it in the `default.ctp` layout file, only allowing clicks on languages other than the current application language.

The current language is set in CakePHP's configure variable, `Config.language`, which is set to a default language (`eng` in our case) in the configuration file `bootstrap.php`. When a language change is needed, this setting should be changed before the first use of a translator function.

To keep a clean controller, we decided to create a component called `Language` to handle language changes. This component will look for a named or URL parameter called `lang`. If no language is specified, the component will look for the current language by looking into a cookie.

If no cookie is set, or if a language change is requested, the component will save the current language in a cookie named `language` that lasts for one year.

10
Testing

In this chapter, we will cover:

- ▶ Setting up the test framework
- ▶ Creating fixtures and testing model methods
- ▶ Testing controller actions and their views
- ▶ Using mocks to test controllers
- ▶ Running tests from the command line

Introduction

This chapter covers one of the most interesting areas of application programming: unit testing through CakePHP's built-in tools, which offers a complete and powerful unit testing framework.

The first recipe shows how to set up the test framework so that we can create our own test cases. The second recipe shows how to create test data (fixtures) and use that data to test model methods. The third and fourth recipes show how to test controller actions, and how to test that our views are showing what we expect. The last recipe shows how to run the test in a non-ordinary fashion.

Setting up the test framework

In this recipe, we will learn how to prepare our CakePHP application with all the elements needed to create our own unit tests, setting up the foundation for the rest of the recipes in this chapter.

Getting ready

To go through the recipes included in this chapter, we need some data to work with. Create the following tables by issuing these SQL statements:

```sql
CREATE TABLE `articles`(
    `id`INT UNSIGNED NOT NULL AUTO_INCREMENT,
    `title` VARCHAR(255) NOT NULL,
    `body` TEXT NOT NULL,
    PRIMARY KEY(`id`)
);

CREATE TABLE `users`(
    `id` INT UNSIGNED NOT NULL AUTO_INCREMENT,
    `username` VARCHAR(255) NOT NULL,
    PRIMARY KEY(`id`)
);

CREATE TABLE `votes`(
    `id` INT UNSIGNED NOT NULL AUTO_INCREMENT,
    `article_id` INT NOT NULL,
    `user_id` INT NOT NULL,
    `vote` INT UNSIGNED NOT NULL,
    PRIMARY KEY(`id`),
    FOREIGN KEY `votes__articles`(`article_id`) REFERENCES
`articles`(`id`),
    FOREIGN KEY `votes__users`(`user_id`) REFERENCES `users`(`id`)
);
```

Create a controller in a file named `articles_controller.php` and place it in your `app/controllers` folder, with the following contents:

```php
<?php
class ArticlesController extends AppController {
    public function vote($id) {
        if (!empty($this->data)) {
            if ($this->Article->vote($id, $this->data)) {
                $this->Session->setFlash('Vote placed');
                return $this->redirect(array('action'=>'index'));
            } else {
                $this->Session->setFlash('Please correct the errors');

            }
        }
    }
```

```php
    public function view($id) {
        $article = $this->Article->get($id);
        if (empty($article)) {
            $this->Session->setFlash('Article not found');
            return $this->redirect(array('action' => 'index'));
        }
        $this->set(compact('article'));
    }
}
?>
```

Create a file named `article.php` and place it in your `app/models` folder, with the following contents:

```php
<?php
class Article extends AppModel
  {
    public $hasMany = array('Vote');

    public function get($id)
      {
        return $this->find('first', array(
        'fields' => array(
                     'Article.*',
                     'AVG(Vote.vote) AS vote'
                ),
                'joins' => array(
                     array(
                          'type' => 'LEFT',
                          'table' => $this->Vote->getDataSource()-
>fullTableName($this->Vote->table),
                          'alias' => 'Vote',
                          'conditions' => array(
                               'Vote.article_id = Article.id'
                          )
                     )
                ),
                'conditions' => array('Article.id' => $id),
                'group' => array(
                     'Article.id'
                ),
                'recursive' => -1
        ));
      }

    public function vote($id, $data = array()) {
            if (empty($data) || empty($data['Vote'])) {
```

```
                    throw new Exception("No data specified");
            }
            $data['Vote']['article_id'] = $id;
            $this->Vote->create($data);
            if (!$this->Vote->validates()) {
                return false;
            }
            $conditions = array(
                'Vote.user_id' => $data['Vote']['user_id'],
                'Vote.article_id' => $data['Vote']['article_id']
            );
            if ($this->Vote->hasAny($conditions)) {
                return false;
            }
            return ($this->Vote->save($data) !== false);
        }
    }
?>
```

Create a file named vote.php and place it in your app/models folder with the following contents:

```php
<?php
class Vote extends AppModel {
    public $belongsTo = array('Article', 'User');
    public $validate = array(
        'article_id' => array('required' => true, 'rule' => 'notEmpty'),
        'user_id' => array('required' => true, 'rule' => 'notEmpty'),
        'vote' => array(
            'required' => array('required' => true, 'rule' =>
'notEmpty'),
            'range' => array(
                'rule' => array('range', 0, 6),
                'allowEmpty' => true
            )
        )
    );
}
?>
```

Create a folder named `articles` and place it in your `app/views` folder. Create a file named `view.ctp` and place it in your `app/views/articles` folder, with the following contents:

```
<h1><?php echo $article['Article']['title']; ?></h1>
Vote: <span id="vote"><?php echo number_format($article[0]['vote'],
1); ?></span>
<p><?php echo $article['Article']['body']; ?></p>
```

How to do it...

1. Download the 1.0.1 SimpleTest release from `https://sourceforge.net/projects/simpletest/files/simpletest/simpletest_1.0.1/simpletest_1.0.1.tar.gz/download`. Uncompress the downloaded file into your `app/vendors` folder. You should now have a folder named `simpletest` in `app/vendors`.

2. If you now browse to `http://localhost/test.php`, you should see the list of test groups available in CakePHP as shown in the next screenshot:

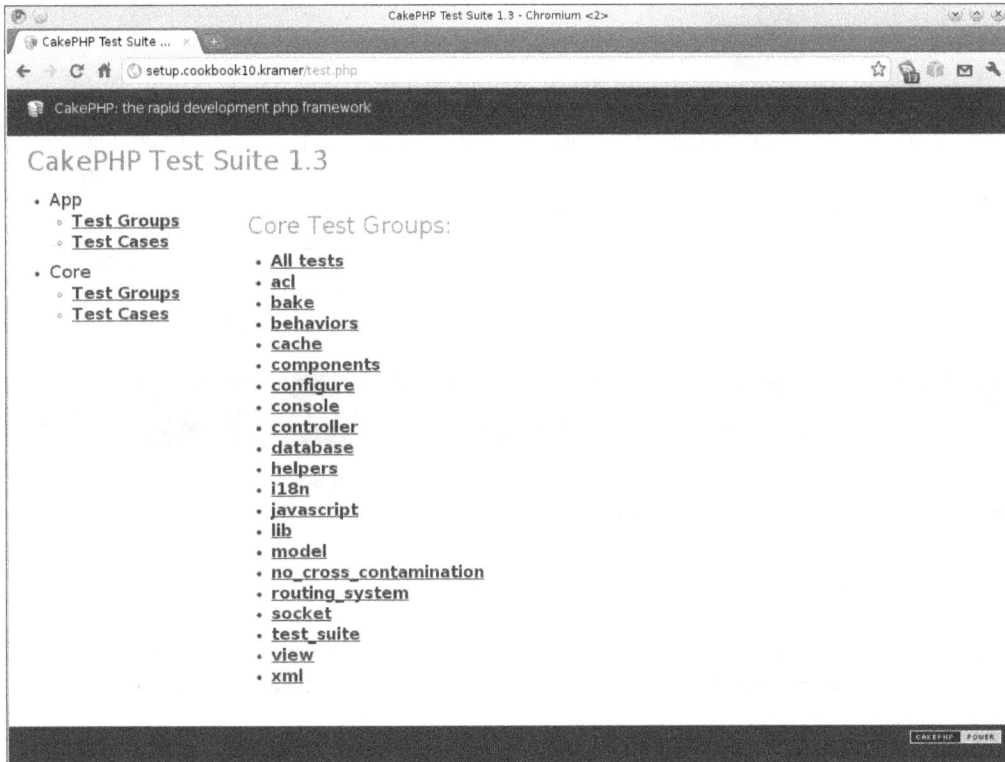

3. Clicking on any of these groups would execute the appropriate unit tests. For example, if you click on the **acl** test group, you should see a green bar indicating that all tests for the selected group succeeded, as shown in the next screenshot:

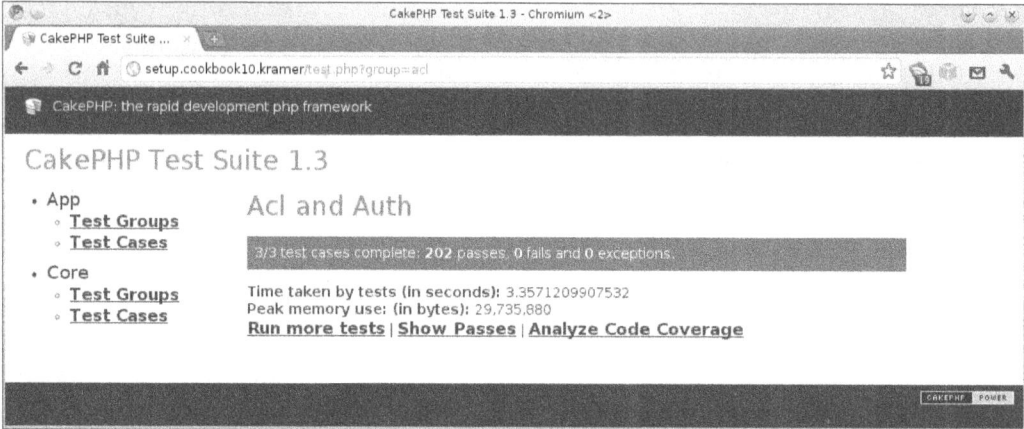

How it works...

CakePHP uses the SimpleTest library as the backbone of its unit testing framework. Unless we have installed SimpleTest on our application, we will be unable to run any unit test. Installing the library is as simple as downloading the appropriate version and extracting its contents into our app/vendors folder.

The framework includes a broad set of unit tests that cover almost every functionality implemented in the core. These unit tests allow the developer to report bugs against core functionality, have them solved, and make sure those bugs do not reappear in future releases.

Creating fixtures and testing model methods

In this recipe, we will learn how to create test data that we can use to test our application without altering real data, and how to create our own unit tests to cover model functionality.

Getting ready

To go through this recipe, we need a basic application skeleton to work with and have the SimpleTest library installed. Go through the entire recipe, *Setting up the test framework*.

How to do it...

1. Create a file named `article_fixture.php` and place it in your `app/tests/fixtures` folder with the following contents:

```php
<?php
class ArticleFixture extends CakeTestFixture {
        public $import = 'Article';
        public $records = array(
            array(
                'id' => 1,
                'title' => 'Article 1',
                'body' => 'Body for Article 1'
            ),
            array(
                'id' => 2,
                'title' => 'Article 2',
                'body' => 'Body for Article 2'
            )
        );
}
?>
```

2. Create a file named `user_fixture.php` and place it in your `app/tests/fixtures` folder with the following contents:

```php
<?php
class UserFixture extends CakeTestFixture {
        public $table = 'users';
        public $import = array('table' => 'users');
        public $records = array(
            array(
                'id' => 1,
                'username' => 'john.doe'
            ),
            array(
                'id' => 2,
                'username' => 'jane.doe'
            ),
            array(
                'id' => 3,
                'username' => 'mark.doe'
            )
        );
}
?>
```

3. Create a file named `vote_fixture.php` and place it in your `app/tests/fixtures` folder, with the following contents:

```php
<?php
class VoteFixture extends CakeTestFixture {
    public $import = 'Vote';
    public $records = array(
        array(
            'article_id' => 1,
            'user_id' => 1,
            'vote' => 4
        ),
        array(
            'article_id' => 1,
            'user_id' => 3,
            'vote' => 5
        ),
        array(
            'article_id' => 1,
            'user_id' => 2,
            'vote' => 4
        ),
        array(
            'article_id' => 2,
            'user_id' => 2,
            'vote' => 3
        ),
        array(
            'article_id' => 2,
            'user_id' => 3,
            'vote' => 4
        )
    );
}
?>
```

4. Create a file named `article.test.php` and place it in your `app/tests/cases/models` folder with the following contents:

```php
<?php
class ArticleTestCase extends CakeTestCase {
    public $fixtures = array('app.article', 'app.user', 'app.vote');

    public function startTest($method) {
        parent::startTest($method);
```

```
            $this->Article = ClassRegistry::init('Article');
    }

    public function endTest($method) {
            parent::endTest($method);
            ClassRegistry::flush();
    }

    public function testGet() {
            $article = $this->Article->get(1);
            $this->assertTrue(!empty($article) &&
!empty($article['Article']));
            $this->assertTrue(!empty($article[0]) &&
!empty($article[0]['vote']));
            $this->assertEqual(number_format($article[0]['vote'],
1), 4.3);

            $article = $this->Article->get(2);
            $this->assertTrue(!empty($article) &&
!empty($article['Article']));
            $this->assertTrue(!empty($article[0]) &&
!empty($article[0]['vote']));
            $this->assertEqual(number_format($article[0]['vote'],
1), 3.5);
    }

    public function testVote() {
            $result = $this->Article->vote(2, array('Vote' =>
array(
                    'user_id' => 2
            )));
            $this->assertFalse($result);
            $this->assertTrue(!empty($this->Article->Vote-
>validationErrors['vote']));
            $result = $this->Article->vote(2, array('Vote' =>
array(
                    'user_id' => 2,
                    'vote' => 6
            )));
            $this->assertFalse($result);
            $this->assertEqual($this->Article->Vote-
>validationErrors['vote'], 'range');
            $result = $this->Article->vote(2, array('Vote' =>
array(
                    'user_id' => 2,
                    'vote' => 1
            )));
            $this->assertFalse($result);

            $result = $this->Article->vote(2, array('Vote' =>
```

```
        array(

                        'user_id' => 1,
                        'vote' => 1
                )));
                $this->assertTrue($result);
                $article = $this->Article->get(2);
                $this->assertTrue(!empty($article[0]) &&
!empty($article[0]['vote']));
                $this->assertEqual(number_format($article[0]['vote'],
1), 2.7);

                $this->expectException();
                $this->Article->vote(2);
        }
    }
?>
```

How it works...

When looking to test model methods, it is very important to know what data is used during testing. Even when it is perfectly possible to test models using real application data, it is often safer (and thus recommendable) to specify the data that will be used for testing. This way, any modification to real data should not affect our tests, and consequently running those tests should not affect real data.

For this very purpose, CakePHP offers the concept of fixtures, which are no more than PHP classes that define the table structure and data used for testing models. These fixtures should have the same name as the model they are providing data for, should extend the base class `CakeTestFixture`, and should end with the word `Fixture`. The file name should be the underscored version of the class name, and should be placed in the `app/tests/fixtures` directory. A fixture may define the following properties:

- `name`: The name of the fixture, used to determine the name of the table this fixture creates. If the table name can be determined by other means, such as by setting the `table` property, or by importing the structure from a model, then this property is optional.

- `table`: The table this fixture creates. If the fixture imports the structure from an existing model, or if the `name` property is specified, then this property is optional.

- `import`: This property is optional and allows the structure, and/or data, to be imported from an existing source. If this property is set to a string, then it is a model name from where to import the structure (not the records.) Otherwise, it should be an array that consists of the following settings:
  - `records`: An optional Boolean setting. If set to `true`, then all records will be imported from the specified source. Defaults to `false`.

- ❑ `model`: The model from where to import the structure, and/or data. If specified, this model must exist.

- ❑ `table`: The table from where to import the structure, and/or data. If the `model` setting is specified, this setting is ignored and thus is optional.

- ❑ `fields`: If `import` is not defined, then this property is mandatory. It should be an array where each key is a field name, and each value the definition of the field, containing settings such as: `type`, `length`, `null`, `default`, and `key`. For more information about these settings, see `http://book. cakephp.org/view/1203/Creating-fixtures`.

- ❑ `records`: An array of records, each record itself being an array where the keys are the field names, and the values their respective values.

We start by creating the following fixtures:

- ▶ `ArticleFixture`: It imports its structure from the `Article` model, and defines two records.

- ▶ `UserFixture`: It imports its structure from the `users` table and defines three records (Notice how we import from a table instead of a model, as we did not create a `User` model).

- ▶ `VoteFixture`: It imports its structure from the `Vote` model, and defines five records.

After creating the fixtures, we proceed to build the test case. A test case is a PHP class without naming restrictions that contains unit tests. It extends from `CakeTestCase`, and is saved in a file ending with the suffix `.test.php` and placed in an appropriate subdirectory of the `app/tests/cases` folder. A unit test is a method of a test case class, but only methods with names starting with the word `test` are considered unit tests and thus run when the test case is executed.

Our test case is named `ArticleTestCase`, and defines the `fixtures` property to specify which fixtures are utilized by the test case. These names should match the fixture file name, without the `_fixture.php` suffix. By means of these fixtures, we provide test data for the models used throughout our test case.

Whenever you instantiate models from a unit test, and unless you specify otherwise through settings sent to the `ClassRegistry::init()` method, CakePHP will automatically set the model's database configuration to be `test_suite`, not only for the directly instantiated models, but for any models instantiated as a result of a binding definition.

The `test_suite` database configuration, unless specifically changed by the developer, will use the same database configuration as defined in the `default` configuration, and will also set `test_suite_` as a table prefix to avoid overwriting existing tables. This means that any models that are instantiated, together with their bindings (including bindings of bindings, and so on) should have a matching fixture, and those fixtures should be added to the test case. If you want to avoid defining fixtures for models you do not intend to test, see the section *Extending models to avoid testing unneeded bindings* in this recipe.

The first two methods in `ArticleTestCase` are implementations of callbacks offered by the parent class `CakeTestCase`. There are four callbacks available:

 ▶ `startCase()`: It executed before the first unit test method is run. This method is executed once per test case.

 ▶ `endCase()`: It executed after the last unit test method was run. This method is executed once per test case.

 ▶ `startTest()`: It executed before each unit test method is run. It receives a single argument, which is the name of the test method that is about to be executed.

 ▶ `endTest()`: It executed after each unit test method was run. It receives a single argument, which is the name of the test method.

We use the `startTest()` callback to instantiate the model we intend to test (`Article` in this case), and the `endTest()` callback to clean up the registry, a step that is not needed for this particular test case but that serves useful in many other scenarios.

We then define two unit test methods: `testGet()` and `testVote()`. The first one is meant to provide testing for the `Article::get()` method, while the later tests the creation of votes through the `Article::vote()` method. In these tests, we issue different calls to the model method we are testing, and then use some of the test case assertion methods to evaluate these calls:

 ▶ `assertTrue()`: Asserts that the provided argument evaluates to `true`.

 ▶ `assertFalse()`: Asserts that the provided argument evaluates to `false`.

 ▶ `assertEqual()`: Asserts that the first argument is equal to the second argument.

 ▶ `expectException()`: Expects the next call to produce an exception. Because of the way exceptions are handled, this assertion should be made last in the test method, as any code within that unit test method that should be executed after the exception is thrown will be ignored. Another approach to avoid this limitation is to use a try-catch block, and manually issue a call to the `fail()` or `pass()` method as a result.

There are other assertion methods that are useful in other scenarios, such as:

- ▸ `assertIsA()`: Asserts that the first argument is an object of the type provided in the second argument.

- ▸ `assertNull()`: Asserts that the provided argument is `null`.

- ▸ `assertPattern()`: Asserts that the second argument matches the regular expression pattern defined in the first argument.

- ▸ `assertTags()`: Asserts that the first argument matches the HTML tags provided in the second argument, without consideration to the order of tag attributes. See recipe *Testing views* for an example use of this assertion method.

There's more...

This recipe has shown us how to easily create fixtures. However, when there are lots of models in our application this can become quite a tedious task. Fortunately, CakePHP's `bake` command offers a task to automatically create fixtures: `fixture`.

It can run in interactive mode where its questions guide us through the steps required, or by using command line parameters. If we wanted to create a fixture for our `Article` model with up to two records, we would do:

On a GNU Linux / Mac / Unix system:

```
../cake/console/cake bake fixture article -count 2
```

On Microsoft Windows:

```
..\cake\console\cake.bat fixture article -count 2
```

This would generate the `article_fixture.php` file in its correct location, with two sample records ready to be used.

Extending models to avoid testing unneeded bindings

In this recipe, we tested code that affects the `Article` and `Vote` models, but none of the functionality that was covered by these unit tests had to interact with the `User` model. Why did we then need to add the `user` fixture? Simply removing this fixture from the `fixtures` property will make CakePHP complain about a missing table (specifically, `test_suite_users`).

To avoid creating fixtures for models we are not testing, we can create modified versions of our model classes by extending them and re-defining their bindings, leaving in only those we intend to test. Let us modify our test case to avoid using the `user` fixture.

Add the following to the beginning of your `app/tests/cases/models/article.test.php` file:

```
App::import('Model', array('Article', 'Vote'));
```

```
class TestArticle extends Article {
        public $belongsTo = array();
        public $hasOne = array();
        public $hasMany = array(
                'Vote' => array('className' => 'TestVote')
        );
        public $hasAndBelongsToMany = array();
        public $alias = 'Article';
        public $useTable = 'articles';
        public $useDbConfig = 'test_suite';
}

class TestVote extends Vote {
        public $belongsTo = array();
        public $hasOne = array();
        public $hasMany = array();
        public $hasAndBelongsToMany = array();
        public $alias = 'Vote';
        public $useTable = 'votes';
        public $useDbConfig = 'test_suite';
}
```

While still editing the `article.test.php file`, change the `fixtures` property of the `ArticleTestCase` class so that the user fixture is no longer loaded:

```
public $fixtures = array('app.article', 'app.vote');
```

Finally, change the instantiation of the `Article` model so that it uses `TestArticle` instead, by making the following changes to the `startTest()` method of the `ArticleTestCase` class:

```
public function startTest($method)
{
        parent::startTest($method);
        $this->Article = ClassRegistry::init('TestArticle');
}
```

Analyzing code coverage

If you have **Xdebug** installed (information about it is available at `http://xdebug.org`) you can find out how much of your application code is covered by your unit tests. This information is a great tool for understanding which parts of your application need more testing.

Once you have run a test case, you will notice a link entitled **Analyze Code Coverage**. After running our test case, click on this link. CakePHP will inform us that we have fully covered (**100%** coverage) our code. If you now comment out the unit test method called `testVote()`, and then run the code coverage analysis, you will notice that this number drops to **47.62%**, and CakePHP also shows us which part of our code has not been covered by unit tests, as shown in the next screenshot:

When you achieve **100%** code coverage, you are not guaranteeing that your code is bug-free, but that all lines of your application code have been reached by at least one unit test.

The more code left out of the reach of unit tests, the more prone to bugs your application becomes.

See also

▶   *Testing controller actions and their views*

Testing controller actions and their views

In this recipe, we will learn how to test controller actions and ensure that their views produce the result we expect.

Getting ready

To go through this recipe we need a basic application skeleton to work with, and have the SimpleTest library installed. Go through the entire recipe *Setting up the test framework*.

We also need test data. Go through the creation of fixtures described in the recipe *Creating fixtures and testing model methods*.

How to do it...

Create a file named `articles_controller.test.php` and place it in your `app/tests/cases/controllers` folder, with the following contents:

```php
<?php
class ArticlesControllerTestCase extends CakeTestCase {
    public $fixtures = array('app.article', 'app.user', 'app.vote');

    public function testView() {

        $result = $this->testAction('/articles/view/1',
array('return'=>'vars'));
        $expected = array(
            'Article' => array(
                'id' => 1,
                'title' => 'Article 1',
                'body' => 'Body for Article 1'
            ),
            0 => array(
                'vote' => 4.3333
            )
        );
        $this->assertTrue(!empty($result['article']));
        $this->assertEqual($result['article'], $expected);

        $result = $this->testAction('/articles/view/1',
array('return'=>'view'));
        $this->assertTags($result, array(
            array('h1' => array()),
            'Article 1',
            '/h1',
```

```
                'Vote:',
                array('span' => array('id'=>'vote')),
                '4.3',
                '/span',
                array('p' => array()),
                'Body for Article 1',
                '/p'
        ));
    }
?>
```

If you now browse to `http://localhost/test.php`, click on the **Test Cases** option under the **App** section in the left menu, and then click on the **controllers / ArticlesController** test case, you should see our unit test succeeding, as shown in the next screenshot:

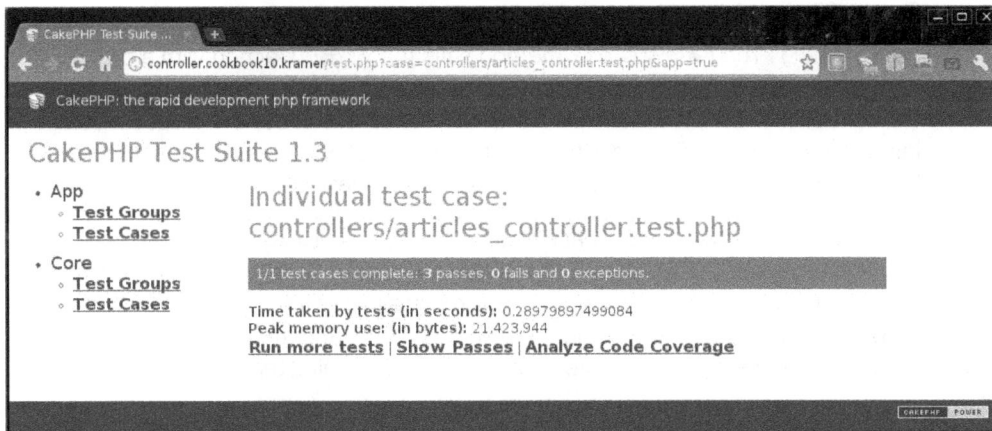

How it works...

We start by creating the test case in a class named `ArticlesControllerTestCase`, and save it in its proper location (`app/tests/cases/controllers`), using the right filename (`articles_controller.test.php`). In this class, we specify which fixtures we need to load, which, just as it was shown in the recipe *Creating fixtures and testing model methods*, consists of fixtures for all the loaded models.

Our test case includes a single unit test method: `testView()`, which intends to unit test the `ArticlesController::view()` action. In this unit test we use the `testAction()` method that is available to all test cases. This method takes two arguments:

> ▶ `url`: This is either a string or an array containing the URL to the controller action we intend to test. If it is an array, it should be in the same format as the format used by CakePHP once a string-based URL has been parsed.

- ▸ `parameters`: This is a set of optional parameters, which can be any of the following:
  - ❑ `connection`: If `fixturize` is set to `true`, it defines the connection from where to import data.
  - ❑ `data`: It is the data to post to the controller.
  - ❑ `fixturize`: If this is set to `true`, then all data from the connection defined in the `connection` setting will be imported into fixtures for all the used models. Defaults to `false`.
- ▸ `method`: This is the method to use when posting the data specified in the `data` setting. Can either be `get` or `post`. Defaults to `post`.
- ▸ `return`: This specifies the type of result that should be returned as a result of a `testAction()` call. If it is set to `result`, which is the default, it will return whatever the controller action returns. If it is set to `vars`, it will return the view variables assigned from the action. If it is `view`, it will return the rendered view without the layout. Finally, if it is set to `contents`, it will return the rendered view within its layout.
- ▸ `testView()`: The `testView()` method calls the `view()` action with a proper ID, and tells the `testAction()` method to return the view variables created in the controller action. We make sure that this variable is set to the proper article information. We then finalize with a call to `testAction()`, using the same URL, but specifying that we want to obtain the rendered view.

To assert that the view has the proper content, we use the `assertTags()` method, which offers a flexible way to check HTML tags. This method takes an array of elements, each element being either a string that represents a static string or a closing tag if the string starts with a forward slash, or an array, where the key is an HTML tag name, and the value is itself an array of attributes (keys being the attribute names, and values being their respective values).

There's more...

We have seen how, by using `testAction()`, we can easily test our controller actions and make assertions on either the action's return value, the view variables, or the view content. However, we have not covered how to test actions that might redirect the user away from the current action, or how to test for session operations. The next recipe shows how to add more complex tests to the unit tests we have just built.

See also

- ▸ *Using mocks to test controllers*

Using mocks to test controllers

In this recipe we will learn how to extend what we have covered in the previous recipe by using mocks, an indispensable tool for building powerful test cases.

Getting ready

To go through this recipe, we need unit tests already in place. Go through the previous recipe.

How to do it...

1. Edit your `app/tests/cases/controllers/articles_controller.test.php` file and place the following code at the beginning, right before the declaration of the class `ArticlesControllerTestCase`:

```
App::import('Controller', 'Articles');

class TestArticlesController extends ArticlesController {
    public $name = 'Articles';
    public $testRedirect = false;

    public function __construct() {
        parent::__construct();
        Configure::write('controllers.'.$this->name, $this);
    }

    public function beforeFilter() {
        if (isset($this->Session)) {
            App::import('Component', 'Session');
            Mock::generate('SessionComponent');
            $this->Session = new MockSessionComponent();
        }

        parent::beforeFilter();
    }

    public function redirect($url, $status = null, $exit = true) {
        $this->testRedirect = compact('url', 'status', 'exit');
        if ($exit) {
            $this->autoRender = false;
        }
    }
}
```

2. While still editing the `articles_controller.test.php` file, add the following code at the beginning of the `ArticlesControllerTestCase` class, right below the declaration of the `fixtures` property:

```
public function testAction($url, $params = array()) {
    $url = preg_replace('/^\/articles\//', '/test_articles/',
$url);
    $result = parent::testAction($url, $params);
    $this->Articles = Configure::read('controllers.Articles');
    return $result;
}
```

3. Add the following code at the beginning of the `testView()` method:

```
$result = $this->testAction('/articles/view/0');
$this->assertTrue(!empty($this->Articles->testRedirect));
$this->assertEqual($this->Articles->testRedirect['url'],
array('action' => 'index'));
```

4. Finally, add the following method to the end of the `ArticlesControllerTestCase` class:

```
public function testVote() {
    $result = $this->testAction('/articles/vote/2', array(
        'data' =>  array(
            'Vote' => array(
                'user_id' => 1,
                'vote' => 1
            )
        )
    ));

    $this->assertTrue(!empty($this->Articles->testRedirect));
    $this->assertEqual($this->Articles->testRedirect['url'],
array('action' => 'index'));

    $this->Articles->Session->expectOnce('setFlash', array('Vote
placed'));

    $article = $this->Articles->Article->get(2);
    $this->assertTrue(!empty($article) &&
!empty($article['Article']));
    $this->assertTrue(!empty($article[0]) && !empty($article[0]
['vote']));
    $this->assertEqual(number_format($article[0]['vote'], 1),
2.7);
}
```

If you now browse to `http://localhost/test.php`, click on the **Test Cases** option under the **App** section in the left menu, and then click on the **controllers / ArticlesController** test case, you should see our unit test succeeding, as shown in the next screenshot:

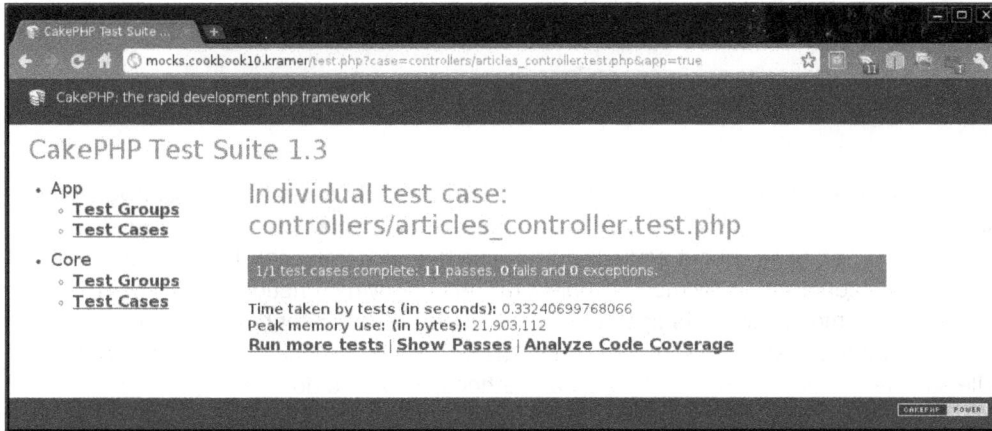

How it works...

We start by extending the controller we intend to test so we can override its `redirect()` method, so that when that method is executed as part of our unit test, the browser is not redirected and we can instead use the redirect information to make our assertions.

If `redirect()` is called, we store the destination in a property named `testRedirect`, and instead of aborting the execution (which would abort the test case) we avoid the view from being rendered. This works properly because every time we called `redirect()` from our `ArticlesController` class, we stopped the action execution by issuing a return statement.

As there is no direct way to get the instance of the controller that was executed from our test case (see the section *There's more* in this recipe for an alternative approach), we need to keep a reference of the controller instance. We use CakePHP's `Configure` class to store the reference, so that it can then be easily obtained.

We also want to avoid using real session data as a result of our unit test. This means that we need to find a way to let CakePHP think that when a controller interacts with its `Session` component, everything behaves as expected, while still not really interacting with the browser session. We also want to be able to assert when a particular method in that component is executed.

Mocks provide a way for us to mimic the way a real object behaves, without actually performing the object's underlying logic. With the following lines of code in the controller's `beforeFilter` callback:

```
if (isset($this->Session)) {
    App::import('Component', 'Session');
    Mock::generate('SessionComponent');
    $this->Session = new MockSessionComponent();
}
```

We are replacing the instance of CakePHP's `Session` component with a mocked version. This mocked version will allow the controller to use all the component's available methods (such as `setFlash()`) without actually performing the underlying call. `Mock::generate()` will by default generate a fully mocked object (all its underlying functionality will be ignored.) If we wanted to mock only parts of an object, we would need to generate a partial mock. For example, if we only wanted to mock the `setFlash()` method of the `Session` component while still maintaining the rest of its original methods, we would do:

```
Mock::generatePartial('SessionComponent', false, array('setFlash'));
```

Once we have a mocked object and a way to access it from our unit tests, we can use any of the following mock assertions methods to test if a method of a mocked object is called as expected:

- ▶ `expectAtLeastOnce()`: Its first argument is the name of the method we expect to have executed, while the second optional argument is an array of parameters we expect that method to have received. This is used when the expected method is to be called at least once, but can still be executed more times.

- ▶ `expectNever()`: Its first mandatory argument is the name of a method that we intend to ensure has not been executed on the mocked object.

- ▶ `expectOnce()`: It behaves exactly as `expectAtLeastOnce()`, but makes sure the method is executed only once.

We proceed by overriding `CakeTestCase`'s `testAction()` method so that whenever an URL for the `ArticlesController` class is requested, we change that URL to use our extended `TestArticlesController` class. Once the proper action is executed, we obtain the instance of the controller class and keep it in a property of the unit test named `Articles` so we can then refer to it.

We are now ready to test. We start by modifying the `testView()` method so we can test a `redirect()` call, by building a test to force an invalid record ID, and asserting that the controller's `testRedirect` property is set to the `index` action.

We finalize the recipe by implementing the `testVote()` method, which gives us a chance to test posting data (using the second argument of the `testAction()` method as described in the previous recipe), and asserting that the mocked `Session` class receives a call to its `setFlash()` method, with the right arguments.

The last part of this unit test uses the main model of our controller to fetch the created article, and make sure that it matches our posted data.

There's more...

While the method shown in this recipe is quite powerful, it is definitely not the only way to test controllers. We can also perform direct calls on the controller actions we intend to test by instantiating the controller class and making a manual call to the action.

However, this is not a straightforward operation, since it would require a proper initialization of our controller by following the same steps than those defined by CakePHP's `Dispatcher` class. Mark Story has produced a thorough article describing this approach at `http://mark-story.com/posts/view/testing-cakephp-controllers-the-hard-way`.

Mark Story has also published a follow-up article on manual testing of controllers, where he introduces mocks. It is definitely a good read, and it is available at `http://mark-story.com/posts/view/testing-cakephp-controllers-mock-objects-edition`.

Running tests from the command line

In this recipe, we will learn how to run our unit tests from the command line, which opens the possibility for automated test reporting.

Getting ready

To go through this recipe we need a basic application skeleton to work with, which should have its own set of unit tests. Go through the entire recipe *Creating fixtures and testing model methods*.

How to do it...

Using your operating system console, switch to your application directory, and run:

If you are on a GNU Linux / Mac / Unix system:

```
../cake/console/cake testsuite app case models/article
```

If you are on Microsoft Windows:

```
..\cake\console\cake.bat testsuite app case models/article
```

The shell should now run the specified unit test and inform us that all unit tests succeeded, as shown in the next screenshot:

How it works...

CakePHP's `testsuite` shell allows us to execute any test case, or group of test cases, from the command line. It offers several ways to specify which unit test to execute by specifying a minimum of two arguments.

The first argument can either be `app`, `core`, or a plugin name. Use `app` when intending to execute a unit test, or group of tests, from your application directory. Use `core` if you wish to run CakePHP's core tests. Finally, if you wish to run tests from a plugin, use the plugin name as the first argument to the `testsuite` shell.

The second argument should specify what type of unit test to run. It can be set to `all`, which runs all tests; `group`, which runs the test group specified in the third argument; or `case`, which runs the test case defined in the third argument.

11
Utility Classes and Tools

In this chapter, we will cover:

- ▸ Working with the Set class
- ▸ Manipulating strings with the String class
- ▸ Sending an e-mail
- ▸ Detecting file types with MagicDb
- ▸ Throwing and handling exceptions

Introduction

This chapter introduces a set of utility classes and helpful techniques that improve the architecture of a CakePHP application.

The first recipe shows how to work with a CakePHP class that optimizes the manipulation of arrays. The second recipe shows how to manipulate strings with CakePHP's `string` class. The third recipe shows how to send an email using the `Email` component. The fourth recipe shows how to use the `MagicDb` class to detect the type of a file.

Working with the Set class

One of the most debated decisions CakePHP has ever made was returning arrays as a result of a model `find` operation. While ORM purists may argue that each returned item should be an instance of a model class, arrays prove themselves very useful, fast, and flexible for manipulating characteristics that can be impossible to achieve with a pure object approach.

The `Set` class was introduced to give the developer even more power when dealing with array based data structures. With a simple method call, we can manipulate an array with ease, avoiding us the pain of having to build long and complex code blocks.

This recipe shows how to use some of the most useful methods this class provides, while introducing other available methods that may be useful under different scenarios.

Getting ready

To go through this recipe, we need some data to work with. Create the following tables, and populate them with data, by issuing these SQL statements:

```sql
CREATE TABLE `students`(
    `id` INT UNSIGNED AUTO_INCREMENT NOT NULL,
    `name` VARCHAR(255) NOT NULL,
    PRIMARY KEY(`id`)
);

CREATE TABLE `categories`(
    `id` INT UNSIGNED AUTO_INCREMENT NOT NULL,
    `name` VARCHAR(255) NOT NULL,
    PRIMARY KEY(`id`)
);

CREATE TABLE `exams`(
    `id` INT UNSIGNED AUTO_INCREMENT NOT NULL,
    `category_id` INT UNSIGNED NOT NULL,
    `name` VARCHAR(255) NOT NULL,
    PRIMARY KEY(`id`),
    FOREIGN KEY `exams__categories`(`category_id`) REFERENCES
`categories`(`id`)
);

CREATE TABLE `grades`(
    `id` INT UNSIGNED AUTO_INCREMENT NOT NULL,
    `student_id` INT UNSIGNED NOT NULL,
    `exam_id` INT UNSIGNED NOT NULL,
    `grade` FLOAT UNSIGNED NOT NULL,
    PRIMARY KEY(`id`),
    FOREIGN KEY `grades__students`(`student_id`) REFERENCES
`students`(`id`),
    FOREIGN KEY `grades__exams`(`exam_id`) REFERENCES `exams`(`id`)
);

INSERT INTO `students`(`id`, `name`) VALUES
    (1, 'John Doe'),
    (2, 'Jane Doe');
```

```
INSERT INTO `categories`(`id`, `name`) VALUES
    (1, 'Programming Language'),
    (2, 'Databases');
INSERT INTO `exams`(`id`, `category_id`, `name`) VALUES
    (1, 1, 'PHP 5.3'),
    (2, 1, 'C++'),
    (3, 1, 'Haskell'),
    (4, 2, 'MySQL'),
    (5, 2, 'MongoDB');
INSERT INTO `grades`(`student_id`, `exam_id`, `grade`) VALUES
    (1, 1, 10),
    (1, 2, 8),
    (1, 3, 7.5),
    (1, 4, 9),
    (1, 5, 6),
    (2, 1, 7),
    (2, 2, 9.5),

    (2, 3, 6),
    (2, 4, 10),
    (2, 5, 9);
```

Create a controller in a file named `exams_controller.php` and place it in your `app/controllers` folder, with the following contents:

```php
<?php
class ExamsController extends AppController {
   public function index() {
   }
}
?>
```

Create a file named `exam.php` and place it in your `app/models` folder, with the following contents:

```php
<?php
class Exam extends AppModel {
   public $belongsTo = array('Category');
   public $hasMany = array('Grade');
}
?>
```

Create a file named `grade.php` and place it in your `app/models` folder, with the following contents:

```php
<?php
class Grade extends AppModel {
    public $belongsTo = array(
        'Exam',
        'Student'
    );
}
?>
```

How to do it...

1. Edit your `app/controllers/exams_controller.php` file and insert the following contents in its `index()` method:

```php
$gradeValues = Set::extract(
    $this->Exam->find('all'),
    '/Grade/grade'
);
$average = array_sum($gradeValues) / count($gradeValues);

$categories = $this->Exam->Category->find('all');
$mappedCategories = Set::combine(
    $categories,
    '/Category/id',
    '/Category/name'
);

$gradeRows = $this->Exam->Grade->find('all', array(
    'recursive' => 2
));

$grades = Set::format(
    $gradeRows,
    '%s got a %-.1f in %s (%s)',
    array(
        '/Student/name',
        '/Grade/grade',
        '/Exam/name',
        '/Exam/Category/name'
    )
);

$categories = Set::map($categories);

$this->set(compact('average', 'grades', 'categories'));
```

2. Create a folder named `exams` and place it in your `app/views` folder. Create a file named `index.ctp` and place it in your `app/views/exams` folder, with the following contents:

```
<h2>Average: <strong><?php echo $average; ?></strong></h2>
<ul>
<?php foreach($grades as $string) { ?>
    <li><?php echo $string; ?></li>
<?php } ?>
</ul>
<h2>Categories:</h2>
<ul>
<?php foreach($categories as $category) { ?>
    <li><?php echo $category->id; ?>: <?php echo $category->name;
?></li>
<?php } ?>
</ul>
```

If you now browse to `http://localhost/exams`, you should see the average grade for all exams, a detailed list of what each student got on each exam, and the list of all categories, as shown in the following screenshot:

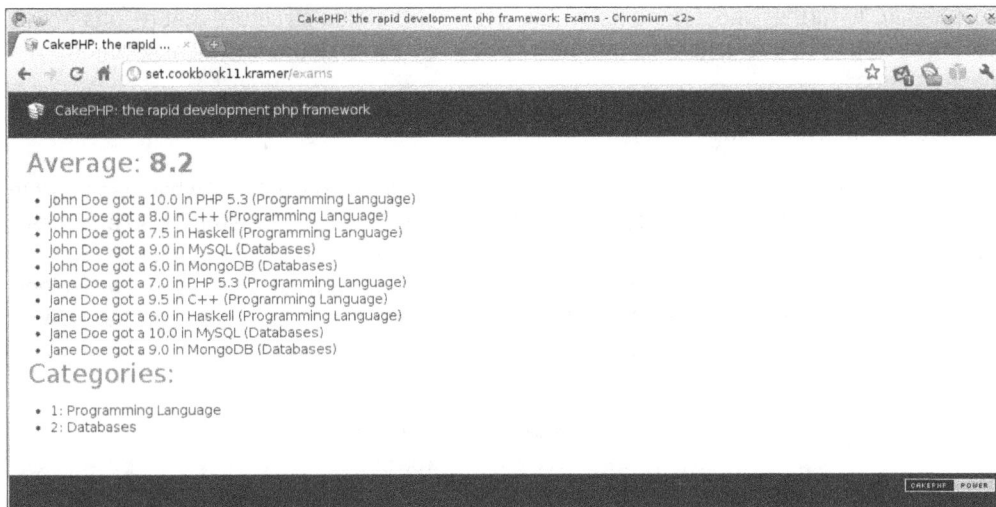

How it works...

We start by using the `Set::extract()` method to extract information out of the result obtained after fetching all rows from the `Exam` model. The information we are interested in retrieving is the list of all grades. The `extract()` method takes up to three arguments:

► `path`: An X-Path 2.0-compatible expression that shows the path to the information that should be extracted.

> The `Set` class supports only a subset of the X-Path 2.0 specification. Expressions such as `//`, which are valid in X-Path, are not available in `Set`. Continue reading this recipe to learn what expressions are supported.

► `data`: The array data structure from which to extract the information.

► `options`: These are optional settings. At the time of this writing, only the option `flatten` (a boolean) is available. Setting it to `false` will return the extracted field as part of the resulting structure. Defaults to `true`.

The `path` argument offers a flexible approach when defining what information we are interested in. To further understand its syntax, consider the data structure that results from fetching all `Exam` records, together with their `Category` information, and all associated `Grade` records:

```
$data = $this->Exam->find('all');
```

In X-Path 2.0, the path is an expression separated by the forward slash (/), while each part in that expression represents a subpath (CakePHP's `Set::extract()` method also enforces a starting slash.) Therefore, the expression `/children` refers to a path that includes only elements named `children`, while the expression `/children/grandchildren` will select items named `grandchildren` that are descendents of items named `children`. When we refer to the name of an item, we are referring to the key in the array structure.

> More information about X-Path 2.0 can be obtained at `http://www.w3.org/TR/xpath20`.

If we intended to grab only the `Exam` fields (thus discarding the information regarding `Category` and `Grade`), we would use the following:

```
Set::extract('/Exam', $data);
```

This would return an array of elements, each element indexed by `Exam`, and having as its value all the fields for the `Exam` key. If we were only interested in the `name` field, we would add another subpath to the expression:

```
Set::extract('/Exam/name', $data);
```

We can also further limit a path by adding conditional expressions. A conditional expression filters the elements (using the `Set::matches()` method), by applying one of the typical comparison operators (`<`, `<=`, `>`, `>=`, `=`, `!=`) to each element that matches the path. To obtain all `Grade` records where the value of the `grade` field is less than 8, we would use the following expression (notice how the conditional expression is applied to a subpath and is surrounded with brackets):

```
Set::extract('/Grade[grade<8]', $data);
```

Instead of a comparison operator, we can use position expressions, which can be any of the following:

- `:first`: Refers to the first matching element.
- `:last`: Refers to the last matching element.
- `number`: Refers to the element located in the position indicated by number, where `number` is a number greater than or equal to 1.
- `start:end`: Refers to all elements starting at position `start`, and ending at position end. Both `start` and end are numbers greater than, or equal to, 1.

To filter the data set so that only the second and third elements of all `Grade` records are returned, using the subset of records where `grade` is greater than or equal to 8, and obtaining only the value for the `grade` field, we would do:

```
Set::extract('/Grade[grade>=8]/grade[2:3]', $data);
```

Going back to the recipe, we started by extracting only the value of the `grade` field for each `Grade` record. This `Set::extract()` call returns an array of `grade` values, so we can then use PHP's `array_sum()` and `count()` functions to calculate the average grading.

> A handful of examples of the `Set::extract()` method, and other `Set` methods, can be obtained from its test case. Look into your CakePHP core folder for the `tests/cases/libs/set.test.php` file and go through the different test cases.

We then use the `Set::combine()` method. This method takes up to four arguments:

- `data`: The array data structure on which to operate.
- `path1`: The X-Path 2.0 path used to fetch the keys of the resulting array.

- ▶ `path2`: The X-Path 2.0 path used to fetch the values of the resulting array. If not specified, the values will be set to `null`.

- ▶ `groupPath`: The X-Path 2.0 path to use when looking to group the resulting items so each item is a subitem of the corresponding group.

Using the `/Category/id` expression as keys and `/Category/name` as values, we obtain an indexed array, where the keys are the `Category` IDs, and the values their respective `Category` names.

The `groupPath` argument can serve useful in many scenarios. Consider the need of obtaining the grades for all exams for a particular student, grouped by the category of the exam. Using the following:

```
$records = $this->Exam->Grade->find('all', array(
    'conditions' => array('Student.id' => 1),
    'recursive' => 2
));
$data = Set::combine(
    $records,
    '/Exam/name',
    '/Grade/grade',
    '/Exam/Category/name'
);
```

We would obtain what we need in an easy to navigate array:

```
array(
    'Programming Language' => array(
        'PHP 5.3' => '10',
        'C++' => '8',
        'Haskell' => '7.5'
    ),
    'Databases' => array(
        'MySQL' => '9',
        'MongoDB' => '6'
    )
)
```

The recipe continues by fetching all grades, and then using the `Set::format()` method to obtain a list of formatted strings. This method takes three arguments:

- ▶ `data`: The data to format.

- ▶ `format`: The `sprintf()`-based string that contains the format to use.

- ▶ `keys`: The array of X-Path 2.0 paths to use when replacing the `sprintf()` conversion specifications included in `format`.

> To learn more about the `sprintf()` based conversion specifications see
> `http://php.net/sprintf`.

`Set::format()` applies the `format` string to each item in the `data` array, and returns an array of formatted strings. In the recipe we used the string `%s got a %-.1f in %s (%s)`. This string contains four conversion specifications: a string, a floating number (which we are forcing to only include one decimal digit), and two other strings. This means that our keys argument should contain four paths. Each of those paths will be used, in sequence to replace their corresponding conversion specification.

The recipe ends by using the `Set::map()` method, which can be useful if you want to deal with objects, rather than arrays. This method takes two optional arguments:

- ▶ `class`: The class name to be used when creating an instance of an object. This argument is normally used to specify the data, and the `tmp` argument is used to specify the class name.
- ▶ `tmp`: If the first argument is an array, then this argument behaves as the `class` argument. Otherwise it is safely ignored.

Simply calling this method with the data to convert will convert that data to a set of generic object instances, recursively. If the `class` argument is used, then the class name specified in that argument will be used when creating the respective object instances.

There's more...

The usefulness of the `Set` class does not end here. There are several other methods that were not covered in this recipe, but can help us when developing our CakePHP applications. Some of these methods are:

- ▶ `merge()`: Acts as a combination of two PHP methods: `array_merge()` and `array_merge_recursive()`, allowing the proper merging of arrays when the same key exists in at least two of the arguments, and they are themselves arrays. In this case, it performs another `Set::merge()` on those elements.
- ▶ `filter()`: Filter empty elements out of an array, leaving in real values that evaluate to empty (0, and `'0'`)
- ▶ `pushDiff()`: Pushes the differences from one array to another, inserting the nonexistent keys from the second argument to the first, recursively.
- ▶ `numeric()`: Determines if the elements in the array contain only numeric values.

▸ `diff()`: Computes and returns the different elements between two arrays.

▸ `reverse()`: Converts an object into an array. This method can be seen as the opposite of the `Set::map()` method.

▸ `sort()`: Sorts an array by the value specified in an X-Path 2.0 compatible path.

Manipulating strings with the String class

String manipulation is probably one of PHP's biggest strengths, as it offers a handful of functions to perform a variety of operations. Even when almost every need can be fulfilled by using PHP's core methods, some forms of string manipulation may prove troublesome.

> To find out more about some of PHP's core string methods see `http://php.net/manual/en/ref.strings.php`.

CakePHP offers a utility class named `String` to help us deal with strings. This recipe introduces the class and its few, yet useful set of methods.

Getting ready

We need a controller to use as placeholder for our code. Create a file named `examples_controller.php` and place it in your `app/controllers` folder, with the following contents:

```php
<?php
class ExamplesController extends AppController {
    public $uses = null;
    public function index() {
        $this->_stop();
    }
}
?>
```

How to do it...

Edit the `app/controllers/examples_controller.php` file and add the following at the beginning of the `index()` method:

```php
$lines = array(
    '"Doe, Jane", jane.doe@email.com',
    '"Doe, John", john.doe@email.com'
);
foreach($lines as $i => $line) {
    $line = String::tokenize($line, ',', '"', '"');
```

```
    $line = array_combine(array('name', 'email'), $line);
    foreach($line as $field => $value) {
        $line[$field] = preg_replace('/^"(.+)"$/', '\\1', $value);
    }
    $line['id'] = String::uuid();
    $lines[$i] = $line;
}

foreach($lines as $line) {
    echo String::insert('[:id] Hello :name! Your email is\\: :email',
$line) . '<br />';
}
```

If you now browse to `http://localhost/examples` you should see a text output similar to the following:

[4d403ee1-6bbc-48c6-a8cc-786894a56bba] Hello Doe, Jane! Your email is: jane.doe@ email.com

[4d403ee1-9e84-487f-95cf-786894a56bba] Hello Doe, John! Your email is: john.doe@ email.com

How it works...

The `String` class offers the following methods for string manipulation:

- `cleanInsert()`: Cleans a string generated via the `String::insert()` method.
- `insert()`: Replaces variable placeholders in a string with a set of values.
- `tokenize()`: Separates a string into parts using a given separator, and ignoring the separator instances that appear between the specified bound strings.
- `uuid()`: Returns a random UUID string.

This recipe starts by defining an array of two strings, each of them following a format similar to what we would find on a CSV (comma-separated values) file. For each of those lines, we use the `String::tokenize()` method to separate the CSV line into a set of values. This method takes up to four arguments:

- `data`: The string to separate.
- `separator`: The token that separates the string. Defaults to `,`.
- `leftBound`: The boundary string that indicates the start of an area where `separator` characters should be ignored. Defaults to `(`.
- `rightBound`: Similar to `leftBound`, but marks the end of that area. Defaults to `)`.

We tell `String::tokenize()` to separate each line taking into account that any expression enclosed between quotes can include the separator character, in which case it should be ignored. We then use PHP's `array_combine()` function so that each line becomes an associative array, indexed by field name and having as its values the corresponding field value.

As the string returned by the `String::tokenize()` method includes the boundary strings defined in the `leftBound` and `rightBound` arguments if they were part of the original string, we proceed to remove them from each line.

We then add a random UUID string as the value for each line's `id` field, using the `String::uuid()` method. This string will be unique to each line, and should never repeat itself, even across separate requests.

> More information about UUIDs can be obtained at `http://en.wikipedia.org/wiki/Universally_unique_identifier`.

Finally, we go through each line and output a dynamically generated string through the `String::insert()` method. This method takes up to three arguments:

- `str`: String that contains the variable placeholders that should be replaced.
- `data`: Associative array in the form `variable => value`, used to replace the variable placeholders with their respective value.
- `options`: Set of options to define how the method should behave. Available options:
  - `before`: String that indicates the start of a variable placeholder. Defaults to `:`.
  - `after`: String that indicates the end of a variable placeholder. Defaults to `null`, which means a placeholder starts with the string defined in `before`, and end where the word ends.
- `escape`: Character to use when looking to escape the string used in the `before` option. Defaults to `\`.
- `format`: Regular expression used to find variable placeholders.
- `clean`: If specified, it will clean the replaced string through the `String::cleanInsert()` method. Defaults to `false`, which means no cleaning is done.

In our example, we use the string `[:id] Hello :name! Your email is\\: :email`. This string contains three variable placeholders: `:id`, `:name`, and `:email`. Each of those get replaced by the respective value in the associative array that is passed as the second argument to the `String::insert()` method.

Sending an e-mail

If there is one task we can hardly avoid when building web applications it is sending out e-mails. It is such a basic need that CakePHP provides us with a ready-to-go component that can send e-mails, either through SMTP, or using PHP's `mail()` function.

In this recipe we will learn how to use the `Email` component to send out e-mails through SMTP using a Google Mail account, and how to use e-mail layouts to proper render the e-mails.

Getting ready

We only need some place to put our code, and that place will be a model-less controller. Create a file named `emails_controller.php` and place it in your `app/controllers` folder, with the following contents:

```
class EmailsController extends AppController {
    public $uses = null;
    public function index() {
        $this->_stop();
    }
}
```

How to do it...

1. Edit your `app/controllers/emails_controller.php` and add the following property to the `EmailsController` class (right below the `uses` property declaration), replacing the `username` and `password` settings highlighted with your Google Mail account, and password:

```
public $components = array(
    'Email' => array(
        'delivery' => 'smtp',
        'smtpOptions' => array(
            'host' => 'ssl://smtp.gmail.com',
            'port' => 465,
            'username' => 'email@gmail.com',
            'password' => 'password'
        )
    )
);
```

2. While still editing the controller, add the following code to its `index()` method, right above the call to the `_stop()` method (replace the `to` property highlighted with the e-mail address where you wish to receive the test e-mail):

```
$this->Email->to = 'Destination <email@gmail.com>';
$this->Email->subject = 'Testing the Email component';
$sent = $this->Email->send('Hello world!');
if (!$sent) {
    echo 'ERROR: ' . $this->Email->smtpError . '<br />';
} else {
    echo 'Email sent!';
}
```

3. If you now browse to `http://localhost/emails`, you should see the message **Email sent!**, and you should then receive the test e-mail message in your inbox, as shown in the following screenshot:

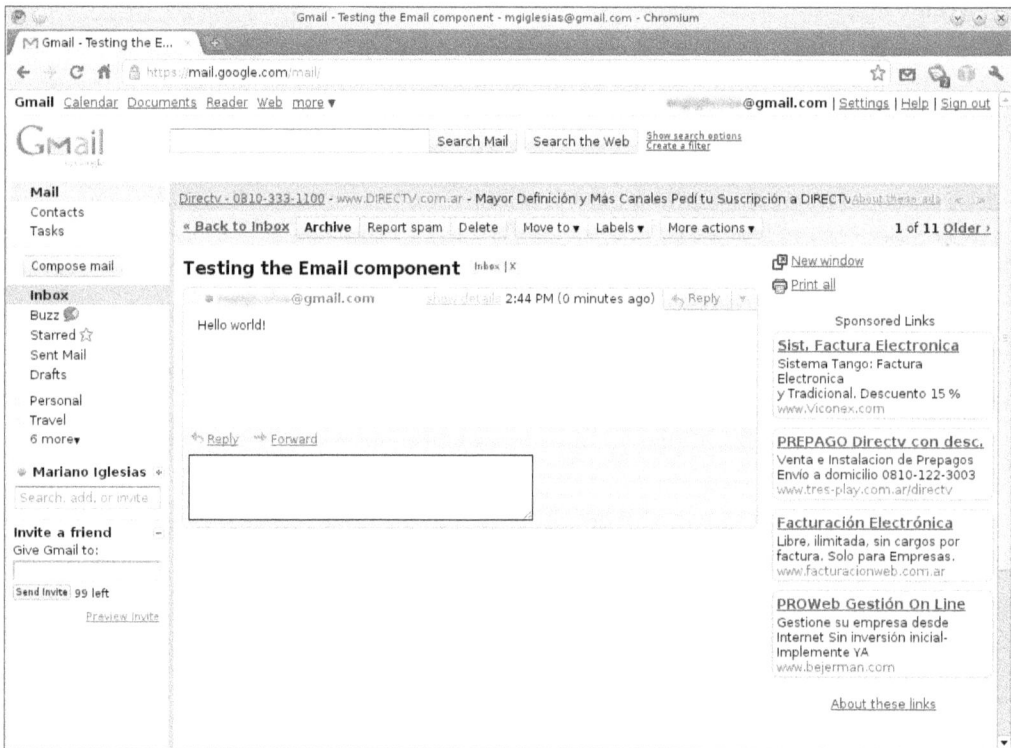

Let us now continue by sending an HTML e-mail, using layouts and templates.

4. Make the following changes to the `index()` method in your `app/controllers/emails_controller.php` file (remember to change the highlighted `to` property to your desired destination e-mail):

```
$this->set(array(
    'name' => 'Mariano Iglesias',
    'url' => Router::url('/', true)
));
$this->Email->to = 'Destination <email@gmail.com>';
$this->Email->subject = 'Testing the Email component';
$this->Email->sendAs = 'both';
$this->Email->template = 'test';
$sent = $this->Email->send();
if (!$sent) {
    echo 'ERROR: ' . $this->Email->smtpError . '<br />';
} else {
    echo 'Email sent!';
}
```

5. Create a file named `default.ctp` and place it in your `app/views/layouts/email/html` folder with the following contents:

```
<html>
<head><title><?php echo $title_for_layout;?></title></head>
<body>
    <?php echo $content_for_layout; ?>
    <p><small>This email was sent on: <?php echo date('F d, Y H:i'); ?></small></p>
</body>
</html>
```

6. Create a file named `default.ctp` and place it in your `app/views/layouts/email/text` folder with the following contents:

```
<?php echo $content_for_layout; ?>
This email was sent on: <?php echo date('F d, Y H:i'); ?>
```

7. Create a file named `test.ctp` and place it in your `app/views/elements/email/html` folder, with the following contents:

```
<p>Hello <?php echo $name; ?>!</p>
<p>This is a test email from <?php echo $this->Html->link('My Test Application', $url); ?></p>
```

8. Create a file named `test.ctp` and place it in your `app/views/elements/email/text` folder, with the following contents:

```
Hello <?php echo $name; ?>!

This is a test email from My Test Application: <?php echo $url; ?>
```

If you now browse to `http://localhost/emails` you should see the message **Email sent!**, and you should then receive the test e-mail message in your inbox in HTML format, and with a link to your web application.

How it works...

We start by adding the `Email` component to our controller's list of components. While adding it, we set the settings required to specify the type of delivery we wish to use. The connection settings available in the `Email` component are:

- ▶ `delivery`: It is the type of delivery to use, and can be either: `mail` (uses PHP's `mail()` function), `smtp` (uses SMTP, and requires proper configuration of the `smtpOptions` setting), and `debug` (which tells the `Email` component to avoid sending the e-mail, and instead create a session flash message with the message contents.)

- ▶ `smtpOptions`: If delivery is set to `smtp`, it defines an array of settings to specify the type of SMTP connection to attempt. Available settings for this setting are:

    - ❑ `protocol`: Protocol to use when connecting. Defaults to `smtp`.

    - ❑ `host`: SMTP host to connect to. Defaults to `localhost`.

    - ❑ `port`: Port to use when connecting to `host`. Defaults to `25`.

    - ❑ `username`: Username.

    - ❑ `password`: Password to use.

    - ❑ `client`: What is the client connecting to the SMTP server. Defaults to the `HTTP_HOST` environment variable.

    - ❑ `timeout`: How many seconds to wait until the attempt to reach the server times out. Defaults to `30`.

We set delivery to `smtp`, and set the `smtpOptions` to what is required when attempting to send e-mails through Google Mail's SMTP server. Once the `Email` component is added to the controller and properly configured, we are ready to build and send e-mails.

The controller's `index()` method builds the e-mail by setting some properties. The `Email` component takes most of its configuration through public properties, some of which are:

- ▶ `to`: Destination, in the form: `name <email>`, where `email` is a valid e-mail address. It can also simply be an email address.

- ▶ `from`: E-mail address that is sending the e-mail. This property uses the same format as the `to` property. Notice that if you use Google Mail's SMTP, only the name part of this setting will be used (as the e-mail address will be set to your Google Mail e-mail address.)

- ▶ `replyTo`: Email address to which responses should be sent to. Same format as the `to` property.

- ▶ `return`: E-mail address to send any delivery errors, sent by the remote mail server. Same format as the `to` property.

- ▶ `readReceipt`: An e-mail address (using the same format as the `to` property) to where to send read receipt e-mails. Defaults to none.

- ▶ `cc`: An array containing the e-mail address to where to send copies of this e-mail. Each e-mail address should be specified using the same format as the `to` property.

- ▶ `bcc`: An array containing e-mail address to send blind copies of this e-mail. Each e-mail address should be specified using the same format as the `to` property.

- ▶ `subject`: Subject for the e-mail.

- ▶ `headers`: An array containing additional headers to send with the e-mail; each of those headers will be prefixed with `X-` as per `RFC 2822`.

- ▶ `attachments`: An array if paths to files that should be attached to the e-mail.

Using the `to` and `subject` property we specify the destination and subject of the e-mail. We did not have to define the `from` property since Google Mail uses the account specified when connecting to the SMTP server.

We then issue a call to the `send()` method, passing the body of the e-mail as its argument, and based on its boolean response we inform if the e-mail was successfully sent or if it failed, in which case we use the `smtpError` property to show the error.

The next part of the recipe uses templates and layouts to properly build the e-mail in two formats: HTML, and text, and uses replacement variables to show the flexibility of the e-mail component. E-mail layouts and templates are no different than controller layouts and views, as they inherit the controller properties (such as its replacement variables, and available helpers.)

E-mail layouts wrap the contents of e-mail templates, by means of their `content_for_layout` variable, just as controllers layouts do. There are two types of email layouts: HTML layouts, stored in `app/views/layouts/email/html`, and text layouts, stored in `app/views/layouts/email/text`. Similarly, you can define templates for HTML emails by storing them in the folder `app/views/elements/emails/html`, and text email templates in `app/views/elements/emails/text`.

We set the layout of the e-mail through the `layout` property of the `Email` component. If no layout is set, the default is used. Therefore, we start by creating the HTML layout in the file `app/views/layouts/email/html/default.ctp`, and the text layout in `app/views/layouts/email/text/default.ctp`.

We create two versions of the same template, called `test`: its HTML version is stored in `app/views/elements/email/html/test.ctp`, and its text version in `app/views/elements/email/html/test.ctp`.

The recipe continues by modifying the `index()` action. We start by defining two replacement variables: `name` and `url`, which are used in the `test` template. We then use the `sendAs` property of the `Email` component to say we are sending an HTML and text friendly e-mail. This property can be set to: `html`, to send HTML only e-mails; `text`, to send text only e-mails; and `both`, to send emails that support HTML and text e-mail clients.

We use the `template` property of the `Email` component to specify that we wish to use our `test` template, and we finalize with a call to the `send()` method to send out the e-mail.

There's more...

A common mistake that web application developers make is sending out e-mails as part of a controller action that is triggered by the visitor. Strictly speaking, e-mail sending is a non-interactive task, and as such should not be tied to the user browsing experience.

It is therefore recommended that the email sending task be performed in a non-interactive manner, which in CakePHP terms means from the console, also known as shell.

To exemplify this solution, consider a subscription website, where users enter their information (including their e-mail address), and, as a result, the application sends out a confirmation e-mail. Instead of sending the e-mail as part of the controller action that is triggered from the submission form, we may set a database field that shows that those users have not yet been sent out the confirmation e-mail, and then have a CakePHP shell periodically check for users that need their confirmation e-mails, sending out those e-mails from the shell.

This means that we find ourselves needing to be able to send e-mails from the shell, a topic covered in the recipe *Sending e-mails from shells* in *Chapter 8, Working with Shells*.

See also

Sending e-mails from shells in *Chapter 8, Working with Shells*.

Detecting file types with MagicDb

When handling file uploads, it is often important to determine the type of file being uploaded. While some files may be easily recognizable based on their contents, others may prove to be hard to identify.

`MagicDb` is a file database that consists of specifications for several file formats. This recipe shows us how to use this database, through CakePHP's `MagicDb` class, to properly identify files uploaded by our users.

The license for the `MagicDb` database file allows its use only on open source or freely available software. If you wish to identify files on commercial applications, you will have to find a different approach.

Getting ready

As we will be working on files uploaded by our users, we need to build a form to upload files. We will store these uploads in a table, so create this table with the following SQL statement:

```
CREATE TABLE `uploads`(
    `id` INT UNSIGNED AUTO_INCREMENT NOT NULL,
    `file` VARCHAR(255) NOT NULL,
    `mime` VARCHAR(255) default NULL,
    `description` TEXT default NULL,
    PRIMARY KEY(`id`)
);
```

Create a file named `uploads_controller.php` and place it in your `app/controllers` folder, with the following contents:

```
class UploadsController extends AppController {
    public function add() {
        if (!empty($this->data)) {
            $this->Upload->create();
            if ($this->Upload->save($this->data)) {
                $this->Session->setFlash('File succesfully uploaded');
                $this->redirect(array('action'=>'view', $this->Upload->id));
            } else {
                $this->Session->setFlash('Please correct the errors marked below');
            }
        }
    }
}
```

Create a folder named `uploads` in your `app/views` folder. Create the view for the `add()` method in a file named `add.ctp` and place it in your `app/views/uploads` folder, with the following contents:

```
<?php
echo $this->Form->create('Upload', array('type'=>'file'));
echo $this->Form->inputs(array(
    'file' => array('type'=>'file')
));
echo $this->Form->end('Upload');
?>
```

How to do it...

1. Download the latest MagicDb database file from `http://www.magicdb.org/magic.db` and place it in your `app/vendors` folder. You should now have a file named `magic.db` in your `app/vendors` folder.

2. Edit your `app/controllers/uploads_controller.php` file and add the following methods right below the `add()` method:

```php
public function view($id) {
    $upload = $this->Upload->find('first', array(
        'conditions' => array('Upload.id' => $id)
    ));
    if (empty($upload)) {
        $this->cakeError('error404');
    }
    $this->set(compact('upload'));
}

public function download($id) {
    $upload = $this->Upload->find('first', array(
        'conditions' => array('Upload.id' => $id)
    ));
    if (empty($upload)) {
        $this->cakeError('error404');
    }
    $path = TMP . $upload['Upload']['file'];

    header('Content-type: '.$upload['Upload']['mime']);
    readfile($path);
    $this->_stop();
}
```

3. Create the view for the `view()` method in a file named `view.ctp` and place it in your `app/views/uploads` folder with the following contents:

```php
<h2><?php echo $upload['Upload']['file']; ?></h2>
<p>
<strong>File</strong>: <?php echo $upload['Upload']['file']; ?><br />
<strong>MIME Type</strong>: <?php echo $upload['Upload']['mime']; ?><br />
<strong>Description</strong>: <?php echo $upload['Upload']['description']; ?>
</p>
<br />
<p>
<?php if (strpos($upload['Upload']['mime'], 'image/') === 0) { ?>
```

```php
    <?php echo $this->Html->image(array('action'=>'download',
$upload['Upload']['id']), array('height'=>200)); ?>
    <?php } else { ?>
    <?php echo $this->Html->link('Download',
array('action'=>'download', $upload['Upload']['id'])); ?>
    <?php } ?>
</p>
```

4. Create the model in a file named `upload.php` and place it in your `app/models` folder with the following contents:

```php
<?php
class Upload extends AppModel {
    protected $magicDb;
    protected function getMagicDb() {
        if (!isset($this->magicDb)) {
            App::import('Core', 'MagicDb');
            $magicDb = new MagicDb();
            if (!$magicDb->read(APP . 'vendors' . DS . 'magic.db')) {
                return null;
            }
            $this->magicDb = $magicDb;
        }
        return $this->magicDb;
    }
}
?>
```

5. While still editing your `app/models/upload.php` file, add the following method to the `Upload` class:

```php
public function beforeValidate($options = array()) {
    $result = parent::beforeValidate($options);

    $data = $this->data[$this->alias];
    if (!empty($data['file'])) {
        if (
            empty($data['file']) ||
            !is_array($data['file']) ||
            empty($data['file']['tmp_name']) ||
            !is_uploaded_file($data['file']['tmp_name'])
        ) {
            $this->invalidate('file', 'No file uploaded');
            return false;
        }
        $magicDb = $this->getMagicDb();
        if (!isset($magicDb)) {
```

```
        $this->invalidate('file', 'Can\'t get instance of MagicDb');
            return false;
        }
        $path = TMP . $data['file']['name'];
        if (!move_uploaded_file($data['file']['tmp_name'], $path)) {
            $this->invalidate('file', 'Could not move uploaded
file');
            return false;
        }
        $data['file'] = basename($path);
        unset($data['mime']);

        $analysis = $magicDb->analyze($path);
        if (!empty($analysis)) {
            $analysis = $analysis[0];
            if (preg_match('/^\[.+?;ext=[^;]+;mime=([^;]+);.*?\]
(.*)$/i', $analysis[3], $match)) {
                $data['mime'] = $match[1];
                if (empty($data['description'])) {
                    $data['description'] = $match[2];
                }
            }
        }

        if (empty($data['mime'])) {
            $this->invalidate('Can\'t recognize file
'.$data['file']);
            return false;
        }
        $this->data[$this->alias] = $data;
    } else {
        $this->invalidate('file', 'This field is required');
        return false;
    }
    return $result;
}
```

If you now browse to `http://localhost/uploads/add`, you will see a form where you can select a file, and then click the button **Upload**. Doing so with a GIF image will produce a result similar to what shown in the following screenshot:

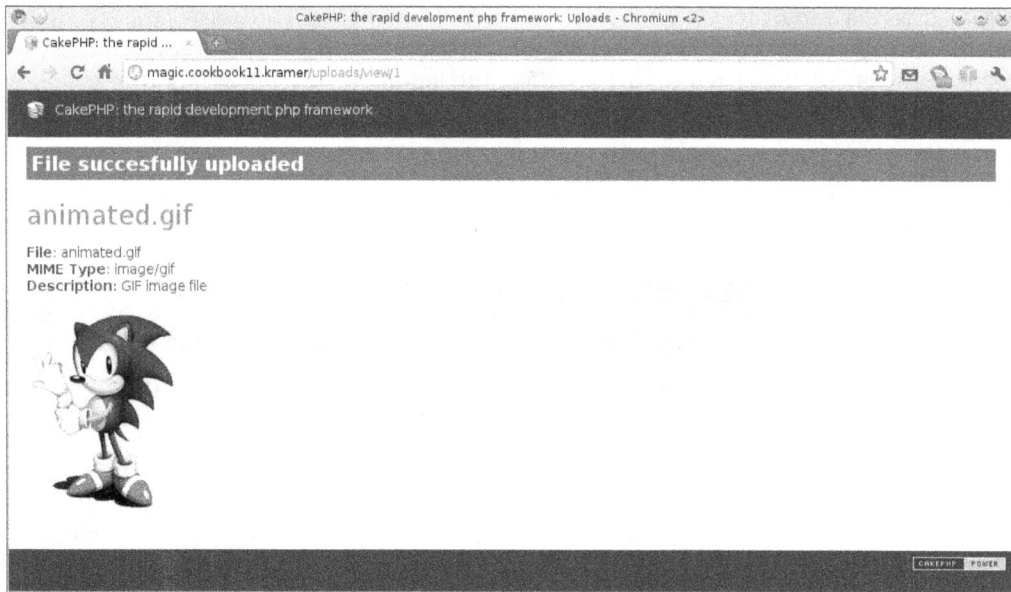

How it works...

The recipe starts by downloading the `MagicDb` file and placing it into the `app/vendors` directory. This file is a text file; containing blocks of identifier file signatures, and for each of these file signature definitions, their respective mime type, and description.

Next, we create the `view()` and `download()` controller actions. Both of them are very similar, except that the `download()` action uses the field `mime` to set the `Content-type` header, thus properly informing the client browser the type of data being sent.

The `download()` action simply sends the contents of the file by using PHP's `readfile()` function, then calling the `_stop()` method (available to all CakePHP classes that descend from `Object`) to stop execution. The `view()` action, on the other hand, requires a view, which prints out the `Upload` record information, showing an image if the file is indeed an image, or showing a link to download the file, in any other case.

The `Upload` model defines two methods: `beforeValidate()`, and `getMagicDb()`. The second method creates an instance of the `MagicDb` class provided by CakePHP, populating it with the contents from the `magic.db` file that was saved in the `app/vendors` directory.

The validation callback `beforeValidate()` starts by making sure that a proper file was uploaded. If so, it moves the uploaded file to the application's temporary directory, and then uses the `analyze()` method of the `MagicDb` class to obtain the file information.

This method will return an empty array if the file was not identified, or a set of file identifications that match the file. These file identifications are themselves arrays, containing information that is defined in the `magic.db` file. The fourth element out of this array contains the information we are looking for: a string that includes the file extension, the mime type, and the file type description.

We extract this information, and we set it so it is saved together with the filename. If the file was not identified, we invalidate the `file` field.

Throwing and handling exceptions

CakePHP 1.3 still offers support for PHP4, yet most CakePHP applications are built exclusively for PHP5. Therefore, it is only expected that our applications use language features only available in PHP5, such as exceptions.

However, there is no built-in support in CakePHP to handle exceptions. This recipe shows us how to create a base exception class that can be used throughout our application, and how to properly recover the application workflow after an exception is thrown.

Getting ready

We need a basic application skeleton to work with. Follow the entire recipe *Detecting file types with MagicDb*.

How to do it...

1. Edit your `app/controllers/uploads_controller.php` file and change the `view()` and `download()` methods, so that where it reads:

   ```
   $this->cakeError('error404');
   ```

   It now reads:

   ```
   throw new AppException('Upload '.$id.' not found');
   ```

2. Create a file named `app_exception.php` and place it in your `app/` folder, with the following contents:

   ```php
   <?php
   class AppException extends Exception {
       public function getInfo() {
           return array(
               'message' => $this->getMessage(),
               'trace' => $this->getStackTrace(),
               'url' => Router::url(null, true),
               'method' => env('REQUEST_METHOD'),
   ```

```php
                'referer' => env('HTTP_REFERER'),
                'POST' => $_POST,
                'GET' => $_GET,
                'SESSION' => $_SESSION
            );
    }

    public function getStackTrace($array = true, $count = 5) {
        if ($array) {
            $trace = $this->getTrace();
            if (!empty($count)) {
                $trace = array_slice($trace, 0, $count);
            }
            foreach($trace as $i => $row) {
                $location = '';
                if (!empty($row['class'])) {
                    $location .= $row['class'] . $row['type'] .
$row['function'] . '()';
                }
                $file = !empty($row['file']) ? str_replace(ROOT.DS,
'', $row['file']) : '';
                if (!empty($file)) {
                    if (!empty($location)) {
                        $location .= ' (' . $file . '@' . $row['line'] .
')';
                    } else {
                        $location .= $file . '@' . $row['line'];
                    }
                }

                $trace[$i]['location'] = $location;
                unset($trace[$i]['args']);
            }
            return $trace;
        }
        return $this->getTraceAsString();
    }
}
?>
```

3. Create a file named `exception_handler.php` and place it in your `app/libs` folder, with the following contents:

```php
<?php
App::import(array('type'=>'File', 'name'=>'AppException',
'file'=>APP.'app_exception.php'));
App::import('Core', 'Controller');

class ExceptionHandler extends Object {

    public static function handleException($exception) {
self::getInstance();
        self::logException($exception);
        self::renderException($exception);
        self::_stop();
    }
}
```

4. While still editing your `app/libs/exception_handler.php` file, add the following methods to the `ExceptionHandler` class:

```php
public function renderException($exception) {
    $Dispatcher = new Dispatcher();
    $Controller = new Controller();

    $Controller->params = array(
        'controller' => 'exceptions',
        'action' => 'exception'
    );

    $Controller->viewPath = 'exceptions';
    if (file_exists(VIEWS.'layouts'.DS.'exception.ctp')) {
        $Controller->layout = 'exception';
    }
    $Controller->base = $Dispatcher->baseUrl();
    $Controller->webroot = $Dispatcher->webroot;
    $Controller->set(compact('exception'));

    $View = new View($Controller);
    if (!file_exists(VIEWS.'exceptions'.DS.'view.ctp')) {
        if (Configure::read('debug') > 0) {
            echo '<strong>Exception</strong>: ';
            echo $exception->getMessage();
            echo '<pre>';
            echo $exception->getStackTrace(false);
            echo '</pre>';
            return;
        }
        return $Controller->redirect(null, 500);
```

```
    }
        echo $View->render('view');
    }

    public function logException($exception) {
        $trace = $exception->getStackTrace();
        $message = get_class($exception) . ' thrown in ' . $trace[0]
    ['location'];
        $message .= ': ' . $exception->getMessage();
        if (is_a($exception, instanceof AppException)) {
            $message .= ' | DEBUG: ' . json_encodevar_export($exception-
    >getInfo(), true);    }
        self::log($message, LOG_ERROR);
    }
```

5. Add the following at the end of your `app/config/bootstrap.php` file (right above the closing PHP tag):

```
App::import('Lib', 'ExceptionHandler');
set_exception_handler(array('ExceptionHandler',
'handleException'));
```

6. Create a folder named `exceptions` in your `app/views` folder. Create a file named `view.ctp` and place it in your `app/views/exceptions` folder, with the following contents:

```
<h2><?php echo $exception->getMessage(); ?></h2>
<?php if (Configure::read('debug') > 0) { ?>
    <ol>
    <?php foreach($exception->getStackTrace() as $trace) { ?>
        <li><?php echo $trace['location']; ?></li>
    <?php } ?>
    </ol>
    <?php if (is_a($exception, 'AppException')) { ?>
        <?php debug(array_diff_key($exception->getInfo(),
array('message'=>null, 'trace'=>null))); ?>
    <?php } ?>
<?php } else { ?>
    <p>An error has been found. It has been logged, and will soon
be fixed.</p>
<?php } ?>
```

If you now force an error by browsing to `http://localhost/uploads/view/xx`, you will see a page describing the exception, its stack trace, and including relevant information, such as the URL, any POST or GET parameters, and session information, as shown in the following screenshot:

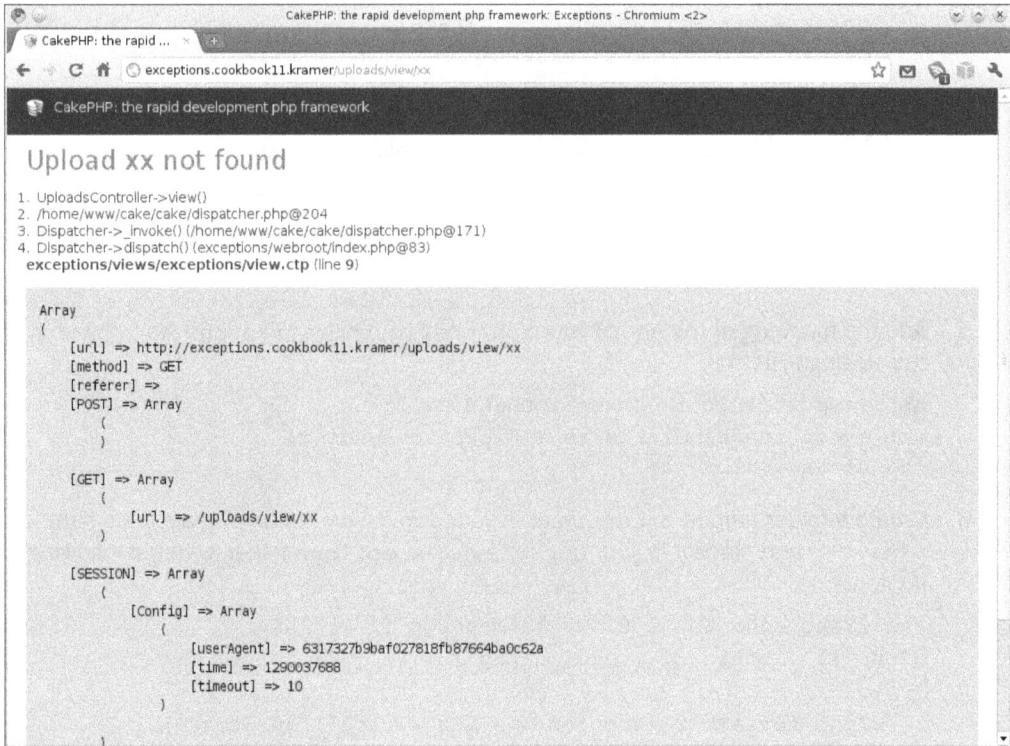

How it works...

We start by using exceptions in our `UploadsController` class, instead of using CakePHP's `cakeError()` method, whenever an `Upload` record is not found. These exceptions are actually instances of `AppException`, but we could have as well created custom exceptions that inherit from `AppException`.

The `AppException` class provides us with a base class from where to extend our application exceptions. This class offers us more contextual information through its `getInfo()` method. This information includes not only the exception message and the stack trace (which is simplified by removing the arguments, and limiting the number of items), but also the URL, method, any POST or GET data, and session information, details that can become valuable when working out the exception.

We still have to add the ability to handle any exceptions that are thrown. For that purpose, we create the `ExceptionHandler` class. Through the code added to the `app/config/bootstrap.php` file, which uses PHP's `set_exception_handler()` function, we tell PHP that whenever an exception is thrown and not caught anywhere, the static `handleException()` method of the `ExceptionHandler` class is to be executed.

This method logs the exception, using the `logException()` method, and renders a friendly page by calling the `renderException()` method. This rendering is performed by creating a dummy controller as an instance of `Controller`, using this controller to render the view `app/views/exceptions.ctp` (optionally using a layout named `exception.ctp` if one is available in `app/views/exceptions`), and setting the view variable `exception` to the exception being handled.

This view shows a simple message if the debug level is set to `0`, or a thorough description of the stack trace and any context information that may be relevant.

Index

[PACKT] PUBLISHING open source *
community experience distilled

Thank you for buying
CakePHP 1.3 Application Development Cookbook

About Packt Publishing

Packt, pronounced 'packed', published its first book "*Mastering phpMyAdmin for Effective MySQL Management*" in April 2004 and subsequently continued to specialize in publishing highly focused books on specific technologies and solutions.

Our books and publications share the experiences of your fellow IT professionals in adapting and customizing today's systems, applications, and frameworks. Our solution based books give you the knowledge and power to customize the software and technologies you're using to get the job done. Packt books are more specific and less general than the IT books you have seen in the past. Our unique business model allows us to bring you more focused information, giving you more of what you need to know, and less of what you don't.

Packt is a modern, yet unique publishing company, which focuses on producing quality, cutting-edge books for communities of developers, administrators, and newbies alike. For more information, please visit our website: www.packtpub.com.

About Packt Open Source

In 2010, Packt launched two new brands, Packt Open Source and Packt Enterprise, in order to continue its focus on specialization. This book is part of the Packt Open Source brand, home to books published on software built around Open Source licences, and offering information to anybody from advanced developers to budding web designers. The Open Source brand also runs Packt's Open Source Royalty Scheme, by which Packt gives a royalty to each Open Source project about whose software a book is sold.

Writing for Packt

We welcome all inquiries from people who are interested in authoring. Book proposals should be sent to author@packtpub.com. If your book idea is still at an early stage and you would like to discuss it first before writing a formal book proposal, contact us; one of our commissioning editors will get in touch with you.

We're not just looking for published authors; if you have strong technical skills but no writing experience, our experienced editors can help you develop a writing career, or simply get some additional reward for your expertise.

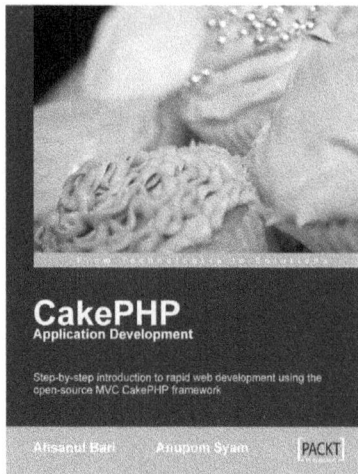

CakePHP Application Development

ISBN: 978-1-847193-89-6   Paperback: 332 pages

Step-by-step introduction to rapid web development using the open-source MVC CakePHP framework

1. Develop cutting-edge Web 2.0 applications, and write PHP code in a faster, more productive way

2. Walk through the creation of a complete CakePHP Web application

3. Customize the look and feel of applications using CakePHP layouts and views

4. Make interactive applications using CakePHP, JavaScript, and AJAX helpers

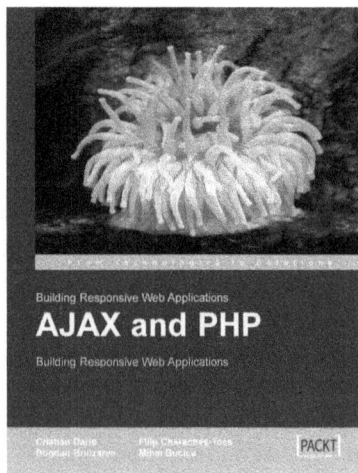

AJAX and PHP: Building Responsive Web Applications

ISBN: 978-1-904811-82-4   Paperback: 284 pages

Enhance the user experience of your PHP website using AJAX with this practical tutorial featuring detailed case studies

1. Build a solid foundation for your next generation of web applications

2. Use better JavaScript code to enable powerful web features

3. Leverage the power of PHP and MySQL to create powerful back-end functionality and make it work in harmony with the smart AJAX client

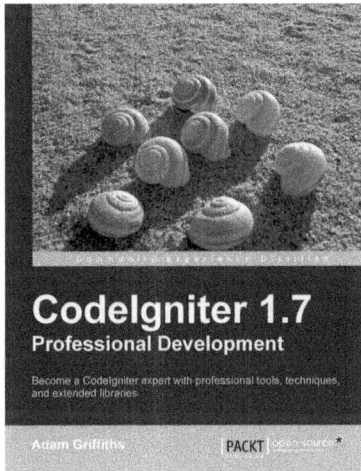

CodeIgniter 1.7 Professional Development

ISBN: 9781849510905   Paperback: 300 pages

Become a CodeIgniter expert with professional tools, techniques and extended libraries

1. Learn expert CodeIgniter techniques and move beyond the realms of the User Guide

2. Create mini-applications that teach you a technique and allow you to easily build extras on top of them

3. Create CodeIgniter Libraries to minimize code bloat and allow for easy transitions across multiple projects

4. A step-by-step, practical guide with examples and screenshots

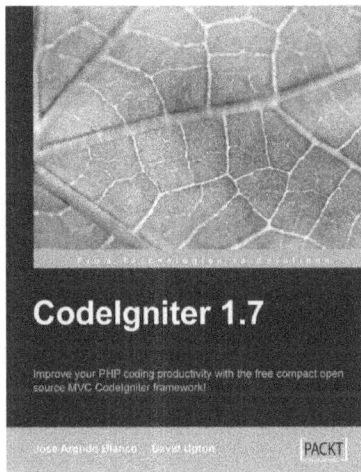

CodeIgniter 1.7

ISBN: 978-1-847199-48-5   Paperback: 300 pages

Improve your PHP coding productivity with the free compact open-source MVC CodeIgniter framework!

1. Clear, structured tutorial on working with CodeIgniter for rapid PHP application development

2. Careful explanation of the basic concepts of CodeIgniter and its MVC architecture

3. Use CodeIgniter with databases, HTML forms, files, images, sessions, and email

Please check **www.PacktPub.com** for information on our titles

www.ingramcontent.com/pod-product-compliance
Lightning Source LLC
Chambersburg PA
CBHW080905220326
41598CB00034B/5481